EXPLORING
YOURSELF

THROUGH VEDIC ASTROLOGY

SANJAY VATTS & NEENA JAIN

BLUEROSE PUBLISHERS
India | U.K.

Copyright © Sanjay Vatts 2024

All rights reserved by author. No part of this publication may be reproduced, stored in a retrieval system or transmitted in any form or by any means, electronic, mechanical, photocopying, recording or otherwise, without the prior permission of the author. Although every precaution has been taken to verify the accuracy of the information contained herein, the publisher assumes no responsibility for any errors or omissions. No liability is assumed for damages that may result from the use of information contained within.

BlueRose Publishers takes no responsibility for any damages, losses, or liabilities that may arise from the use or misuse of the information, products, or services provided in this publication.

For permissions requests or inquiries regarding this publication,
please contact:

BLUEROSE PUBLISHERS
www.BlueRoseONE.com
info@bluerosepublishers.com
+91 8882 898 898
+4407342408967

ISBN: 978-93-5989-813-1

Cover design: Shivam
Typesetting: Namrata Saini

First Edition: January 2024

Foreword

I have been associated with holistic wellness for so many years. Holistic wellness and astrology are connected through the belief that cosmic energies and celestial movements can influence an individual's well-being. Vedic astrology, an ancient Indian system, holds a significant place in the realm of holistic wellness. Rooted in the Vedas, the sacred texts of ancient India, Vedic astrology is based on the belief that celestial movements and  positions can influence human affairs and natural phenomena. In the context of holistic wellness, Vedic astrology is viewed as a guiding light, offering insights into an individual's physical, mental, and spiritual well-being.

In the scriptures of ancient India, or Bharat, are found folds of wisdom with deep knowledge of Vedic astrology. Rooted in the timeless tradition of the Vedas, this ancient celestial science reveals the cosmic structure that creates our destiny and illuminates our path in life.

In the mysterious dance of planets and stars, Vedic astrology shows not only the power of the earth but also the essence of our lives. This book, "Explore Yourself with Vedic Astrology," is the door to a fascinating world where you could learn things not only about yourself but also about your loved ones from the eyes of the cosmos. Vedic astrology also delves into the spiritual dimension of holistic wellness. It explores the concept of karma, suggesting that our actions in past lives influence our current circumstances. By understanding one's karmic patterns, individuals can gain insights into their life's purpose and spiritual journey.

In these pages, you will discover about the Nakshatras, or the lunar mansions, that hold the key to our emotional and spiritual depths. You will also delve deeper into the complexities of planetary influences, understanding their benevolent blessings as well as their difficult challenges. The authors have explained Zodiac Signs, Planets, Houses, Vimshottari Dahas, Nakshatras, and Remedies in simple but effective words.

In embracing the wisdom of the ancients, the authors of this book, Sanjay Vatts and Neena Jain, invite the readers to embark on a transformative journey to learn about this ancient science and help themselves and their loved ones. A journey that transcends the boundaries of time and space, offering profound insights into the very fabric of our existence. As we unravel the mysteries of the celestial realm, may this book serve as a guiding light, illuminating your path and unveiling the secrets of your soul, as written in the stars.

Dr. Bharat Bhushan Sharma

Ph.D. (Hon.) Holistic Wellness

Foreword

It gives me immense pleasure to inform you that the Authors of the book "Explore Yourself with Vedic Astrology" have brought out this book that will surely help people understand this Vedic Ancient Science and serve Society better by becoming better human beings.

By the grace of God, I have been blessed to serve people and Society by being associated with Shri Mata Vaishno Devi Shrine Board and various other religious holy shrines. Due to proximity with various holy shrines especially Mata Vaishno Devi, I find this exploration of Vedic Astrology to be a harmonious blend of cosmic guidance and practical wisdom. I firmly believe that stars have a deep connection with humans. Humans should have a proper understanding of this vast Universe as well as about themselves and after going through this book, anyone can understand about their strengths as well as weaknesses.

For me, this book unfolds the ancient wisdom that has guided seekers for centuries. I hope that the book helps you to illuminate your understanding and inspire a deeper connection with this Universe so that the entire World becomes a better place to live. Both the authors, Sh. Sanjay Vatts and Ms. Neena Jain, have explained the connection between a human being with Zodiac Signs, Planets, Houses, Dashas, and, Nakshatras in words that every human being can understand. May the wisdom within these pages guide the spiritual seeker and the dynamic mind toward a balanced and purposeful existence.

K.K. Sharma,

Member, Shri Mata Vaishno Devi Shrine Board

Chairman & Managing Director, AIMIL Pharmaceuticals (India) Ltd

From Authors of this Book
to
Our Esteemed Reader

We firmly believe this book is in your hands for a reason, and probably this was destined to happen at this time. This is the time when people like you have started to explore our ancient science. In the country where Vedic astrology originated, Bharat or India, where Jyotish was and is proudly known as a Vedanga, the government was never able to give any place higher than a traditionally 'low' occupation to any astrologer. This may be due to several reasons that are not relevant to be discussed as of now. In the present time, many well-qualified people have analyzed Vedic astrology and are trying their best to impart the knowledge gained to people about this ancient science.

This book has been written to educate people on the fundamentals of Vedic astrology so that they can understand themselves and the people around them in a better way. The contents of the books are compilations of information that has been gathered from different sources and also through our own experiences, and we in no way try to make readers believe anything. While writing this book, we have endeavored to attempt to adopt a format similar to that found in textbooks related to mathematics and physics that are commonly read in schools. Additionally, the text has been tested to ensure that it is concise and to the point. It is important to note that this book does not purport to be an encyclopaedia, nor does it claim to provide comprehensive knowledge of astrology that has been developed over the past more than 5000 years. Even if this book were to be 100 times longer than the current volume, it would still not be sufficient to understand all the concepts and nitty-gritty of Vedic astrology. Instead, this book serves as a comprehensive, single-source guide to the fundamentals of astrology that have been collected, compiled, and written based on our understanding and experience. Furthermore, it is important to remember that astrology cannot transform one's life; only one can do so. Astrology cannot alter the course of one's life; however, it can provide insight into how to manage one's life and offer information and guidance. We hope this book will provide readers with a better understanding of the fundamentals of astronomy and help them improve their lives.

Sanjay Vatts

Neena Jain

Contents

1. Introduction to Astrology 1
2. Vedic Astrology 6
3. Vedic Astrology and Planets 11
4. Houses 107
5. Zodiac 125
6. Vimshottari Dasha System 140
7. Nakshatras 153
8. Remedial Measures 241
9. Conclusion 271

Introduction to Astrology

Om Ganeshay Namah

Before embarking on this new mission of understanding Vedic astrology, let's pray to Lord Ganesha, the first god to be worshiped. Ganeshji is the son of Lord Shiva and Mother Goddess Paravati. He is the harbinger of success, wisdom, luck, and wisdom, and he is also considered the best god who removes all obstacles. Lord Ganesha is widely worshiped all over the world. Ganesha is said to be our life, and astrology is the mirror of life.

Through astrology, Lord Ganesha guides us with light so that we do not lose it in our lives. Ganesha holds all the planets as he is Supreme and has a special ability to speak to planets that we recur in our lives through his astrology. Astrology is a difficult and vast study. It has an ancient history, and people are still trying to understand it. Becoming a professional astrologer requires many years of study, and the discipline is so broad that it is impossible to know everything about it in one lifetime. Many texts link the history of Indian astrology to various gods and saints.

The most popular texts have been written by Rishis like Parashara, Varahamihira, Garga, Jaimini, and their followers. The credit for explaining almost all aspects of Indian astrology belongs to Rishi Parashara in his great book Brihat Parashara Hora Shastra. According to legend, he was the grandson of Rishi Vasistha (one of the seven sages, the seer of Rigveda, and the great seeker of the Gayatri Mantra) and father of Rishi Veda Vyasa (who wrote 18 Puranas, including the great epic Mahabharata, which includes the famous Bhagavat Geeta, the Brahma Sutras, and the Uttara Mimansa).

Rishi Parashar's father's name was Shaktimuni, and his mother's name was Adyashyanti. Parashara was a disciple of Baskala and Yajnavalkya. Rishi Parashara is considered to be the twenty-sixth incarnation of Lord Shiva. The depth of his astrological knowledge was so great that one day, while crossing a river in a boat, he casually looked at his favorite stars in heaven and realized that if a child is conceived at that moment, he will be an expert in Shastras. So, he told this to the lady rowing the boat and requested that she marry him. She agreed, and so their son, Veda Vyasa, was born. He also wrote Parashara Samhita and Parashara Smriti.

According to one theory, Brahma taught the Vedas and Jyotisha to his son, Narada. Narada taught these to Rishi Saunaka. Parashara was a disciple of Rishi Saunaka. Brihat Parashara Hora Shastra is a kind of dialogue between Rishi Parashara and his student Maitreya; they ask questions, and Parashara explains the points. Even after 5,000 years, it is the best classic of astrology. The exact period of existence of Parashara is difficult to ascertain, but it is widely believed that he lived during Mahabharataharata period, around 3200 BC.

Modern Indian astrology is based on the theory of destiny. Good and bad karma in past lives determines your destiny or karma in this life, and your karma in this life determines your future karma.

According to Indian astrology, a person's destiny is calculated according to the movement of the stars in the sky when he is born at a particular place, on that day, and at that hour. However, Indian astrology doesn't teach you to be dependent on fate. Indian astrology allows you to know about your birth, abilities, limitations, strengths, and weaknesses. It also shows the expectations of what kind of life and work are good for you. It also recommends a variety of treatments to prevent adverse effects and improve outcomes. According to Indian Vedic astrology, a horoscope is a roadmap for your destiny, but your fate is in your hands.

Various religious scriptures also tell us what is good and what is bad; what to do and what not to do; how to do and how not to do. It is similar in that you have an acre of land and seeds to plant. You are responsible for how much energy you put in, how much fertilizer and water you add, and when you harvest your crops. So, you have to do it with your knowledge, intelligence, skills, insights, and experience. Astrology argues that people are influenced not only by genetics and the environment but also by the state of the sun and planets at the time of their birth. Planets are seen as the main force of life, the tools we rely on for survival, and the basis of our day-to-day instances in life. The planetary combinations use different types depending on where they are in the zodiac and how they relate to each other. The factors created by the planet define these relationships, and the positions of the planets according to their birthplaces tell us how they behave in the living spaces defined by the different astrological houses.

According to Vedic astrology, the ascendant, or Lagna, extends for a period of two hours. Thousands of people throughout the world are born with the same planetary combination in various regions of the world during these two hours, and they cannot have the same fate or destiny. Therefore, their estimates are based only on the location of planets, and they may not be accurate. Due to the nature of astrological signs, they are somewhat accurate, but they get nowhere when it comes to predicting events and times in people's lives. You don't need an astrologer to tell you; for example, if you're a Scorpio, you tend to be jealous and creative. Vedic Hindu astrology uses a four-dimensional approach.

Firstly, in Vedic astrology, we have a divisional chart system called the Varga system. Thereafter, sixteen divisional charts are prepared by dividing the degrees of the planets at the time of birth. These divisional charts are studied to determine the strength of planets and houses and to examine many aspects of a person's life. For example, the ninth division, called Navamsa, is used to study marriage and married life; the 10th division is used to study careers and work; the 7th division is used to study children; etc. The final Varga, called Shodashamsha, is prepared by dividing the degrees of the planet by one 6th division.

Thereafter, there is the Dasha system. It is based on the degree of moon of the native at the time of birth. We calculate the Dashas (main dasha), Antardashas (sub period, of planet), or Pratyantar Dasha (sub-sub period, of planet), or period of rules of various planets that keep on changing over a person's life. Gochara, or transit of planets, is the 3rd element of Vedic astrology. Planets passing through different houses give different results. But the planet takes significant time to travel through a house; e.g., Saturn changes the house or signs after a span of two and a half years. All the while, the results cannot be all good or all bad.

Vedic astrology points to good and bad times even when going through the zodiac sign. We have the systems of Ashtakavarga and Prastharasthakavarga, which divide the transits of planets in a star into eight parts and show which are good and which are bad. Finally, in Vedic astrology, there is a Prasna Kundali system or chart based on that time. This is reviewed as an additional guide to provide predictions. By describing and combining the roles and attributes (elements, signs, and houses) of the actors (planets), astrology can present a complete and comprehensive picture of a person and his potential based on one's natal chart.

Today's scientists do not accept the horoscope or the birth chart. But we all know that the planets are related to us and have an effect on us. Almost all psychiatrists agree that mental patients do not behave the same way during the full moon and new moon periods. The police collect and record the same habits for many criminals. Today, scientists are aware of some of the effects of the sun's ultraviolet, gamma, and beta rays. But unfortunately, they don't have the wisdom of our elders; they just knew all the effects.

Why to understand Astrology?

The best part of wisdom is accepting things beyond our control. Think of sailors on the high seas—they can't control the wind, but they can adjust their sails at any moment. Traveling the world is much easier with the insight of astrology. It can affect our decisions more profoundly than the weather or daily news updates.

A person's horoscope contains many details about them, such as their deep aspirations, career, marital status, wealth, funny facts, fears, pain, and actions. By knowing the horoscope of the person, you can decide whether you can agree with them or not.

You can use astrology in many ways. But the most effective way is to clear your path and take steps to improve your life. That is the main goal of understanding astrology. By reading and analyzing your horoscope, you will be able to identify the areas where you need to improve. You can also work on the weak areas of your life. You can also perform effective astrological remedies. Moreover, it gives you an exclusive hobby, and you can stand out from the crowd.

Vedic Astrology

Vedic astrology is derived from the Sanskrit word Vedic, which translates to "divine knowledge." Vedic astrology also translates to "the study of light." Vedic astrology has its origins in the religious literature known as the Vedas, which was written by Bhrigu, one of the most influential Vedic astrologers of the era.

This ancient Indian science explains the movement and position of the planets, as well as the influence of time on people and the world around them. There are various reasons why some people are successful and some people are unhappy.

Early Vedic astrology relied solely on the movements of the stars relative to the planets. However, later, Vedic astrology began to include the zodiac signs in it.

There are twenty-seven constellations, or nakshatras, each of which contains twelve signs, nine planets, and twelve houses. Each house and planet represent a specific aspect of a person's life. The twelve zodiac signs of a person are divided into twelve houses based on the time of birth. Nine planets are divided among the twelve zodiac signs and placed in twelve houses. The visual representation of the signs and snapshots of the planets is called a horoscope.

The primary purpose of Vedic astrology is to elucidate the significance of these patterns and explain them in relation to individuals and other entities.

Types of Vedic Astrology

Vedic Astrology is basically composed of the following six branches:

(i)   **Gola:** Positional astronomy
(ii) **Ganita:** Mathematical calculations to find Gola
(iii) **Jataka:** Natal astrology
(iv) **Prasna:** Where predictions are made based on the time of asking the question.
(v)   **Muhurta:** The most favourable and auspicious time to start something new.
(vi) **Nimitta:** Good omens and portents

Types of Indian Vedic Astrology

Below are the three types of Indian Vedic Astrology:

(i) **Siddhanta (Astronomy):** Where astronomy is applied to astrology.
(ii) **Samhita (Mundane astrology):** In Mundane astrology, important events of countries like wars, political events, natural disasters like earthquakes, floods, etc. are all predicted. In addition, Astro - meteorology, financial situations, housing and construction problems, Vaastu Shastra, omens, etc. are included in Samhita astrology.
(iii) **Hora (Predictive astrology):** Vedic astrology defines each hour of the day as 'Hora' similar to the Western clock, there are 24 horas, beginning from dawn to sunset in the Hindu Vedic calendar. Hora is a branch of the Indian system of astrology that deals with the finer points of predictive techniques. A Hora is of an approximate one-hour duration and is ruled with a specific planet and relying on the attributes of this planet; horas may be beneficial or inimical.

Difference between Jyotish and Western Astrology

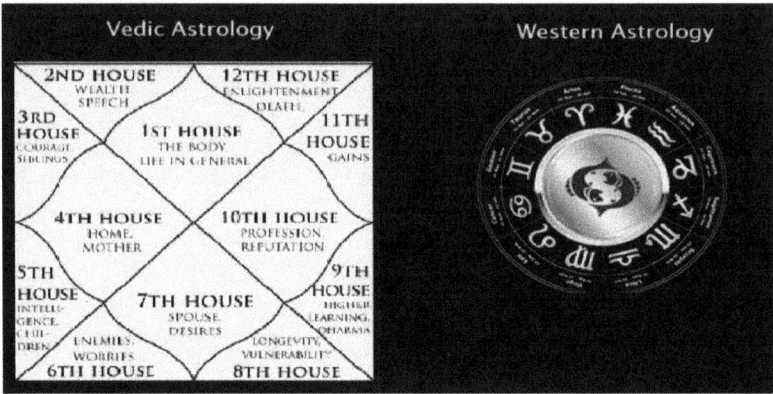

Jyotish is different from astrology practiced in the West. The difference is that in Jyotish, we use the celestial zodiac, which is based on the fixed, observable positions of the stars as we see them in the sky. In contrast, Western astrology uses so-called tropical zodiac signs. The tropical zodiac does not depend on the fixed and visible positions of the stars, but on the relative and differential positions of the sun.

Due to a phenomenon called "echinoid precession" and the oscillations of the Earth's axis of rotation, the positions of the Tropics gradually move away from the constellation at a rate of about 1 degree every 72 years.

When most of us were born, the temperature, and thus the sun, had shifted about 24 degrees from its fixed and visible position. In short, there are many differences between the two astrological systems. Due to the precession of the equinox, this difference only became apparent over time, several centuries later. At the same time, the two systems are identical, but the origin of the star spans a change of 22 degrees or days, making the position of the earth in the previous sign to the west about 80% of the time.

In Jyotish, we don't think of people according to their sun sign, as in tropical astrology. Instead, we enter the chart of "Ascendant", the star that is rising on the eastern horizon when a person is born. This establishes the relationship between the natal planets and the natal conditions, and gives clues about his personality, body, and how he presents himself to the world. First, we look at the Ascendant to know about the person.

Vedic astrology describes the movements of the planets and their positions relative to time and space. The word Jyotish in Sanskrit means "science of light" and refers to the mathematical and esoteric complex of astrology rooted in the Vedic tradition of India. Jyotish, sometimes called Vedic Astrology, describes the patterns of the world into which we are born and can provide us with important information for understanding our way of life. By carefully considering these cosmic influences, Jyotish can help us make a realistic assessment of our strengths and challenges in realizing our potential. Jyotish can also allow us to be more selective in predicting changes and times in our lives. It offers solutions to simple problems, gives us the confidence to see our true destiny, and creates success, happiness, and harmony on all levels.

Scientific Basis of Vedic Astrology

Ancient Indian literature is filled with stories about zodiac signs, nakshatras, and planets that explain many astrological rules. However, the general opinion is that these stories are a tool used by our ancient masters or gurus to explain some complex laws of physics that are beyond everyone's understanding. Unfortunately, even today's science cannot fully understand the laws of physics behind this ancient method, despite its rapid development. Our current understanding of the science of astrology is based on statistics and probability. Statistics is a branch of mathematics that deals with the relationship between two or more seemingly independent phenomena without knowing the reason for that relationship.

If there is the same sign in the images of 1000 people, you can see that certain astrological rules apply to 70–80% of people. Statistically, we can say that an event occurring in one's life is "meaningful" when there is a connection between different beings in the world. Suppose you toss a coin 1000 times; the probability of "heads" is always close to 50%. Now, let's say you're looking at the results of a coin toss at sunset and sunrise. If, after a year of testing, you find that the probability that the sun is "in the lead" is actually 70% at sunrise, not the expected 50%, then if you toss a coin at sunrise, most likely you are going to have a "head"

Vedic astrology can be interpreted in a similar way. Some combinations in the chart estimate 70–80% of the chart with combinations. We may not be able to explain why this happens, but there is very solid evidence that events can be predicted with a high degree of importance.

Vedic Astrology and Planets

In Vedic astrology, each planet represents something specific to your lifestyle, from love to intelligence. The positions of these nine planets determine your 12 zodiac signs and personal horoscope.

Human thinking is inspired by the planets that are compatible with their inherent inclinations and the ways in which they affect every way of life. The good aspects produce the desired influence, while the bad aspects are seen in the bad or afflictive aspects; a planet in the bad aspect is called the afflicted or affected planet.

Seven of the nine planets, the Sun, the Moon, Mars, Mercury, Jupiter, Venus, and Saturn, are named as the planets of the solar system, but the planets Rahu and Ketu are also considered to be the planets in Vedic Astrology. Rahu and Ketu are grahas with no real mass. They represent two points in space where the orbits of the sun and moon intersect. Due to the fact that eclipses block light and occur in relation to intersections, Rahu and Ketu are often referred to as "shadow planets" and often indicate negative effects.

The planets on which Vedic astrology is entirely based are called "navagrahas", which means "9" (nava) in Sanskrit + "catch or hold" (grahas). Each planet "holds" a problem in your way of life. The planets are called grahas because they are the holders and givers of life's lessons due to karma, and they can be the evolutionary force that teaches us to grow and be in harmony with the cosmic order. According to astrology, everything in this universe has an impact on others. Astrology is based on the notion that celestial bodies influence the entire universe, from the smallest to the greatest, including humans.

Each navgraha has the ability to influence some elements of our existence.

- The position and strength of each of these grahas at the time of your birth will determine your horoscope and influence where you will succeed and where you will encounter conflicts in your life.
- Some grahas rule several zodiac signs, while Rahu and Ketu do not rule any because they are not actual masses but astronomical points.

Benefic and Malefic planets in astrology

The nine planets, or grahas, in Vedic astrology can be categorized into two categories:

Benefic planets: Moon, Mercury, Venus, and Jupiter

Malefic planets: Sun, Mars, Saturn, Rahu, and Ketu

Jupiter and Venus are natural benefics (saumya grahas or shubha grahas). Mercury becomes a natural benefic when alone or with more natural benefics. Waxing moon of Shukla paksha is a natural benefic.

The Sun, Mars, Rahu, and Ketu are natural malefics (kroora grahas or paapa grahas). Mercury becomes a natural malefic when it is connected with more natural malefics. The waning moon of Krishna Paksha is a natural malefic. This information is important because the results given by the planets are based on their inherent nature.

Also, keep in mind that a bad planet doesn't always bring bad results. Again, the good and bad effects of the planets depend on many different factors.

Avastha or States of Planets

According to the great Rishi Parasara, before judging the results of any planet, the avasthas or states of the planets must be looked at. Planets have five different states:

1. Baalaadhi – maturity
2. Jagradadi – alertness
3. Deeptaadi – status
4. Lajjitaadi – mood (such as proud, shy etc.)
5. Shayanaadi – condition of activity

1. Baaladhi Avasthas

This state reflects the maturity of the planet and comes in five categories listed in the table below. The planet that is in the first six degrees of an odd sign is called Bala (child). It will only give 25% of its results. The table below shows the states of the planets according to the different signs and orders. Note that the results are reversed for even signs.

	Odd Sign	Results	Even Sign	Results
0-6	Bala (Infant)	25%	Mitra	Nil
6-12	Kumara (Adolescent)	50%	Vridha	Very Little
12-18	Yuva (Youth)	100%	Yuva	100%
18-24	Vridha (Mature)	Very Little	Kumara	50%
24-36	Mrita (dead or static)	Nil	Bala	25%

Planets like the Sun and Mars are said to work best in Balaavastha (childhood), Jupiter and Venus in Yuva (Youth), Moon and Saturn in Vriddha (old age). Mercury always gives good results.

2. Jagratadi Avasthas

Jagratadi avasthas are related to the planets state of alertness. These states are based on the positions of the planets in a sign that depend on friendship and enemity between them. There are three different states under Jagratadi avasthas. This condition indicates the general alertness of the planet and is of three types. When a planet in its own sign or exaltation, it is called Wake or Jagrit. In the waking state, the planet is fully aware of the physical, mental, and emotional world and how it functions. A planet in a dream state or Swapna avastha is very emotional and lives in reality due to one's situation and mind projection. A planet that is in a deep sleep aka "shushupti" and is unaware to what is happening in the outside world. It is natural that this planet is not useful for acquiring material wealth.

Condition of the Graha	Avastha	Meaning	Results
Own sign or Exaltation Rasi	Jagrit	Wake	Full
Friend or Neutral	Swapna	Dreamer	Medium
Enemy Rasi or debilitation	Sushupti	Deep Sleep	Nil

3. Deeptaadi Avasthas

This avastha reflects the status or dignity of the planets and has a total of 10 categories. Deepthadi avasthas are related to the attitudes of the planets. They are based on a planet's position in the horoscope. Avasthas help determine the strength or weakness of a planet, which is important for the judgment of a horoscope. In addition, readers should be aware of the terms used to describe the various Avasthas as they may come across references to them while reading astrological articles. The 10 avasthas and the results that the various planets produce while in these Avasthas are as follows:

(i) Deepta (Planet in Exaltation): Benefits from vehicle for comfortable travel, fame, wealth, gain of respect from elders and lucky descendants.

(ii) Swastha or Swakshetra (in own house): Happiness, good children, fame, wealth, high status, land and other possessions.

(iii) Mudita (in the house of a friendly planet): happy, confident and optimistic

(iv) Santha (in auspicious Vargas or subdivisions): Courageous, dynamic, motivated, benevolent, relaxed and happy.

(v) Sakta (Retrogression) :Courage, fame, wealth and good children

(vi) Peediya (In the last quarter of a sign): Criminal prosecution, imprisonment, looting and leaving the home land to another country

(vii) Deena (Not in a friendly house): Anxiety, mental confusion, illness and deprave.

(viii) Vikala (Combust): Losing wife and children, getting sick and becoming an orphan.

(ix) Khala or Neecha (Debilitated): Imprisonment, irreligious, loss, inferiority, friction with parents and relationships.

(x) Bhita: sufferings, torture, many enemies, many bad habits, and dangers in foreign lands.

4. Lajjitaadi Avasthas

This avastha conveys the mood of planet. The various conditions and the results are as mentioned below.

Graha	Condition	Meaning	Results
Situated in the 5th house with Rahu, Ketu or conjunct with Sun, Saturn or Mars	Lajita	Shy, Ashamed	God Aversion
Exalted or Mooltrikona	Garvita	Proud	Happiness and gains
Enemy Rasi, conjunct with or aspected by Enemy, or Saturn	Kshudhita	Hungry	Grief
In Water sign, aspected by enemy without benefic aspect	Trashita	Thirsty	Losses, Wicked deeds
Friend's Rasi, or conjunct with or aspected by Friend or Jupiter	Mudita	Delighted	Gains
Conjunction with Sun and aspected by malefics and enemy	Kshobhita	Agitated	Penury

5. Shayanaadi Avasthas

This avastha relates to the condition of various activities and are arrived at by carrying out calculations that involve taking into account the serial number of planet, of nakshatra the planet is in, the navamsha planet is in and the ishta gathi of the native. The various Shayanadi avasthas are as below.

1	Shayana	Resting, Lying down
2	Upaveshana	Sitting down
3	Netrapani	Leading
4	Prakashana	Illuminating
5	Gamana	Coming
6	Agamana	Coming and going
7	Sabha	In the audience
8	Aagama	Flowing
9	Bhojana	Eating
10	Nrityalipsa	Dancing
11	Kautuka	Desiring
12	Nidra	Sleeping

It should be noted that when evaluating results, planets with auspicious avastha give excellent results but are influenced by Chesthas (awakening state). They come by additional calculations involving taking into account the first letter or name of the person and the previously obtained avatha.

Dhrishti Chestha gives mediocre results, Chestha gives full results and Vicheshta (still) gives very little results. Conversely, if the planets are in a bad state, the adverse effects of the planets will be reduced to moderate, completely reduced or insignificantly reduced.

In conclusion, we can say that the effects of avasthas should not be considered in isolation, but should apply specifically to yoga and the associations and judgments of the planets in the various houses, conjunctions, planetary signs and dashas.

Position of Planets – Own House/Exalted/Debilitated/ MoolTrikona According to Vedic astrology, the positions of the planets in the zodiac are considered important in determining their influence on human life and events. The positions of the planets can be described as Exalted, Debilitated or neutral, and these are based on the positions of the planets in relation to the zodiac signs.

Based on Exalted, Debilitated or neutral positions of the planet, astrologers predict and give their astrological advice. There are number of other factors that are considered by an astrologer before arriving at any conclusion.

The Exalted planets are considered to be in the strongest and most active positions. When a planet is in its exalted state, it is said to produce positive effects and effects, and is said to have a beneficial effect on the individual's life. For example, when the Sun is in Aries, it is considered to be in a state of exaltation and is said to bring success, confidence and positive energy to the individual.

On the other hand, debilitated planets are considered to be in the weakest and most negative positions. When a planet is in a debilitated state, it is believed to produce negative effects and influences, and is said to hurt the individual's life. For example, when the Moon is in Scorpio, it is considered debilitated and is said to bring emotional instability and negativity to the individual.

Neutral planets are not considered to have significant strengths or weaknesses. When a planet is in a neutral position, it is said to produce neither positive nor negative results, and its influence on the individual's life is considered moderate.

For all planets except Mercury, the signs of exaltation are different from those that are ruled by each planet. As for Mercury, Virgo is the sign of exaltation and is also ruled by Mercury.

Each planet, except for the Sun and Moon, rules two houses. Out of the signs a planet has, whichever one the planet feels most comfortable with or most closely resembles the planet's nature that sign will become its Moola Trikona sign. For example, Venus rules Taurus and Libra, and Saturn rules Capricorn and Aquarius. Now, out of these two signs, the planet has one which is the Mool-Trikona sign. In other words, it's his main/permanent home. This is the house in which the planet feels most comfortable and therefore stronger than the others. As for the Sun and Moon, since they have only one sign as their ruling house, they have no other choice.

The other house can be considered his vacation house. Therefore, if Mercury is placed in your 2nd house, it will be more responsible for the 12th house because Virgo is Mercury's Mooltrikona house.

Table Showing Exaltation/Debilitation/Own Rashi/Mool Trikona

Planet	Peak Exaltation Point	Peak Debilitation Point	Moola Trikona	Own Rashi
Sun	Aries (0° – 10°)	Libra (0° – 10°)	Aries (0° – 20°) Leo (0° – 20°)	Leo (20° – 30°)
Moon	Taurus (0° – 3°)	Scorpio (0° – 3°)	Taurus (3° – 30°) Cancer (0° – 10°)	Cancer (10° – 30°)
Mars	Capricorn (0° – 28°)	Cancer (0° – 28°)	Capricorn (28° – 30°) Aries (0° – 12°)	Aries (12° – 30°) & Scorpio

				(0° – 30°)
Mercury	Virgo (0° – 15°)	Pisces (0° – 15°)	Virgo (16° – 20°)	Virgo (20° – 30°) &Gemini (0° – 30°)
Jupiter	Cancer (0° – 5°)[1]	Capricorn (0° – 5°)	Cancer (5° – 30°) Sagittarius (0° – 10°)	Sagittarius (10° – 30°) & Pisces (0° – 30°)
Venus	Pisces (0° – 27°)[1]	Virgo (0° – 27°)	Libra (0° – 15°)[2] Pisces (27° – 30°)[3]	Libra (15° – 30°)[4] & Taurus (0° – 30°)[5]
Saturn	Libra (0° – 20°)	Aries (0° – 20°)	Libra (20° – 30°) Aquarius (0° – 20°)	Aquarius (20° – 30°) & Capricorn (0° – 30°)
Rahu	Gemini Taurus	Sagittarius Scorpio	Virgo	Aquarius
Ketu	Sagittarius Scorpio	Gemini Taurus	Pisces	Scorpio

PLANETS IN VEDIC ASTROLOGY

Now let's study about the nine planets that are mentioned in Vedic Astrology.

(i) Surya : Represent planet Sun

Rules: Leo

Exalted: Aries

Debilitated: Libra

Exalted / Debilitated Degree: 10°

Mahadasha period: 06 years

Principle: vitality, sense of individuality; creative energy; radiant inner self (attainments of sour); essential values.

Urges represented: urge to be and to create.

Needs symbolized: Needs to be recognized and to express self.

Positive expression: Radiation of spirit; creative and loving pouring of self.

Negative expressions: Pride, Arrogance; Excessive desire to be special.

The sun, which is the life-giving heart of our solar system, rules both will and individuality. It conveys your capability and uniqueness as an individual—who you are and what you are about. It represents the primary path and recognition you need in your life and your dedication to performing what you set out to do. The sun's position and strength in your horoscope demonstrate the intensity of your honesty and integrity, the capacity to command, recognize, and use authority, and have an effect on others.

Surya, the solar god, is the foremost of the Navagrahas. The sun represents the self and has masculine strength. He is the ruler of the zodiac sign Leo and is the lord of the Krittika, Uttaraphalguni, and Uttarashada Nakshatras. The sun takes a month's time to navigate through every zodiac sign, and it takes 12 months to come back around all 12 zodiac signs. Its motion is pretty fixed, and many Indian festivals are celebrated as per the entry of the sun in different zodiac signs; e.g., on January 14th, the sun enters Makara, and this day is celebrated as Makar Sankranti. On April 13 or 14th, it enters Mesha, and these days are well known as Baisakhi. The change in seasons is likewise related to the entry of the sun in different signs and nakshatra (constellations).

Sun is also recognized by different names like Mitra, Ravi, Bhanu, Khaga, Pushan, Marichi, Aditya, Savitha, Arka, and Bhaskara. He is also called Ajan, which means self-created.

The Sun is a majestic graha possessing the qualities of conscience, intelligence, individuality, bravery, authority, royalty, higher office, devotion to God, leadership, ability to withstand struggles, immunity, fame, self-reliance, liberal mindset, honor, and trustworthiness.

He signifies father, and the fame of the king; he holds energy and authority and rules over respiration, the mouth, throat, and spleen in a human physique. It represents the soul, strength of mind, father, paternal relations, the king, or excessive officials. It is warm and angry. The color is red, the metal is gold, and the gem is a ruby, which represents the east.

Surya, the sun, is depicted with four arms, having a lotus flower, a conch, a chakra, a discus, and a gada, the mace. The sun is usually portrayed as sitting on a chariot that is being driven by seven horses.

These seven horses represent the seven colors of the rainbow, red, green, orange, yellow, blue, indigo, and violet. The seven horses are also represented as the seven chakra centers within the subtle human body and the seven days of the week.

If the sun is well positioned inside the horoscope, the native is likely to be bestowed with intelligence, sturdy will, vitality, energy, authority, bravery, leadership, and courage. At the same time, if the sun is just too strongly located, it brings pride, ego, overconfidence, self-centered nature, outshining anyone else, etc., but a weakly-positioned solar may turn someone right into a weak being due to a lack of self-belief, low self-esteem, meekness, being likely to be dominated by others, and having a lack of enthusiasm.

Aditya Hridayam Stotram is the sacred textual content of Surya and is a hymn in glorification and praise of him, considering him the ruler of the universe, the remover of all illnesses, and the repository of peace. This prayer is considered the best among the numerous verses of Surya. Devotees have faith that regular chanting of the hymn may help wash away all sins, dispel all doubts, getting rid of concerns and sorrows, and offering the benefits of whole prosperity.

Natural Friends of Sun: The Moon, Mars, and Jupiter

Neutral: Mercury

Natural Enemies of Sun: Venus, Saturn, Rahu, and Ketu

Effect of Sun in different Houses: There are many things to evaluate while giving predictions about placement of Sun in horoscope like sign of the house, conjunction of other planet(s), aspects of other planet(s), degree of Sun, the condition of house lord etc. However, the general predictions about placement of Sun in different Houses of a horoscope are as below:

1st House: The sun in the ascendant, lagna, or 1st house of the horoscope blesses a person with leadership, a striking personality, and passion. He will be an obedient, respectful person to his father. On the contrary, anger, violence, and laziness might prevail. He considers himself superior. This person is very aggressive. This position of the sun also indicates the leadership of this person. Sometimes it demands more authority than responsibility. The presence of the sun in the ascendant makes one egocentric. Therefore, it helps to have the sun in the 1st house, where leadership is needed with authorities, government, and especially in professional life. But on the other side, it may create problems in your private life; you may have children and family problems. Overconfidence sometimes pushes people over the edge in money-related matters too. The sun in the 1st house can make a person emotional and selfish, but they care about others as well as the sun. Also, people whose sun is in the first house can be talkative and extroverts. This type of behavior is not necessarily good at many stages of life.

2nd House: The 2nd house is related to finances, family, nourishment, etc. The native likes to be financially autonomous and will gain finances from business or from the government. The individual may end up as a representative or spokesperson for the government. The individual may like to eat illustrious nourishment or like to eat different and royal foods. A solid craving for riches can be seen. In the event that the sun is weak or frail in the horoscope, at that point, natives may have issues or problems related to the eyes or issues related to the facial region, like scars or burns. Native may have problems related to speech or stammering. The placement of the sun in this house might make the individual fickle-minded. His intellect may be slanted towards logical and scientific subjects. The individual gains finances through hard work. He may get entrapped in court cases and have the propensity to resist the older folks. The person's wellbeing may diminish.

3rd House: The Sun in the 3rd house in the horoscope helps natives become powerful, influential, politicians, and have a courageous nature. This position of the sun bestows luxury, and such individuals can be relied upon. The location of the sun in the 3rd house tells us that the native loves talking and is likely to be a customary speaker. He'll have accomplishments in the fields of editing, printing, and distributing. This positioning, however, places the association with a more youthful brother or sister beside other relatives. The more youthful brothers, sisters, neighbors, or co-workers may achieve higher positions in their lives. The native will be blessed, extraordinary-looking, well-taught, effective, shrewd, courageous, and in an authoritative position. They adore voyaging and might travel a lot as a part of their career. The native is wise and shares his wisdom. The sun in the 3rd house can make an individual great at communicating, distributing, and altering work. An individual with the sun in the 3rd house may have a striking identity and favor great fortune. But some of the time it makes a native drifter as well as much more open in talking. Some of the time, these individuals can deliver additional comfort to their subordinates. This position of Sun, however, can deny an individual the backs of colleagues, and the individual can be inclined to misuse, backbite, and extort. Now and then, the best of their efforts are not recognized, and they might feel low and deprived.

4th House: The 4th house is the house of family, possessions, properties, and so on. The placement of the sun in the 4th house means that the native takes a lot of interest in matters concerning the domestic side of his or her life. It's about the homeland; it's about the mother's nourishment that you get in the home. They take good care of the family's welfare and social status. The native identifies himself by what he loves and feels like home is where the heart is. The person may own property as an heir. They have more introverted personalities and love being inside the home. The sun in the 4th house also gives the natives increased energy and strength in the latter half of life. These people usually find success later on in their lives because the sun is the vitality of your soul, the engine that fuels you, and it wasn't there when you were born. But the sun rises, and when it rises, it brightens up your life. The person with the sun in the 4th house in his horoscope can be heartless and selfish by nature. He may also deceive others into going ahead. He may suffer from blood pressure disorders.

5th House: According to Vedic astrology, the 5th house is the natural home of the sun. Leo is the 5th Zodiac sign. This house is associated with creative abilities, academic education, creativity, happiness, business, the stock market, film, acting, stage, academic education, cultural education, etc. When the sun enters the 5th house, everything lights up. Natives love to talk about politics, creative ideas, philosophy, and ancient texts, scriptures, and books. They want to be part of these creative aspects of life so that they can put them into practice. In terms of academic career, people with this place of the sun are very daring;

they like to be the center of attention. This is where their ego is located, in education and self-expression.

They love to share their knowledge, creativity, and business skills. They share a good relationship with their father. They respect and care for their elders. They have good intellectual ability. They have good political skills. They have honorable and successful attachments. They have a social and pleasure-loving personality. They are intelligent and gain through judicious speculation. They are easily moved. They have a loveable and sincere personality. They are generous and sincere. They have good travel habits. They are smart and intelligent. They are well-versed in the Shastra. They enjoy manipulating others. They accumulate wealth. They are careless and negligent. They might suffer from the denial of children. Chest pain is the probable cause of death.

Phaladeepika says that such a person will suffer the denial of children. However, we do not agree with this statement. It depends on the sign of the child, nature of the 5th house sign, lord of the sign, aspects of the sign, etc. However, one thing is proven by our experience: natives suffer from first sons.

6th House: The sun in this house is also known as Ripu Hanta, Shatru Hanta, and Shatari. It is believed that the sun in the 6th house protects individuals from enemies, sickness, sorrows, and debts. It is also associated with greed, passion, strength, gentleness, and the role of king, general, or judge. It is not considered good for my maternal uncle and his family. Native may encounter accidents involving cows, buffalo, or sharp-horned animals, and chances of robbery are also there. In this position, the sun is a powerful Shatru Nashak. Generally, the 6th house has a weak constitution; however, if it is surrounded by benefic planets, health can be improved, but it must be safeguarded. In the business world, one gains when they associate with a companion. It is commonly believed that the 6th House of the Sun is bad; however, many savants consider it to be beneficial, as the 6th House is posited by the maleficent planet Sun. According to the teachings of the Satyacharyas, the 6th Sun has the power to destroy enemies positively.

The 6th house of astrology is also associated with servitude, loss, hostility, illness, and conflict. This indicates a person who is more inclined to assist others than themselves or their family. Additionally, they possess analytical skills for resolving issues. Generally, when the sun is in a favorable alignment, a person can become wealthy, attractive, healthy, able to overcome adversity, wise, and helpful to others, as well as accumulate wealth. Additionally, a favorable aspect of Mars, Jupiter, or Venus can bring about good health, prosperity, and success through the assistance of subordinates, staff, promotion, and luck. This person is also known for their administrative abilities, as well as their courage and ability to maintain a positive relationship with relatives. Ultimately, success is achieved through hard work.

7th House: The 7th House is considered the house of marital bliss; it has a great impact on a native's personal and married life. The 7th house represents the commitment and legal binding of marriage, business partnerships, and sexual relationships. A negative sun in the 7th house indicates that the person is having a difficult marital life. It also indicates that the spouse is more egoistic, aggressive, or full of anger at times. On the other hand, a positive sun in the 7th house indicates the person to be motivated, take care of their wife, improve romance and love life, and keep the person away from disease. Because of the energy of the sun, it can bless a person with a good career, a high position, and a position in the government. A positive and balanced sun is needed for the best marital life. A strong sun is needed to achieve career success, especially in the organization, but after facing competition, the person may have several marriages. His married life is not peaceful and happy. The life partner is very ambitious. Here, the person will strive to be better than others, and it will lead to conflict between them. The person will face lots of opposition from 'others'. An exalted sun gives people leadership qualities and makes them judges and lawyers.

8th House: The 8th house is associated with transformation and change. It also deals with fear, death, witchcraft, insurance, etc. The 8th house also deals with wills, greed, dowry, chronic diseases, loss of fortune, extravagance, suit and quarrel, death, witchcraft, and co-workers.

Natives can expect to gain from wives and partnerships, ancestral wealth, steady fortune after marriage, and fame late in life. They are interested in culture, science, and success and are very famous. Only when the sun is well aspected in the 8th house can it boost vigor and offer long life.

The native is handsome but lazy, rich but thrifty, travels a lot, but also quarrels with some people. He might have bad eyesight. Natives are likely to be violent and have fewer progeny. He is fickle-minded, generous, talkative, and long-lived. He has little happiness from the Son, if not denied. He will not get respect from the government. He will try for a government job but fail repeatedly. This will lead to frustration and disappointment. He may have differences with his father. He may suffer from some diseases. He will inherit from his father. He is interested in occult sciences like astrology or searching for the unknown. He has a spiritual inclination. He will have a liberal mindset and will talk more about philosophy.

9th House: This house stands for law, your father, your instructors' home, religion, and spirituality. Your soul, ego, self-worth, vigor, father figure, and authority are all represented by the sun. People tend to obey the rules and are heavily influenced by their fathers. Such natives are in constant search for wisdom.

Additionally, it represents luck, riches, and lengthy travels like pilgrimages. The sun's ego therefore grows as it enters the 9th house. At this point, the native's father's guidance and teachings have a significant impact on him. Your sense of self-worth and ego will entirely be based on what your father and teachers have taught you.

As a result, this individual is limited by what he has learned during his life. From this placement, one can view attorneys, judges, professors, and clergy. They like enforcing restrictions on others. Because it is so difficult to crush this person's ego, they may engage in ego conflicts with their dads. These are the folks who, when they travel, want their adventure to have a purpose and provide them with some learning.

10th House: The sun in the 10th house is in an advantageous position as it is in its strongest position in this place. The 10th house is concerned with karma, career, and concerned activities. Natives are born leaders and are likely to act as leaders for others. Most of the time, the native doesn't like to be bossed around. He either works for the government or starts his own business. Because the 10th house represents the highest part of the visible zodiac, it's related to public life. The sun forces the natives to spend the entire day outdoors. He doesn't enjoy being alone and prefers to be around people like kings and politicians. He will be hurt if he's left out or ignored. People with the sun in the 10th house hold positions of power in the private and public sectors. This means executive jobs, professional growth, and government jobs. If the sun in the 10th house is in your house, then you will only succeed if you put in a lot of work and learn new skills. The high level in your profession is achieved by the native with the sun in this house. He puts his name and recognition first. Athletes, fighters, soldiers, CEOs, and presidents often have this placement of the sun in this house because it's the house of the presidency.

11th House: The 11th house represents gains in different areas of your growth, prosperity, objectives, etc. The most significant house of prosperity is the 11th house. Strong indicators of income, unanticipated wealth, success, and prosperity can be seen from this house. Your social circle and business contacts are at home. This is Saturn's original home, so when the Sun moves into it, it causes a lot of discomfort.

Both Saturn and the Sun don't get along well since they both have different temperaments. This disposition makes people want more attractive things. A better degree of collaboration is what it seeks to establish. Such natives may not enjoy socializing with socially disadvantaged individuals. Livelihood or financial gains are not the native's primary goals. He thinks about the higher purpose of existence.

Native may think about starting a company that employs many people or overhauling society as a whole. One can easily become the group's leader and get the respect of others because the house represents the group or groups. He will have a long life and be wealthy. It is effective in higher positions. His companions might interfere. He will need less energy to gather beneficial presents.

He is capable of working in more senior roles. His pals may have an impact. The connection with one's elder brothers would be strained. He will be able to earn a lot of money with little effort.

12th House: The 12th house is the house of hidden talents, hidden enemies, hidden treasures, spirituality, and beliefs. The sun in this house enhances the ability to recognize hidden enemies and hidden skills. Native have a good sense of art. This house helps establish international relations or foreign trade with other countries. The sun in the 12th house can harm human life.

The sun in the 12th house shows occult and psychic tendencies and different tastes and preferences. Natives can fight their enemies and excel in medicine, occult science, chemistry, etc. Native might hate his father. If the sun is eclipsed here, the eyesight will not be good. A person can have many evils. Native enjoy long journeys to foreign countries and are likely to succeed there.

Festivals like Pongal or Makara Sankranti, Rathasaptami, Chath, and Samba Dasami are important Indian festivals committed to Lord Surya. There are various temples dedicated to the sun, e.g., the Suryanar Temple in the southern part of India and the Konark Solar Temple in the northeast part of India.

Sunday is the day of the week for the sun; the valuable gem is ruby; the flowers are the red lotus, hibiscus, and red oleander; and wheat, or broken wheat, is the grain for the sun. The sun is continually draped in red shade cloth.

According to Hindu mythology, the renowned progenies of Surya are Shani (Saturn), Yama (God of Death), and Karna (Kunti Putra in Mahabharatha). To gain the blessings of the sun, one need to worship him every day in the morning after having a bath, look at the early morning sun, provide water to him, and pay salutations by chanting the Gayatri Mantra or Aditya Hrudaya Mantra.

(ii) Chandra: Represents planet Moon

Rules: Cancer

Exalted: Taurus

Debilitated: Scorpio

Exalted / Debilitated Degree: 3°

Mahadasha Period: 10 years

Principle: Reaction, Subconscious predisposition, Feeling about self (self-image), Conditional Responses.

Urges represented: Urge to feel inner support; Domestic and Emotional Security.

Needs symbolized: Need for emotional Tranquility and sense of belonging, Need to feel right about self.

Positive Expression: Responsiveness, inner contentment; flowing; adaptable sense of self. Negative expression: over sensitivity; insecurity, inaccurate; inhibits self of self.

Chandra, also known as the Moon, is 2nd among the Navagrahas, or the nine planets. Chandra is considered a lunar god and is also known by the name of Soma. He is portrayed as youthful, wonderful, reasonable, two-armed, and having a club and a lotus in his hands. He rides his chariot (the moon) over the sky each night, pulled by ten white horses.

He is associated with dew and is one of the gods responsible for fertility. He is additionally called Nishadipati (Nisha=night; Adipathi=Lord) and Kshuparaka (one who lights up the night). He, as Soma, presides over Somvar, or Monday. He is of Sattva Guna and connected with the mind and the thoughts.

Chandra is a royal planet and the queen of astrology. It is associated with the mind, emotions, and sensitivity; motherhood; home and domestic comfort; milk; the sea; and all related industries related to the sea, including hotels, food, textiles, and apparel. Its color is white, its direction is north-west, its metal is silver, and its gem is a pearl. The Moon is the fastest-moving of the nine planets, taking approximately two and a-half days to traverse a sign.

The Moon is the ruler of the 4th house in the zodiac chart, i.e., Cancer, and its presiding deity is the Divine Goddess Parvati. The moon is associated with feminine creative energy and is responsible for regulating the state of mind, emotions, and intuition. It is also responsible for influencing one's attachment to things, people, and how they influence others, their moods, and their character. Additionally, the Moon gives birth, pregnancy, childbirth, and fertility to the Lord Chandra, who is also the Lord of Plants and Vegetables. In Hindu mythology, the Lord Chandra is depicted as a fair and young man, wearing a club and carrying a lotus in his hands. He rides a chariot through the sky each night, accompanied by a dozen white horses or antelope. He is also referred to by various names, such as 'Soma', 'Rajanipati', 'Kushuparaka', 'Indu', and 'Chandra'.

Hindu mythology tells us that Lord Chandra arrived from the ocean during the time when the ocean was being churned. He's the one who gave birth to Budha (the planet Mercury). He married Lord Daksha's 27 daughters. The name of 27 Nakshatras is as per the names of 27 wives of Lord Chandra.

The 100 names of Lord Chandra are found in the sacred text, namely Ashtottara Shatanamavali. The moon is praised as the Lord of the wise men and the Lord of all sorrows. It also removes the affliction caused by the sins of the ancestors. The text also conveys that the moon is also a fulfiller of wishes and dreams. The worship of Lord Chandra brings relief from all sorrows. It also increases mental and emotional power. Lord Chandra worships Lord Shiva's head. The most effective way to get his blessing is to worship Lord Chandra on Mondays.

When the Sun is in the same sign as the Moon, the day is referred to as Amavasya, or the New Moon day, or the first day of the dark fortnight. The number of lunar days, or Tithi, varies with each 12-degree variation between the Sun and Moon. Conversely, when the Sun and Moon reside in the opposite sign or are 180 degrees apart from each other, the day is known as Poornima, or the Full Moon Day, or the First Day of the Bright Fortnight. The moon is the matra karaka, or planet connected with the mother.

When the moon is placed in a strong position, it is associated with qualities such as encouragement, care, sensitivity, and receptivity, as well as emotional maturity, mental strength, responsibility, and being beneficial to others. Conversely, when the moon is placed poorly or is associated with a planet that has negative energy, it is referred to as an afflicted moon. An afflicted moon can lead to mental disorders, emotional instability, confusion, poor judgment, and personality disorders. The Moon is susceptible to the energy of other planets and is associated with relationships and communication with other people. There are a number of slokas and mantras attributed to Lord Chandra, such as Chandra Gayatri, Chandra Kavacham, and Sri Chandra Stotram.

Where the moon is placed in your birth chart, it is called your Janma Rashi or Moon Sign, and the constellation in which the moon is placed is called your Janma Nakshatra.

Natural Friends of Moon: Sun and Mercury

Neutral: Mars, Jupiter, Venus, Saturn, Rahu, and Ketu

Natural Enemies of Moon: None

Effect of Moon in different Houses: There are many things to evaluate while giving predictions about placement of Moon in horoscope like sign of the house, conjunction of other planet(s), aspects of other planet(s), degree of Moon, the condition of house lord etc.

However the general predictions about placement of Moon in different Houses of a horoscope are as below:

1st House: When the moon is in the 1st house of your chart, you will be able to predict two aspects of your life at the same time: one from the ascendant position and the other from the moon. The first house represents yourself and your individuality. The moon represents your mind, your emotions, and your inner core. In general, people in the first house are beautiful, handsome, young, and energetic. They are also very emotional and sensitive. They are very polite and have nice manners. They prioritize emotions and feelings over practicality and logic. They love beauty in all things. Their mother is a big influence on them. They inherit these qualities from their mother. Aries, Leo, or Sagittarius in the first house gives you a focused, ambitious, goal-oriented mind with defined principles and goals in life. In the 1st house of Cancer, Scorpius, or Pisces in your horoscope, you will have a secretive, sensitive, emotional, and sensitive personality, especially in love and relationships. The 1st house of your horoscope gives you a bit of emotional instability, moodiness, and a fickle mind.

The combination of the moon in the 1st house of Libra or Aquarius makes the natives successful in career and marriage and keeps them happy and balanced. The moon in the ascendant house of Taurus, Gemini, Virgo, Capricorn, etc. makes the native's rich in life, but with a certain delay. The combination of the moon and the first house of Aquarius give the natives artistic and creative talents and make them successful in their early years. If afflicted with the moon, they will have many problems with it. They dream of the sea, the water, the river, etc. The natives are very creative and intuitive. The problem is that they are unable to fix anything. They are emotionally charged up, very quick to react, mood swings quickly, and restless. The natives may take up occupations related to sea and water products, sports, psychology, etc.

2nd House: The 2nd house in astrology is responsible for money, values, and material things. When the moon is in the 2nd house, it has a big impact on an individual's financial security and material attachment. Those with the Moon in the 2nd house tend to look for emotional security through money and often look for comfort in material things. The 2nd house of wealth creates the habit of charity in the person. The person's face is attractive. The person is always trying to be happy. The person is very attached to the family. The person is a nature lover and spends time appreciating the beauty of nature. The person's personality is calm and polite. He is a rational and reliable person in his personal life. The person loves to work for the public's welfare. A person's emotional security is directly linked to their financial security.

Due to the presence of the moon in the 2nd house of astrology, the natives of this house tend to spend too much money, which can lead to financial difficulties. They get so attached to their property that they lose their family life. Since the 2nd house is a permanent house of Venus, it continues to affect the Moon's performance in this house. The friendly support of Venus means that the Moon always gives good results to the natives of this house. Most likely, you will not have a sister, but you will have brothers. Even if your wife does not have brothers, you will often get your share of the parents' property. There are strong chances of having a male child and a native getting a good education, which will help them excel in their profession.

3rd **House:** When the Moon is in the 3rd house of the Natal chart, people have great communication abilities and strong emotional bonds with siblings. They are able to express their thoughts and feelings with great clarity and sensitivity, which makes them good communicators and compassionate listeners. The Moon's influence in the 3rd House also increases their ability to empathize with others on a deeper level.

The 3rd House in astrology symbolizes communication, intelligence, and the environment around us. When the Moon is in the 3rd House of Natives' chart, it accentuates an individual's emotional communication skills, intellectual interests, and bond with siblings or neighbors. This person has the ability to influence others through their speech and written work. They travel a lot and are less talkative, as they tend to make less use of words. They also have a curious nature.

4th **House:** The 4th house of the moon will bring a lot of comfort and luxury to your life. Your mother will be happy, but there may be health problems. Natives will be very calm and naturally emotionally balanced. This person can become rich at the age of 27. The 4th house will bring good career opportunities and prosperity to your hometown or birthplace. A native person can become a politician or a freelancer.

The position in the 4th house makes a native very attached to his family, especially his mother. Family is very important to them, and they act as protectors of their family. Such kinds of people have a generous, loving, and caring personality.

5th House: The 5th house represents wisdom, offspring, love, creativity, etc. Because the Moon is a planet of sensitivity and expression, the native will become quite passionate and emotional when it comes to matters of the heart. They might date frequently. The moon will greatly enhance the person's inventiveness in this house of creativity. They will be at ease and have the ability to sense. They may be insightful and possess a strong imagination. Past lives are shown in the 5th house. It makes someone more jovial. He has a strong desire to find a romantic partner. One of his interests is investing in the stock market. He naturally shows an interest in creative fields. They would receive highly favorable outcomes from their past karma, which again depends on the 5th lord, if the moon is in a favorable position in the chart. They'll be quite cognizant of their subconscious mind. They will have a great influence on kids. There could be more daughters. They'll be enthusiastic about music, particularly about musical instruments. They get wealthy as a result of the moon's karakas being in their 5th house and interacting with their 11th house.

6th House: The 6th house is known in astrology as the first negative house. It's about work, health, daily life, service, responsibilities, and many other negative things, while the moon represents emotions, habits, nurturing, and comfort. The Moon is a very soft planet and hates being indoors, but this proves difficult. The moon shows emotion, so the person is busy dealing with all things in the 6th house. In traditional astrology, the moon in the 6th house is considered a sign of psychological problems. When the Moon is in a bad place, aspect, or conjunction, Native has to take medicine.

The moon is a maternal omen, and the mother is indivisible from the moon. The Jatakas with the Moon in the 6th house will find employment caring for the underprivileged. These people are primarily able to work in the medical or paramedic professions. They don't like changes in their routine. Failure to do so may affect their well-being. These people are close to the maternal relatives, as the 6th house shows the maternal relatives. The downside is that these people will always have their own livelihood and career insecurity. Women will be their main enemies. You have an emotional need to be useful, to be productive, to be organized, to stay on top of things, and to live a healthy life. To feel happy, you need variety in your work, and you need to be inspired. Some people change jobs frequently. They find it difficult to accept that all jobs require a certain level of routine.

They are very sensitive and perceive mostly minor health problems and body pain. Some people show symptoms of hypochondria. Some people try to get away from things they don't want to do by overemphasizing their health problems or illnesses in order to gain sympathy. But at best, they are people who are always willing to help and show affection to others in practical ways to solve problems and improve their lives.

7th House: The 7th house signifies marriage, partnership, other people, etc. Here, the moon makes a person emotionally attached to their mate. They will become dependent on others. Their spouse will be young and full of energy. They may have many relationships. They will take ample time to find their soul mate. They will be very confused about the matter of marriage, but they will have an early marriage. This person's life partner is handsome and obedient. Material affluence is there. He is very popular with the people around him. In addition, he is praised anywhere and anytime in the group, wherever he is present. He can achieve prosperity through his hard work. He cooperates with people when he is with them. They can do business with women. They will be frequent travelers and enjoy seeing different places. Travel will also be for business purposes. Determination and frankness are their strengths. They have a benevolent attitude toward those close to them. On a professional level, any uncertainty is unlikely to stop them from progressing. They will minimize their workload and do their work systematically and efficiently. Here, the Moon also aspects the first house, so if the Moon is benefic, it will be of great help to the destiny. of native

8th House: The 8th house is one of the least auspicious houses in the horoscope, and a planet usually loses all its auspicious meaning when placed in this house. The 8th house is the 12th house (house of loss) to the 9th house, which signifies luck and prosperity. Therefore, the moon in this house will damage one's possessions and comfort. He will be deprived of the comfort of transportation because the moon means traffic in the 8th place. The 8th house is a strong sign of an accident. Since the Moon is a watery planet, drowning would be life-threatening. The moon in the 8th house will separate the native from his relationships for the sake of his wife, as the 8th house is his wife's Kutumba sthana. It is especially a bad position for the moon, as it damages the relationship with the mother. The mother may have a secretive nature, or she will have a lot of struggles and conflicts in her life. It will be difficult for the native to understand his mother. It is also the house of transformation. Such native's will be attracted to mysticism and occult science. They may have some sort of intuitive power. They will become healers. Due to dark experiences in life, they will turn to meditation. When the moon faces the 2nd house, they will have difficulty getting along with family members. Their financial situation will fluctuate. The moon in the 8th house causes 'Balarishta' to disturb the child in all forms, such as illness, etc. This is primarily a bad position for the moon in most cases. This moon becomes the reason for divorce or relationship breakdown.

9th House: The 9th house deals with fortune, luck, religion, morality, father, teacher, etc. Natives with the moon in the 9th house are likely to have good luck in most areas. They will have a strong mindset and a strong belief system in religious matters. They will have the power to imagine and also be intuitive. They will have a lot of luck in matters of monetary gain. The mind will always think about higher learning and intellectual expansion. They can travel to places related to religion or philosophy. Mothers play a more important role in their lives than fathers. Most likely, the mother will be extroverted and also interested in financial matters. Prosperity can also be seen in agriculture, medicine, especially vanaspati and herbal medicine, liquid chemistry, etc. The moon in 9th house makes one a religious individual. Natives are experts in their fields. He may have to change careers. He may have to travel a lot in his life. Natives will have a comfortable and long service life. He is philosophical and also curious about the world. Their interest in learning new languages and getting to know different cultures will force them to travel to different places. The influence of the moon in the 9th house will grant the natives extra special abilities.

10th House: The 10th house denotes occupation, current karma, public life, etc. Their main motivations for a native with the Moon in the 10th house are authority, power, and achievement. There is a strong need for a positive public image and a desire to communicate with the public. They will achieve material success. They will bond emotionally with their co-workers. They will easily make friends at work. They will also be subject to office politics. This position is good for all planets, and in the 10th house, the moon gives most people a career in the medical or hospitality sector, especially if it is in Cancer, Libra, or Pisces. The 10th house is the house of career, profession, honor, etc. If there is no adverse effect on the moon and the owner of the house is well, it will bring beneficial results to all meanings of this house. Indigenous people will do good deeds and are very smart and kind. Since the moon will aspect the native's 3rd house, he will gain a high level of education. The moon signifies fluctuations, so a career will have fluctuations. These people will find it difficult to control their emotions. They will openly express their feelings, which can be a problem for them. The moon signifies the spirit, and those with the moon in the 10th house will also work on their imaginative skills. The 10th house signifies the wealth of the father, so jathakas in this position will be proud of their father. Fathers will have a huge influence in their lives. With bad influences on the moon, the meaning of the 10th house will be ruined, and the native will fall into sinful acts of all kinds, and his life will be full of obstacles. If the Moon is in its own Cancer sign (the ascendant will be Libra), the lord of the 10th house will be in the 10th house, creating a powerful Raj yoga and bestowing name, fame, and honor on the natives.

11th House: The 11th house deals with gains of all types, networks of people, etc. The position of the moon in this house is very favorable if placed positively. This position of the moon indicates an emotional need for a sense of belonging, support from friends, and affiliation with groups. Such people will look to acquaintances for help and reciprocate the same. An altered or unstable social life may be a reflection of inner emotional turmoil. Emotional ups and downs for others can cause problems in their relationships. A native is a person filled with many dreams, desires, and hopes for the future, and most of them are selfless and kind wishes. They will be much respected personality in society. They will have many friends, especially women. They will be very expressive and enjoy being around people. They may be emotionally attached to older siblings. Usually, they will have more sisters than brothers. Since the 11th house is one of the houses of 'Kama trikona', they will be very passionate and eager. There may be a strong need for material possessions, love, sex, etc. They seem very attractive to the opposite sex. They can also be selfish at times. As aspects of the 5th house of the moon, they are artistically gifted. However, indigenous people can change their aspirations often due to mood swings, and it is difficult to set goals to achieve accordingly. Such people succeed easily. He helps his friends a lot and has many friends. He is lucky.

12th House: The 12th house talks about deliverance, loss, hospitals, strangers, etc. Since the 12th house talks about loss, here the mind will lose its emotions and its sensitivity. Natives with their moon in the 12th house are usually very harsh, rude, and feel isolated. They can become very selfish. Favorable planetary aspects on the moon would be an advantage. Otherwise, it will be difficult for them to balance. This position of the moon shows an emotional attachment and sensitivity to all that is ethereal, groundless, and eternal. The 12th house is about spirituality and liberation. Here, the mind will oscillate towards the spirit. If the other planets, especially the Sun and the 12th Lord, don't help, they feel discouraged. They will go through turmoil. Their mother will be in a lot of trouble. They may spend a lot of time alone. Weakness of vision and a lack of closeness to the mother may occur. They often have problems in their married lives. They often suffer from loss of money, loss of reputation, high spending, and confusion. Sometimes this moon gives the habit of drinking as a habit. This position produces very talented writers, healers, and spiritual personalities. This location allows foreign visitors from the sea and may even offer the opportunity to settle permanently abroad. If the moon in the 12th house is weak, the natives are lazy and prone to emotional disturbances, lack of confidence, poor morals, and poor eyesight. Indigenous people will encounter limitations, will be unstable, and can be easily taken away. Native people will probably always be restless and may face large expenditures.

(iii) **Mangala : Represents planet Mars**

Rules: Aries & Scorpio

Exalted: Taurus

Debilitated: Scorpio

Exalted / Debilitated Degree: 3°

Mahadasha Period: 07 years

Principle desire: Wills towards actions, Initiative, Physical energy, Drive.

Urge represented: Self-assertive and aggressive urge; Sex urge, urge to act decisively. Asserts self through direct physical action; Initiative and outgoing radiation of energy, Uses power and Initiative. Physical energy stimulated by constant movement, Confident Enthusiasm and Dynamic action.

Positive expression: Courage, Initiative, Will power consciously directed towards legitimate aim.

Negative expression: Impatience, Violence, Improper use of force or threat.

Mangala, or Kuja, is the commander in astrology. It represents energy, courage, boys and girls, armed forces, police forces, commanders, managers, people in high positions, earth, engineering, metal, real estate agents, and surgery. It also describes preparation for action, how one does things, and simple aggression.

Its metal is copper, and its gem is coral; its color is red, and its direction is south. Mars takes about 45 days to pass through a sign. He is a Bhatra Karaka, or brother-related planet.

Mars is the 4th planet from the Sun. It is red and is a fiery planet. His energy is masculine. Tuesday is his day, and he rules over the zodiac signs Aries and Scorpio, as well as the stars Mrigashira, Chitra, and Dhanishtha. The transit time of the planet Mars from one sign to another is usually 45 days. However, this is unpredictable because sometimes Mars stays stable in a zodiac sign, even for 6 months. The presiding deity of the planet is Lord Murugan.

He is the god of war and is celibate. He is considered the son of Prithvi or Bhumi, the Goddess of the Earth. He is the owner of the signs Aries and Scorpio, as well as a teacher of occult science (Ruchaka Mahapurusha Yoga). He is the god of war and is celibate. It is Tamas Guna in nature and represents action filled with energy, confidence, and ego.

It also describes preparation for action, how one does things, and simple aggression.

Mars is a powerful planet and symbolises desire, boldness, adventure, physical strength, primal inclinations, self-reliance, strength to resist stress, and nature. Independent, yearning for position, and energy warrior because it is the commander of the divine army. The energy of Mars can be both constructive and destructive, and you must be extremely vigilant.

Angaraka is depicted with four arms, carrying a trident, a mace, a lotus, and a spear. Dressed in red, he usually rides on a ram or goat.

The male energy of Mars shows the projection of our vital and emotional energies, and it shows our passion, drive, and determination. A strong Mars will indicate qualities like vitality, strength, endurance, motivation, courage, etc. In addition, when Mars is in a favourable position, it brings confidence, strong will, insight, and discernment. However, misplaced Mars can cause violence, control, domination, injury, accidents, anger, war, criticism, marriage delays, relationship struggles, etc. The day of the week for Mars is Tuesday, the gem is coral, and the most important flowers are red oleander and red rose. Thuvar Dhal is the grain of Mars. Since Mars color is red, he is always wrapped in a red cloth.

The power point of Mars is Vaitheeswaran Koil, south of Tamil Nadu. Worshipping Mars on Tuesday and its presiding deity, Lord Murugan, removes all afflictions caused by the wrong placement of the planet Mars. He is painted red or fire, has four arms, and carries a trident, a mace, a lotus, and a spear. His Vahana (mountain) is a ram. He presides over 'Mangal-war' or Tuesdays.

Friendly planets of Mars: Sun, Moon, Jupiter

Neutral planets: Venus, Saturn, Rahu, and Ketu

Enemy planets of Mars: Mercury

Effect of Mars in different Houses: There are many things to evaluate while giving predictions about placement of Mars in horoscope like sign of the house, conjunction of other planet(s), aspects of other planet(s), degree of Mars, the condition of house lord etc. However the general predictions about placement of Mars in different Houses of a horoscope are as below:

1st House: The 1st house symbolises physique and self-expression. Since Mars is an aggressive planet, this makes the natives hyperactive. They are very competitive and action-oriented. Their only goal will be to win, no matter what. One can be strong and brave. He will be very impulsive, angry, and explosive. He may be an athlete and practice many different sports, but he only benefits from doing so in the sense of

Eastern martial arts, where natives can learn endurance, attention, and patience. Mars in the first house can also cause a sick ego, aggression, overconfidence, and a dominant attitude towards people. It is very important for him to learn how to maintain his balance.

Such a person would rather be their own boss than follow orders. Mars in the 1st house allows people to stay active in their profession with many ongoing projects. Mars in Ascendant brings a lot of energy and enthusiasm. These energetic people have a clear path, and they will follow it wholeheartedly. When it comes to side effects, like Mars in the first house, people make rash decisions, which can be harmful. Even when being very aggressive, there are problems from time to time. They may possess an aggressive nature and often make their own decisions without consulting others. This position of Mars also causes wounds and burns on the head. Recklessness should be avoided, as it can also lead to accidents.

2nd House: The 2nd house is mainly concerned with family, wealth, words, eating habits, etc. Generally, natives with Mars in the 2nd house rush in financial matters and are not good savers. They should not make important financial decisions independently and should consult with advisors. They will have sharp tongues and reckless use of language unless there is a beneficial edge. They will have an authoritative voice. If Mars is placed in a negative position, they even say insults and add enemies. They may want to dominate the family, and some family members may not like them. They like hot and spicy food. In general, they are natural meat lovers. Since they have a commanding voice, they will do well in commanding roles in the military, police, and security agencies. If the lord of the 2nd house is malefic or placed in 6th, 8th, or 12th houses, the marriage can be delayed or denied. A person under the influence of negative emotions may use vulgar language, causing pain to the interlocutor. Indigenous families can also be deconstructive, emotional, and conflicting, so that natives can foster a similar pattern of behaviour within themselves. Since Mars exposes a person to risk, he can make money on speculation. Such people can spend their savings quite quickly and recklessly. Such a person must work hard and learn to save, because luxury can lead to financial problems. He should strive to develop his oratory skills and influence the masses through his speech to lead a more affluent and fulfilling life.

3rd House: The 3rd house signifies courage, personal effort, communication, brotherhood, etc. Mars in the 3rd house is very suitable. But it must be placed very favourably with the favourable aspect. Mars in this house makes them brave communicators, helping the press, police, and secret services. They will be good at debates. Mars in the 3rd house can make a person confident, bold, and courageous in their communication and intellect. It can give them the motivation to pursue their interests and succeed in their studies and careers. Idealistic spirit, independent vision, and selfishness Wealth will be achieved through courageous action, energy, recklessness, intelligence, determination, management, and education. The risk of accidents is there while driving. Natives are generous, favoured by the emperor, have good health with a toned body, and are gentle.

If Mars is exalted, the native is happy and in love. If debilitated or placed in a sign of an enemy, one suffers from lack, discontent, no friends, and no family life. If Mars conjuncts or is aspected by a malefic planet, the first child is likely to be female. If Mars is in Capricorn or Aquarius, abortion is possible. Exalted Mars, as noted above, is the most auspicious, but if juxtaposed with Saturn or Mercury, it develops creative abilities. Afflicted Mars develops suicidal tendencies. If Mars is in a friendly sign with a malefic, the native is patient.

If Mars is in the 3rd house, it shows that education up to high school might not be smooth. Nature will rebel against the government. Travel accidents also indicate suicidal or violent tendencies. If associated with Rahu, the native abandons his wife, commits adultery with other women, is bold, cruel (to enemies), and has great friends and relations. Mars in Scorpio brings very little wealth.

4th House: The 4th house deals with happiness, houses, vehicles, earth, mother, etc. The 4th house is in the invisible half of the zodiac, and it is a hidden house. Mars is not very comfortable in this house. Mars in the 4th house can make a person assertive and confident in family life. It can make them want to succeed in their home and family lives. It can also give them the ability to protect their family and home. On the negative side, Mars in the 4th house can make a person aggressive, brash, and confrontational in family life. It can also cause conflicts and disagreements with family members.

A person can be demanding with their family members, which can lead to constant tension and passion between the walls in the home. An indigenous mother can be a domineering and ruthless woman or a strong and courageous woman. It is extremely necessary for the owner of the union to increase the level of patience in order to establish a warm relationship with all family members. He may also often leave his home. These people need a place or a method where they can release their excess energy for a more balanced life. They can be involved in construction, working with real estate. It's good to deal with this situation by going to the gym, running a marathon, and having your own sports community and friends in mind.

5th House: The 5th house is associated with intelligence and creativity, as well as education, children, and investment. It is likely to create a bold and creative individual with a lot of action and creativity. However, this is not a comfortable environment for Mars Energy, as it may not be conducive to education and may lead to a lack of focus on studies. It is likely that the individual is passionate and has an increased attraction to the opposite sex, making it difficult for them to control their excess sexual energy. Depending on the intensity of Mars, the individual may either be a gambler or a speculator, depending on the strength of Mars. The individual may also be interested in creative activities related to movement, such as sports. Children of the house, particularly the first, will have a tendency towards characteristics of Mars such as a short temper and egoism, as well as being extremely active, liberal, and native, and might face conflict with children. The 5th house is also associated with emotions, intellect, and mental horizons, making the individual either hyper or dull.

6th House: The 6th house is associated with diseases, conflict, enemies, debts, competition, etc. This house is like a battlefield, and Mars is very content here. For sports players, this position is good because it will help them win the competition. The killer instinct will help them overpower their opponents. The 6th house goes well with the 10th house and complements it.

The house of service is where the person will be most active and competitive in the workplace. It may be difficult for others to compete with him. He may try to control others. He may not like it when others try to teach him. Natives with Mars in the 6th house have the physical strength to do very hard work. He puts a lot of effort and energy into his work. He can be a great manager because he is able to organise, rearrange, sort, classify, and analyse things.

On the other hand, when Mars enters the 6th house, it is easy for him to get impatient and aggressive if others are not working as quickly as him. He may get frustrated if things don't go his way. He may get angry if someone criticises him or disturbs his work.

7th House: Mars in the 7th house can make a person passionate, energetic, and assertive in their relationships. It can give them the drive to pursue their romantic interests and assert their needs in partnerships. Chances of two wives or friction with the wife, dropsy, rash speculations, unsuccessful, intelligent, tactless, stubborn, idiosyncratic, peevish, passionate, tension in married life A person will compete for primacy with all partners in a relationship if they are too emotional and self-centered but he will also look for a partner who is the same: confident, strong, and active. In the 7th house, Mars also gives immense strength and aggression. The 7th house belongs to married life and its pleasures. Mars here may make a person impatient and violent, which may have an adverse effect on his married life relations. He may have immense sexual energy with a touch of impatience and aggression if Mars in the 7th house has the aspect of negative planets. Married couples may face problems and difficulties in maintaining smooth and strong conjugal relations. A person with Mars in the 7th house will try to keep the upper hand in all matters by entering into unnecessary hot arguments.

The 7th house of Mars makes the native Manglik. This house of Mars is also associated with obstructing or delaying marriage. This can lead to misunderstandings and differences of point of view between the husband and wife. It has been observed that the ego issues of both parties can make the situation unpleasant and difficult. It is desirable for a Manglik boy to get married to a Manglik girl, or vice versa, to offset the negative energy released by Mars.

The 7th house also refers to other relationships, including professional ones. In the field of business, the planets also represent partners, and their strength is placed in the 7th house. An afflicted Mars will lead to a disturbed relationship between partners. Such a native may also face difficulties in his professional life or workplace.

For those who work in marketing, the 7th house placement will lead to good results. Salesmanship requires energy and a lot of hustle and bustle. It also leads to a passionate and temperamental relationship. It is also likely that a person will quickly decide to get married. In the combination of the 7th house and the planets, it is very important for a person to be loyal to his partner and not waste his sexual energy on all things sexual. A person in the 7th house of Mars is likely to be quarrelsome, aggressive, confrontational, and quarrelsome. It can lead to conflict and disagreement with partners.

8th House: The 8th house is associated with longevity, change, conflict, etc. The placement of Mars in the 8th house of the astrological chart is not considered favourable unless it is placed in its own or exalted sign. This house gives power and determination to the natives. The 8th house is 2nd to the 7th house, so the pleasures of married life are also seen in this house. The presence of Mars in this house may lead to a problem in the relationship with the spouse because of a lack of understanding. The problem may be caused by the ego problem of the partner. People with Mars in the 8th house are passionate and energetic but are very unstable too; it will be hard for them to regulate their emotions. They are interested in occult sciences such as yantras, mantras, etc. They may speak rashly. Natives with such placement of Mars usually don't care about morality. They want to prove their superiority, and they won't hesitate to hurt others. In the horoscope of Kalpurush, Mars is the lord of the 8th house.

Natives don't use the energy for good things like sports; they use it for bad things like crime, drugs, etc. However, if there is any good influence from other planets, the negative effects of Mars will be greatly reduced. Therefore, we should be very cautious when studying Mars' position.

8th house means loss, loss of faith, loss of loyalty in married life relations, which creates a difficult situation for whole family. This house also houses the native Manglik. It has been observed that the ego problems of both parties can make the situation worse. Therefore, it is desirable for a Manglik boy to get married to a Manglik girl, or vice versa, to reduce the negative effects of energy released by Mars. Mars is associated with younger brothers, and its placement in the 8th house may lead to issues with younger brothers, or relationships with them may not be harmonious. Furthermore, the presence of Mars in the 8th house can lead to strong desires for worldly luxuries, which the native is usually provided with due to his hard work and determination. Furthermore, cheating on one's spouse may lead to revengeful feelings. The 8th house has a special meaning for married women, which is why astrologers are highly concerned about the power and position of the 8th house. Additionally, the presence of evil planets in the 8th house could lead to issues regarding the longevity of the husband.

9th House: The 9th house represents luck, wisdom, teaching, fatherhood, etc. Natives are very ambitious and are likely to excel in society. Such people are brave and help those in need. They love to travel long distances. They may use crude methods to teach others to follow law and order. They do not hesitate to punish others who break the law. In religious matters, they may act differently. They may not be very religious, but they want to practice the good things of their religion. With Mars aspecting, they use their imagination in writing. They can become fiction writers and crime writers. Fathers may be irritable or impatient. This is the house where Mars feels comfortable when placed in its own sign, exalted, or on friendly planets such as Jupiter, the Moon, and the Sun. A native will be a free man without any fear. He can express his own point of view and does not need guidance from others. This is a blessing that God has given him. Such a placement of Mars gives a person a unique and charming personality from birth. He may be lucky and reach high positions at a young age, especially in administration and sales management. He has the persuasive power to achieve the desired benefits at work and in the company. Jupiter's blessing gives him unique persuasiveness and ideas for finding solutions to problems he may face at times in his life. Mars in the 9th house can make a person more passionate, driven, and adventurous in their pursuit of knowledge, education, and spirituality. It also gives you the courage to take risks and pursue your dreams. Mars in the 9th house can make a person dogmatic, aggressive, and confrontational in their beliefs and ideologies. It can also lead to conflicts and disagreements with teachers, leaders, and authority figures.

10th House: The 10th house in the horoscope is related to occupations and jobs to secure a living. If Mars is strong here, it has positive consequences. A native is a hard worker, and his only goal is to reach the top of his profession through his own strength and diligence. He may also employ some key tactics to achieve the desired position. His childhood also reflects this personality trait. He will shine in life, and his family can be proud of his status, successes, and accomplishments. He wants to be a leader. Some prominent politicians have strong Mars in the 10th House.

The 10th house indicates karma, activity, career, etc. Mars likes the 10th house. Here, Mars acts with complete freedom and maximum potential. People with Mars in the 10th house love activity. They are the type of people who don't want to sit around doing nothing. They prefer outdoor activities. Even professionally, they prefer a job that involves a lot of travel. Natives are enthusiastic and energetic at work and ambitious in their career. However, a native's career may not be very stable. In their work, they have to face many conflicts and enemies. They may try to dominate at work, but this is a hindrance to their growth. As a boss, it becomes difficult for subordinates to work under him. They are quick-tempered and ferocious, and they expect the same from others. They are not afraid to impose punishment when someone makes a mistake. Sometimes such natives don't even give others time to explain. Occupations that may help locals include mechanical, electrical, industrial, metallurgical, nuclear, soil mechanics, chemical, and surgical. Such natives can also excel in the police, security services, sports, and vigilance departments.

Such a person may start from a low position, but his efforts will soon lead him to a high position in the workplace. He wants a job that is challenging and requires a lot of physical strength. He excels when left to work independently. This type of personality can also have adversaries and hidden enemies at work that can make them restless. Others may become jealous of him and try to get in his way. But such natives don't care and will continue to strive to achieve or maintain the goals they have already set. At times, he may feel superior or in control. If he maintains friendly relations with others, then other people's opinions will also prove useful to him.

11th House: The 11th house is associated with wealth, ambition, success, etc. In general, all the 11th house planets are good in terms of wealth. The 11th house is good for material success. The people in this house are energetic and passionate. They are very confident and think that nothing can be impossible for them. They are also very arrogant, and if they can control their arrogance, they will do well in their careers. These people have excellent qualities. They are courageous, rich, and happy. They are brave, have no sorrow, and have good character. They fulfil their dreams and their hopes. They have real friends. They are social and win over their opponents. The 11th house of Mars can make people passionate, driven, and assertive. It can help them pursue their dreams and goals with the support of their friends. Disagreements with friends, social life, unpopularity, and contentment will be overcome by thoughtful actions. Avoid extravagance. The person in this house is invincible. He is loud, sexy, wealthy, and honest. He is easily excited. He starts acquiring wealth at 24 years of age. He has good relations with his friends and gains from them. He has a love for truth. If Mars is surrounded by good planets, it means good relationships with friends and the gains from them. There is love for the truth. If Mars is afflicted, it means unfaithful companions and the loss of them. If Mars is afflicted by the planets Saturn and Mercury, it means a breach of friendship or some kind of conspiracy. By Jupiter and the sun, it means difficulties due to bad advice, legal problems, financial loss, etc. By Venus and the moon, it means overindulgence with friends and the loss of it.

12th House: Mars in the 12th house can make those seeking solitude, meditation, and introspection brave, strong, and spiritual. It can give them the courage to face their subconscious fears and overcome their limitations. Mars does not like addiction. This also applies to natives with Mars in the 12th house. He is confident enough and believes in his ability to achieve his life goals. In general, he does not express his opinion openly and does not like to easily share secrets with others. He tries to be modest. But at the same time, he is very selfish and does not hesitate to ask for help from others if he needs it.

In his workplace, he has to face strong resistance from his peers and colleagues. In order to deal with this situation, he has to put in extra effort and sometimes feels exhausted. It has also been observed that such natives have an unfavourable atmosphere at work and may be forced to make frequent changes. He may also be suffering from low energy levels.

12th house also indicate a loss of respect. He may have to face several false charges in his life and needs the support of his loved ones at this time. His extravagance goes unchecked, sometimes forcing him to take out a loan. With Mars in the 12th house, you are prone to accidents, injuries, and hospitalizations. Conflicts and power struggles with hidden enemies and obstacles can also occur.

(iv)Budha : Represent planet Mercury

Rules: Gemini & Virgo.

Exalted: Virgo.

Debilitated: Pisces.

Exalted/ Debilitated Degree: 15º

Mahadasha Period: 17 years

Principle: Communication, Conscious mind (i.e., logical or rational, mind)

Urge represented: Urge to express one's perceptions & Intelligence through skill or speech. Needs symbolized: Need to establish connections with others, need to learn. Positive Expression: Creative use of skill or intelligence, reason and power of discrimination used to serve higher ideals; ability to come to agreement through objective understanding and clear verbal expression.

Negative Expression: Misuse of skill or intelligence; amorality through rationalization of anything; opinionated and one-sided "communication".

Mercury, also known as Budha, is the Prince of Astrology and is associated with speech, intelligence, maternal uncles, short journeys, the medical profession, trade, computers and the web, astrology, and knowledge of the scriptures, accounts, mathematics, journalism, printing, and publishing. Mercury is considered to be the son of Chandra (the moon) and Tara (Taraka). He is also known as the God of Merchandise and the Protector of Merchants. Buddha has Rajas Guna and is also associated with communication.

His character is characterized by being mild and eloquent; his color is greenish; his metal is bronze; and his gem is merald. He is typically depicted in the form of a winged lion holding a scimitar, club, and shield. In a few other paintings, Buddha is shown riding a carpet, an eagle, or a carriage drawn by lions. In other depictions, he is depicted holding a sceptre and lotus and riding a chariot drawn by lions.

Mercury takes about a month to travel a sign. It is always within a 27-degree distance from the sun, as per the astrological point of view.

Mercury represents reason and rationality (common sense). It represents the processes of spoken and written language, ordering, weighing, and evaluation, learning, and competence. Mercury acts as a mouthpiece, showing how we speak and communicate and what we want to say about it. This is how we function mentally: what we perceive, how we perceive it, our critical skills, our ability to reason, and how we take in and process information. Schools, colleges, learning, libraries, books, magazines, newspapers, and social networks are all under the auspices of this planet.

Sign equivalents: Gemini and Virgo

Budha presides over 'Budh-war' or Wednesday. In modern Hindi, Telugu, Bengali, Marathi, Kannada, and Gujarati, Wednesday is called Budhvara; in Tamil and Malayalam, it is Budhan.

Sign equivalents: Gemini and Virgo

Friendly planets of Mercury: Sun and Venus

Neutral planets: Saturn, Mars and Jupiter

Enemy planets of Mercury: Moon

Effect of Mercury in different Houses: There are many things to evaluate while giving predictions about placement of Mercury in horoscope like sign of the house, conjunction of other planet(s), aspects of other planet(s), degree of Mercury, the condition of house lord etc. However the general predictions about placement of Mercury in different Houses of a horoscope are as below:

1st House: The 1st is the personality of the person. It represents the inner character, such as nature and mindset, as well as the outer character, such as the physical characteristics of the person. Mercury in the first house shows the intelligence and wit of the person. He wants to learn and discover more. It gives him a lively personality. It also helps him to be full of ideas and information. He is very versatile, flexible, and adaptable.

When Mercury is placed in the first house in its own or highest sign, it forms Bhadra Raj Yoga. It gives the natives excellent trade and mathematical abilities. Mercury in the first house has a slender physique. The native has small eyes, an expressive face, a long nose, and a high forehead.

In the first house, Mercury has a philosophical but indecisive mind. Afflicted Mercury in the 1st house may lead to depression and a lack of moral values. It may lead to a life of confusion as the person wants to learn new things all the time but doesn't have any continuity. They are usually not attentive and have loud voices.

2nd House: The 2nd house is linked to wealth, success, language, spirituality, education, family, and the food habits of the indigenous person. The 2nd house represents all that we possess, including material items, wealth, and possessions, but these are not only physical possessions. It also encompasses our emotions, our younger siblings, and our relationship with them. With Mercury in the 2nd house, one may have power over their financial situation. They may be able to find various ways to make money. This placement is likely to lead to a career in teaching, management, or consulting. Financial success and business success can be anticipated. The native person has a strong capacity for communication and negotiation, as well as good organizational abilities and attention to details. The native person may have a natural aptitude for writing and speaking, as well as a tendency to be excessively talkative and quarrelsome. They may have difficulty controlling their spending habits and may be overly critical and judgmental.

3rd House: In Vedic astrology, the 3rd house represents short trips, siblings, friends, neighbors, relatives, tendencies or hobbies, courage, and communication. Mercury in the 3rd house is the perfect placement for this. Mercury is Karaka, and the 3rd house is the house of communication. Here, Mercury makes natives influential speakers, writers, and highly social figures. You are multitasking and keen on reading, teaching, speaking, exchanging ideas, checking the daily news, and perhaps gossiping. These restless minds are quick learners and readily share their knowledge with others. The person may work in fields such as astrology, publishing, education, the internet, writing, mass media, web design, consulting, speaking, or travel. Under the influence of Mercury in the 3rd house, you can be harsh in your language. Locals can trick others with their manipulative speech. He has difficulty traveling, and his education is being adversely affected. Mercury in the 3rd house gives natives a sense of curiosity and inquisitiveness. These locals are interested in different events happening in their world. People with Mercury in the 3rd house explore different topics and have different hobbies. So you can be a jack of all trades, but not a master of all. This can cause frustration.

4th House: The 4th house is ruled by the Moon, the enemy of Mercury. So this combination may not be beneficial to the natives. This position of Mercury could damage your relationship with your mother, or you could get into family arguments. When mercury reaches the 4th house, the 1st mercury affects the 4th house of such things as family manufacturing businesses, travel businesses, import and export businesses, rulers of land, politicians, and cultivate patient people like doctors or nurses, guide people like guides, manage the 4th house of things, so managers, even a management position in an IT company to manage their clients and secure their own business. Provides protection if associated with Mars. Mercury in the 4th house also affects the 10th house of occupation. Indigenous people can take on any career-related choices as indicated by the planet Mercury. All types of psychic healers, tantrics, and even astrologers are seen by this placement in the 4th house of mercury. A good or bad relationship with the mother depends on the good or bad placement of mercury in the 4th house. We all know Mercury is very business-oriented, and the 4th house represents earth and home. So it represents jobs related to houses or land. If the 4th house sign is a sign of air or water, or if the 12th lord is related to the 4th house, it is very likely that it is an import-export business or a transport, travel, and tourism company. Such people are likely to be busy with research duties and may also choose to work from home.

5th House: The 5th house of the horoscope represents the birth of a child, entertainment, sports, romantic relationships, creative skills, intelligence, higher education, speculation, etc. The 5th house is also associated with progeny and knowledge. If Mercury sits in this room, you will be good at communicating with others. Your actions can speak louder than your words. If a baby is born in an exalted Virgo or Gemini, that baby may possess an intelligent mind during birth. It is also the home of Purva Punya, which is the merit of past lives. Mercury in the 5th house gives natives very impressive intellectual and communication skills. The natives here receive a good education, great intelligence, writing, and poetry. Mercury in the 5th house in different signs offers the following career options: Fiery Sign: Mathematics,

Astrology, Vedic Knowledge, Politics, and Choreography Earth Signs: Physics, Grammar, Magic, Air Signs: Journalism, Sports, Speaker, Writer, Water Signs: Literature, Linguistics, and Administration Mercury in the 5th house gives birth to an intelligent and multi-talented first child. Afflicted Mercury in the 5th house gives the person a restless, confused, and indecisive mind.

6th House: If Mercury occupies the 6th house, natives will always succeed in legal matters and disputes, suffer from illness and insolence, do not get angry easily, and use harsh words and speech. People with Mercury in the 6th house can be very active-minded, and they tend to remember things that other people tend to forget easily. In addition, they are very good at organizing things and making lists and associations. Mercury in the 6th house gives you the intelligence and ingenuity to resolve conflicts, whether professional or other people's affairs. Positive Mercury in the 6th Bhava can lead you to a happy married life, and your children can grow up to be smart, successful, and intelligent people. Mercury entering the 6th house unduly affects their health. They may have headaches, and the pain may get worse. Many of their health problems are caused by stress. Mercury retrograde in the 6th house can make you super argumentative and judgmental in everyday personal and professional matters, which will be detrimental to you in the long run. Your co-workers or employees may be angry with you. Due to this placement, your communication skills can get you into trouble in your career. This position at Mercury can bring you small business benefits. You can still have health problems, especially those related to the nervous system.

7th House: The 7th house is the house of marriage, husband and wife, all kinds of partnerships, sex life, daily work, and relationships with life and business partners. Mercury in the 7th house makes the native an excellent business partner, and he tends to think about his wife and marriage. Mercury in the 7th house also brings intelligent life and a business partner. Natives like people who are insightful, knowledgeable, and funny. If a person has Mercury in the 7th house, his or her spouse may be a good writer, poet, financial advisor, or may be related to other Mercury career attributes. People with Mercury in the 7th house will enjoy lasting happiness in marriage and business partnerships. The realistic look at their relationship greatly enhances their compatibility. Both partners believe in forgiving each other and moving on. Arguing over little things for hours on end is not their style. Mercury retrograde in the 7th house can cause misunderstandings and arguments in marriages and business partnerships. Legal movement should be strictly prohibited in the event of a fight. The bad influence of Mercury in the 7th house leaves individuals with a lack of decision-making power. This can harm their image at home and at work.

8th House: The 8th House is known for its knowledge of the underworld, government taxes, and secret government policies. It is the home of unexpected events, unexpected surgery, unexpected accidents, or unexpected deaths. Sometimes surprises include good things like suddenly winning the lottery or suddenly getting a house or a job. People with Mercury in the 8th house use intelligence and logical thinking to dig for objects. Indigenous people can be palaeontologists, archaeologists, or experts in any related field as they dig deep to find out, observe, or analyze something because data analysis comes with wisdom. The 8th house is also significant in terms of family history and lineage. The native, by digging into his family history, gets to know his family and makes them resourceful. Mercury in the 8th house is important for speech and improves speech. Indigenous people can be very open with parents-in-law and family, but communication with family will be poor if the planets are shifted. The ability to communicate with native speakers goes deeper into the philosophy of life. Curiosity to know and learn new things in the 8th house can lead natives to dig into intellectual things. It can be troublesome to turn to family matters because family problems are not so intellectual. Mercury in the 8th house makes a person intelligent, because in order for a person to be able to communicate well, one must be intelligent.

Mercury also represents the management and business skills of the natives due to their calculating nature, logic, and love for the market. Mercury in astrology represents speech. It also governs the logical and intellectual aspects of the mind, the thinking process before speech, the ability to communicate, and everything related to language, whether using symbols, logic, processing information, or making connections with people or things.

9th House: The 9th house is the house of pilgrimage, or spiritual journeys. On the other hand, the planet Mercury signifies communication. This means that whenever planet Mercury is placed in the 9th house, the native will have a good inclination towards spiritual learning and may also become a spiritual seeker. Mercury placement in this house also indicates that the person may go for higher studies. This person even has great chances to go abroad regarding his or her studies. They also seem to have a good interest in foreign cultures. These people have good moral values; they may also be poets, singers, editors, writers, astrologers, or seem like businessmen. They do something for their society.

10th House: This house is the house for karma, or profession. When Mercury has a good placement in this house, the native has a strong inclination to go into a profession related to communication. This means he can become a speaker or a journalist. They always succeed in whichever field they are in. These people are studious and obedient to their parents. Usually, they opt for the fields they are studying.

11th House: This is the house of gains and profits. This house also indicates friendship. Mercury's placement might indicate a sudden gain related to any communication pursuit. He will also make a lot of friends due to his communication skills. Career-wise, the IT sector or anything related to science or math suits these people well. These people are wealthy, honest, and have an attractive appearance. They are long-lived. They are into charitable work.

12th House: House of foreign land, jail, hospital, etc. When Mercury is placed here, the native can become an explorer. He will unravel the mysteries of life. There is also a high chance that he may go very deep into learning spiritual knowledge. They seem to have a good interest in poetry writing, have knowledge of Vedanta, and learn about shashtras. Speaking about their health status, their immune system may get lower with age, further causing skin as well as digestive issues.

(v) Brihaspati : Represents planet Jupiter

Rules: Sagittarius & Pisces

Exalted: Cancer

Debilitated: Capricorn

Exalted / Debilitated Degree: 5°

Mahadasha Period: 16 years

Principle: Expansion, Grace

Urges represented: Urge towards a larger order or to connect self, Need to improve self.

Needs symbolized: Need for faith, trust and confidence in life and self, Need to improve self.

Positive expression: Faith, Reliance on higher power or greater plan; Openness to grace; Optimism, Openness to self's need for improvement.

Negative expression: Overconfidence; laziness; scattering energy; leaving the work to others; irresponsibility; overextending self or promising too much.

Jupiter, also called the Guru, is the chief of prayers and sacrifice. He takes us from the darkness of ignorance to the brightness of wisdom. Brihaspati is also known as the 'Purohit' or the 'Guru of Devas', unlike Shukracharya, who is known as 'the Guru of the 'Danavas'. Jupiter is associated with knowledge, spirituality, and religion. It is also associated with higher learning and research, as well as with philosophy, optimism, and much more. It is associated with children, spiritual knowledge, moksha (saved) or salvation, and education related to "higher learning," "research," "Philosophy," and "Optimism." This is why Jupiter is assigned to the 9th or 12th house of the natural zodiac (Kalapurusha), which symbolizes "dharmic" and "spiritual" knowledge. Jupiter is one of the luckiest, most beneficial, and most auspicious planets in the zodiac. It brings prosperity, growth, and abundance to native life. Jupiter rules two signs: Sagittarius and Pisces.

His Tattva (element) is Akasha (ether), and his direction is north-east. He is depicted as yellow or golden in color with a stick, lotus, and beads. Jupiter is also known as "Devaguru" and presides over "Guru-War" "Brhaspati War" or "Thursday". It symbolizes higher knowledge and spirituality, priest, temple, teacher, researcher and scientist, lawyer and judge, child, and understanding of Shastras and astrology. Its gem is yellow sapphire. It takes about 1 year to travel through a sign, is the planet associated with children, and is called Putra Karaka.

Friendly planets of Jupiter: Sun, Moon, Mars

Neutral planets: Saturn and Ketu

Enemy planets of Jupiter: Mercury, Venus and Rahu

Effect of Jupiter in different Houses: There are many things to evaluate while giving predictions about placement of Jupiter in horoscope like sign of the house, conjunction of other planet(s), aspects of other planet(s), degree of Jupiter, the condition of house lord etc. However the general predictions about placement of Jupiter in different Houses of a horoscope are as below:

1st House: The 1st house, or ascendant, is primarily concerned with the native's physical appearance, health, and how he or she looks to the outside world. It is the most significant part of the birth chart, as it determines the houses in which the other signs and planets will reside. The placement of Jupiter in this house increases the native's desire to travel, read, and basically explore. It makes the person happy, content, and kind. It encourages good health and longevity. It strengthens the person's belief in spirituality and faith. It provides financial stability and success in a career. Jupiter in the first house grants a lot of prosperity, wealth, and success in life, especially after 45 years. Guru in the first house blesses good and prosperous kids in life. The native may become popular and successful in a career after 40 years. The fortune and prosperity of the natives will increase after marriage. When in Lagna, Jupiter protects the native from bad situations in life. A person with Jupiter in the first house will have an abundance of blessings from a very early age, and the inclination of the native towards spirituality will increase from a very early age.

2nd House: The 2nd house refers to the native's assets and wealth. It is likely that the native was born into a well-off family and grew up without any financial problems. This position ensures the native's financial stability for the rest of their life. The 2nd house of Jupiter indicates that the native has a lot of influence in society. They have a wide circle of friends, which gives them authority and leadership.

Since the 2nd house also controls the neck area, the natives in this house will be blessed with a sweet and beautiful voice and will have a good chance of singing. Since Jupiter is a planet of growth, if it has bad aspects, it can make the natives spend excessively. However, this planet is fortunate that it can still help the natives regain their financial stability. When Jupiter is in this place, it ensures that natives have an inborn passion for acquiring knowledge and education. This position of Jupiter can lead to an individual's tendency to become overweight or obese.

3rd House: The 3rd house is the house of communication and short trips. This house also signifies our relationships. When Jupiter is placed in this house, it means that the native will take short trips to enhance his intellectual knowledge. He will also have a very good relationship with the people close to him. These people can also include colleagues, neighbors, friends, etc. It gives fame, analytical ability, predictability, a good planner, a traditionalist who follows rituals), makes the person wise, and such people easily absorb knowledge. new consciousness. They are good planners. They can also be a good writer or in the literary field, or they can also be a good speaker. It leads to a successful career. That person can advance his career through his passion. They are mentally strong and motivated for their work. They are blessed with much wealth. These people often have strong personalities.

4th House: The 4th house is related to motherhood, property, and luxury items. Whenever Jupiter is placed in this house, it means that the person will have a good relationship with his mother, but the mother can suffer from any illness. Good Sanskar and deeds of his mother's will be transferred to the native. When Jupiter is placed in the 4th house, it brings all kinds of happiness and prosperity. I am always lucky to have a lot of wealth and property. Since Jupiter is a slow planet and also means Guru, the native will have luxuries around him but will not indulge them too much. These people are generally satisfied with their lives in any situation. They are practical and witty. They are quite responsible when it comes to their family. They have good family ties and are lucky enough to have children. They do well in whatever careers they choose.

5th House: The 5th house is related to children and also signifies higher studies. When Jupiter is placed in this house, it can lead the person to higher studies. Such people will also be inclined to learn about their religion and other artistic studies. These people can also become good astrologers, financiers, advisors, and consultants and are very popular in their field of work. They have very strong intuition. Usually, these people specialize in betting, lotteries, and the stock market. They enjoy life to the fullest. Initially, they tended to encounter some obstacles in their higher education, but they overcame them and succeeded.

6th House: Natives with Jupiter in the 6th house can excel in their profession and have a good success rate. Although many factors depend on the outcome of placing Jupiter in the 6th house, for example, which planet is aspecting this house, which planets conjuct with Jupiter, etc., to give a general idea, the native will not engage in anything illegal and will do his best to be fair and honest with himself and his society. They have some internal enemies, but placing this planet in the 6th house has brought them victory. They have a workaholic nature. Tends to have a weak digestive system and may also suffer from liver disease.

7th House: The spouse of a native with Jupiter in the 7th house will be a devout person and will also come from a wealthy family. Their marital relationship will be based on loyalty and trust, which in turn leads to a happy married life. In terms of business relations, it is also a very good investment. These people tend to be healthy. They are lucky to get along with their respective partners. They are blessed with a son. It gives strength to the lagan or ascendant (first house), and thus the person is blessed in any way, i.e., he has a strong personality both physically and mentally.

8th House: People with Jupiter in the 8th house will have an excellent understanding of matters related to the occult and mystical sciences. If Jupiter is strongly placed in this house, the natives will also enjoy good health. People can take advantage of such a native, but despite this, the person will have a strong will and a strong tendency towards spiritual development. They live a long life. They receive an inheritance. They like to spend their money on religious matters. These people have kind hearts and are pilgrims.

9th House: Jupiter in the 9th house blesses you with the divine spirit and directs you towards religious goals. In this house, Jupiter is considered "Karaka" and brings auspicious results. Bless you with a good reputation, and your actions will uplift the poor and needy. It will make you have a peaceful and loving home life. You will be very close to your family. Such people will become very noble, follow their traditional values, culture, and religion, and also gain a considerable amount of wealth during their lifetime through the pursuit of good deeds. When Jupiter is placed in this house, the person is very religious. Either these people hold a high position in their work or they are successful businessmen. They have a remarkable power of intuition. They are very possessive of their children. They live like saints. They are men of honor.

Jupiter in the 9th house develops spiritual desires in you and makes you very religious. This creates opportunities for overseas travel and brings you closer to your father, and a native will be inclined to share feelings with him and get advice on all important matters of life. This connection will give you great strength and bring you peace and mental stability. The 9th house deals with life events and actions that bring about spiritual transformation within you. You become motivated to pursue spirituality with your greatest strength and energy. There will often be opportunities to travel abroad for work or personal reasons. It will bring good benefits that will have a lasting impact on your life.

Jupiter tilts you here to gain knowledge on your chosen subject; you will pursue higher education. You will always want to learn new things; topics related to religion and spirituality will appeal to you the most. You will always be willing to participate in religious activities or organize such activities with your family, relatives, or friends. People will also admire you for such actions and will follow or help you organize these activities.

Positive Jupiter in the 9th house makes you very mentally active; you have a strong desire to pursue higher education, and your wise decisions will bring positive results in life. Zodiac sign, accuracy, conjunction, and influence of other planets on your Jupiter determine a Jupiter pole.

Negative Jupiter in the 9th house can keep you away from family and loved ones for long periods of time due to travel and cause problems in your relationships. Overindulgence in spiritual activities can take you away from family life. Zodiac signs, accuracy, conjunctions, and influence of other planets on your Jupiter identify a Jupiter pole as negative.

10th House: The 10th house covers areas like career, position in society, social status, material success, etc. The strength of this house and the inner transition planets better define the professional life of the native. For your convenience, Jupiter in the 10th house means Jupiter transits your career sign, which may require you to walk on strings.

Strong Jupiter in the 10th house can help you choose the right career path and can provide you with many opportunities to become a teacher, businessman, or judge. But the natives may not receive its blessings if Jupiter is associated with Rahu or Ketu, as these planets will form obstacles in their way. They can be leaders at home and at work because the people around them can recognize their worth.

Such people are virtuous, mature, and resourceful. They are more or less serious in life. In addition, they are grateful to those who help them in difficult times. These natives value place and status in life. They can achieve much success and fame in their business or profession. They are also recognized for their efforts in their social and professional circles. Such natives are generally generous and compassionate people. They are very reliable, so people trust them a lot and help them in difficult times. This sense of trust makes them popular among the masses. Their marriage can also go well because they are not so focused on their careers.

Such natives are very wise and understanding. These natives are very determined and dedicated to pursuing their goals and seeing them. Of course, the position of Jupiter in the 10th house helps natives progress in their respective professions. In addition, the influence of Jupiter in the 10th house makes the natives need to be more lenient with others. They shouldn't think they're always right. They should also consider the advice and suggestions of others. This will only add to their greatness and leadership qualities.

On the other hand, such natives must be careful not to exceed their limits. While advancing in their career and other aspects of life, they should not be too preoccupied with their goals. Given the position of Jupiter, the planet of benevolence and wealth, that's unlikely, but it's best to stay on the safe side.

Also, people with Jupiter in the 10th house are good workers, but they have to learn the art of being more team players. The self-interest place should be very small. Indigenous people need to make sure that the goals are important and that it is the achievement of them that is important, not a small but potentially dangerous ego problem.

11th House: Jupiter is the karaka of this house. People with Jupiter in the 11th house may be religious and philosophical. They can be creative and expressive in their speech. They can have fun even in adverse conditions and have many friends to support them when needed. These people will gain a lot of wealth through legal means. They will also find themselves with a very good network of people around them who will support the natives. Overall, they are good entrepreneurs who never face financial problems in life. They experience an unexpected gain in life. They get achievements and any kind of awards or scholarships in their lives. They are fortunate to have a younger brother and a son. They have a good group of friends. They tend to seek the blessings of their ancestors. They have God's grace in their lives. The son's wife is seen from this house.

Here, Jupiter affects the outcome of your social interactions and social activities, what it means to you, and the benefits it can bring you. Jupiter allows you to expand your social circle with new relationships that develop over time.

Jupiter brings good interaction with your siblings and improves your relationship with them; it brings you closer to them and creates a deep bond with them. Your siblings will take care of you and help you when you need it. You always have someone you can share your feelings with and someone you can trust to help and support you.

Positive Jupiter in the 11th house will expand your social circles, connect deeply with older siblings, and give you power. Zodiac sign, accuracy, conjunction, and influence of other planets on your Jupiter determine a Jupiter pole.

Negative Jupiter in the 11th house can lead to irregular income, even though your income increases. Zodiac signs, accuracy, conjunctions, and influence of other planets on your Jupiter identify a Jupiter pole as negative.

12th House: The 12th house is representative of hidden talents, spirituality, other dimensions, secrets, and foreign lands. The 12th house is the house of losses in money, health, or energy. It is also known as a charity house because it seeks to give to others. Jupiter's position here is unique. It can lead the individual to the path of moksha, or the best word for it is to pursue the path of moksha. He can also travel to distant countries and foreign countries to acquire spiritual knowledge and fulfil his life mission, that is, spreading values and knowledge that he acquired during his lifetime to those who needed it most. If Jupiter is placed in the 12th house, it also brings the person foreign relationships, foreign education, and settlement. These people make money abroad in various ways, such as through import and export businesses. They live like Yogis. There is a useful character. They love to travel, even over long distances.

Now while Jupiter is in the 12th house—from the 12th house, aspect of Jupiter is on the 4th, 6th, and 8th houses. The aspect of Jupiter above the 4th house shows heavy spending (12) on amenities and transportation (4). If Jupiter is well placed, it will be endowed with comforts, transportation, and a beautiful home abroad. Since the 4th house belongs to the triangle of salvation (Moksha Trikona), it favors becoming spiritual. You find mental peace through spirituality and meditation.

The aspect of Jupiter in the 6th house protects against secret enemies (12) (6). You are usually benevolent and learn from your enemies instead of punishing them. The aspect considered also protects against diseases (6) and obstacles (6); natives usually have a relatively easy life with little struggle and chaos.

(vi) Shukra : Represents planet Venus.

Rules: Taurus & Libra

Exalted: Pisces

Debilitated: Virgo

Exalted / Debilitated Degree: 27°

Mahadasha Period: 20 years

Principle: Emotionally colored tastes; values. Exchange of energy with others through giving of self and receiving from others, sharing.

Urges Represented: Social and love urge; urge to express affection; urge for pleasures.

Needs Symbolized: need to feel close to one another, need to feel comfort and harmony, need to give self's emotion. Feels love and closeness with another through sharing vigorous activities and mutual aspirations and enthusiasm

Positive expression: Love - Give and take with others, Sharing, Generosity of spirit. Negative expression: affection and appreciation are expressed energetically, directly and grandly.

Shukra (Sanskrit for "clear, pure" or "bright, clearness") is the name given by Bhrigu and Ushana to their son and the preceptor of Daityas or Danvas. He is also known as the "Guru of the Demons" and the "Asura-Guru" and is represented as Shukracharya. Shukra rules over 'Shukra war' or 'Friday'. Venus is Rajas in nature.

It is the planet of wealth, pleasure, and reproduction. It completes the cycle of the zodiac within 12 months and takes about one month to travel in a sign. Venus is always within 48 degrees of the sun. It is the planet connected to the spouse. Venus is the symbol of marriage, sex, kidneys, and sex organs. It is also the symbol of dance, music, and the arts. It is the symbol of wine, bars, and gambling places.

Silver is the metal of Venus. The gem is a diamond. The direction is southeast.

He carries a stick, pearls, lotuses, and sometimes arrows. He is white-skinned and middle-aged. He has a pleasant face. He is seen riding a camel, horse, crocodile, etc. He carries a stick, pearls, and sometimes arrows.

There is a planetary period in astrology called Shukra Mahadasha. This period is active for 20 years in a person's horoscope. It is believed to bring more wealth, luck, and luxury to your life if you have Shukra in a good position in your horoscope. Shukra is an important planet in your horoscope because it is a benefic planet.

Friendly planets of Venus: Saturn, Mercury

Neutral planets: Jupiter, Mars

Enemy planets of Venus: Sun, Moon, Rahu, Ketu

Effect of Venus in different Houses: There are many things to evaluate while giving predictions about placement of Venus in horoscope like sign of the house, conjunction of other planet(s), aspects of other planet(s), degree of Venus, the condition of house lord etc. However, the general predictions about placement of Venus in different Houses of a horoscope are as below:

Venus Result in Different Houses

1st House: The 1st house is related to the native's physical appearance, health, personality, temperament, strengths, and weaknesses. Most of the focus of the first house is on one's public image. Venus' presence in the first house shows that the native is an artist with a touch of sensuality in her personality. Native people love music, poetry, and all forms of art, as well as beautiful surroundings. Natives also have an excellent sense of aesthetics. With Venus in the first house, the Natives are well-bred individuals with an erotic flair to their character. They are charming, attractive, and charismatic. The Natives are attracted to luxurious and comfortable lifestyles. They are prone to luxury and excessive spending. The Natives create a need for love and erotic pleasures. Such natives may also indicate a need for beauty and fashion. However, if afflicted with Venus in the First House, the Natives may feel self-conscious about their looks. Such natives want to be accepted and loved by all those around them. They may delay marriage and have multiple partners if Venus in the First House is weak.

2nd House: The 2nd house is related to the property and wealth of the natural person. This position indicates the natural person's ability to earn money as well as their ability to manage money. Venus is the feminine planet that attracts money and finances. The natural person's cash flow increases, and they spend a lot of money on art, beauty, and fun. A good Venus makes the natural person balanced, gentle, and peaceful. They know when to say what and choose their words wisely. Their words make a difference in people's lives. The 2nd house is also associated with language, affluence, family, and dietary habits. It is characterized by attractive features, a harmonious voice, and a sweet personality. Women with a placement of Venus in the 2nd house tend to take a great deal of care with their appearance. Generally, such natives have a collection of jewelry or fashionable apparel. They lead a lavish lifestyle, are deeply attached to their family, and enjoy quality food. Additionally, they enjoy indulging in chocolate, ice cream, and dry fruits. They may generate income through art, clothing, musical performances, creative pursuits, and work related to flowers like floral artistry, floriculture, etc.

3rd **House:** The 3rd house of Venus is associated with courage, self-effort, communication, and brothers. It is believed to stimulate the creative mind of the native, leading to a passionate and creative nature. This is a favorable position for those wishing to become writers. It is particularly associated with creativity in the areas of writing, craftsmanship, and art. Venus is associated with the arts, music, dancing, fine art, fashion, decor, beauty, and films. This house encourages the native to pursue any of these activities, which may lead to a serious income-generating venture. In the men's chart, the native's wife is likely to be courageous and artistic, and the spouse is likely to be supportive. On the other hand, Venus in the 3rd house can lead to excessive sexual behavior, a high level of ambition in life, a struggle in career and finance at a young age, and a lack of stability in adulthood. The natives may attain financial stability after reaching the age of 39. The 3rd house of Venus, on the other hand, is associated with good communication and optimism. A native may become an expert in marketing, media, and journalism due to the presence of Venus in the 3rd house. This position can also lead to the emergence of a television or radio presenter. Venus in the 3rd house can cause a native to avoid religion and spirituality. Additionally, a native may become popular by serving the public. On the other hand, Venus in the 3rd house can lead to a late marriage and subsequent success in life. Furthermore, a native may find themselves married to a domineering and egoistic spouse.

4th House: The 4th house represents the home, the childhood, the mother, the relationship between the native and the mother, the early childhood, and the way the native is likely to act towards the family. When Venus is in the 4th house, the native is extra sensitive and affectionate towards his parents. He had a childhood filled with beautiful and fond memories. The native loves to be a great host. He has a sense of aesthetics that is evident in his homes. It gives him a sense of productivity and inner joy. He is likely to benefit financially from his family matters. Venus in the 4th house gives you the opportunity to emotionally bond with your mother. These people are overprotective and nostalgic for their childhood. People with Venus in the 4th house are born hosts, and their houses can be seen for their style and decor. They can also get financial benefits from their families. If Venus is in the 4th house, their tireless efforts to please their family are overlooked, especially when Venus is afflicted. Apart from this, if Venus is afflicted in the 4th house, then the couple may have to break up after a few years of their married lives.

5th House: The 5th house is associated with intelligence and creativity, past actions, education, children, speculations, etc. The placement of Venus in the 5th house proves to be beneficial. The native is fortunate to have this house in his natal chart. Venus feels comfortable in this house. It gives the natives creative power. It gives him ambition and positive thinking. It makes him or her very intelligent. When Venus is in the 5th house, the native is creative. He or she has artistic skills like painting or dancing. He or she loves children and wants a happy family life. He or she is prone to sensual indulgence. He or she may have a taste for gambling or taking risks. Natives create a desire for affection and admiration and will accumulate huge wealth if Venus is not afflicted. A Venus afflicted in the 5th house causes the native to be promiscuous and flirtatious. Children are beautiful and highly successful. A native may have many relationships in life, especially secret relationships. With Venus in the 5th house, the natives tend to have a female first child and may have a beautiful first child.

6th House: The 6th house indicates service, diseases, conflict, enemies, debts, competition, etc. The house of Venus gives mixed results. Venus and the characteristics of the 6th house don't match well. They are well-known in their profession and well-liked by their peers. Generally, they have fewer enemies in life. For men, it is best to avoid confrontation with women. If they try to provoke, they may face problems. They are interested in social services and may look after some pets. This position may lead to a loss of marital happiness for the native. Due to some dissatisfaction at home, he may spend his time outdoors. He may have illicit relations (depending on the position of Venus). He may have diabetes, kidney problems, virility, sex diseases, and other troubles for the lady in the first month of pregnancy. This placement gives rise to good hairdressers, fitness trainers, beauty or cosmetics specialists, dance trainers, and so on. At a young age, a native will suffer from financial deprivation. He or she may face debt and litigation later in life. He or she will lose some of his or her wealth and property. He or she will face controversies and scandals related to the opposite sex. He or she won't find peace in his or her personal or professional life at such a young age. Natives will start to see growth in their lives after attaining the age of 48.

7th House: The 7th house is the most important house of all; it's the house of partnership, whether it's in business or in life; it represents marriage, spouse, partnership, etc. Natives in this house will be beautiful, passionate, and ambitious. Venus' presence in this house is good for marriage; it will give the native a beautiful, rich, and attractive partner to live with and enjoy the luxuries of life. The native is likely to thrive in business; they are usually blessed with a partner who is not only their business partner but also their friend, which makes the business environment comfortable. This placement is good for love and relationships; natives are attracted to beautiful and luxurious partners and tend to overindulge in sensual pleasure. They may experience relationship ups and downs or difficulty sustaining long-term relationships. Natives are expected to achieve success in their careers after reaching the age of 26. A very strong Venus or an afflicted Venus without a positive association is not desirable. Consequently, they may experience dissatisfaction with their marital life over the course of the years. Additionally, they may attempt to engage in other relationships, which may lead to tension in their lives. A debilitated Venus in the 7th house may have a partner who is lazy and possesses bad behavior.

8th House: The 8th house of Venus is associated with longevity, change, sudden occurrences, corporate resources, and inherited property. It is also the house of concealed matters, occultism, mysticism, mortality, and rebirth. The presence of Venus in this house may lead to a desire to study deeply and acquire knowledge. The opposite sex may find the native attractive, have a sweet and melodic voice, and gain from marriage, particularly for males. There may be some hidden money or unexpected income from the wife, and the native may be very secretive. There is a possibility of secret love affairs as well as uncontrolled sexual impulses with the native. If placed incorrectly, Venus may harm their marital life. The placement of Venus alone in this house is not a suitable one, as it must have some control from another planet. The association of Venus and Mercury, Saturn, or Ketu can affect the sperm count in the men's chart. If Venus is afflicted in this house, the native may become lethargic and imprudent. The natives may also experience dissatisfaction in their romantic relationships. Planet Venus presence in this house attracts the natives to those who possess a dark and mysterious energy.

9th House: Since Venus signifies a luxurious lifestyle, placement in this house indicates the seeker will be traveling to a lot of destinations to understand the culture and heritage of that place. These people are religious-minded, clever, and have a happy family life. People with Venus in the 9th house are likely to be carefree. They are good at mediating in cases where objective advice is needed. The presence of Venus in the 9th house indicates that there are chances of a love marriage. Close relationships with spouses and in-laws have proven to be beneficial for locals, especially with female relatives. Venus in this position will make people happier and more optimistic. The need for personal freedom and creative expression is heightened when Venus is retrograde.

Such people are attracted to or tend to attract people from different cultures. Their interests lie in areas such as philosophy, religion, and higher education. They want a partner with a sense of adventure. They are not particularly clingy and expect some form of freedom in a relationship. They want to grow as individuals and will not be happy in a restrictive relationship. In fact, these natives have a great love for freedom.

A lot is going on in the world that people with Venus in the 9th house want to experience and explore. They may want to take in a lot—much more than they can digest. Moreover, they can fall in love easily because they are very quick to make decisions with only some facts. But their definition of love is also different; they will not let their personalities affect the relationship.

They will inadvertently pull people away because they don't put much emotion into their words or actions. At the same time, they must be careful not to break the romantic dreams of others with a bad attitude towards love. Their inappropriate behavior with different lovers can get them in trouble if they are constantly looking for something better somewhere else.

10th House: This person will be artistic in nature and may select professions related to name and fame. If Venus has a good placement in this house, then this person can also go into the media line or professions related to entertainment like acting, singing, playing instruments, etc. These people are highly fond of pleasure; they love to own high-end vehicles. They are quite rich and popular in their field of work. They are very passionate and love to have fame. These people also have an artistic nature. They seem to have a good interest in painting or sketching.

Most cheerful, energetic people with magnetic personalities have Venus in the 10th house. At work or at social gatherings, they are the center of attention. People with Venus in the 10th house are appreciated for their positivity and easy-going nature. They are also blessed with great opportunities thanks to these charming qualities.

People with Venus in the 10th house share a great and strong bond with their father. Debate, music, and politics may be a strange combination, but this is their first love. But if Venus in the 10th house is troubled, the native's public image will be seriously disturbed. People with Venus in the 10th house can also make money using these talents selfishly.

11th House: It's a house of gains (any kind) and achievements. Natives will be goal-oriented and ambitious. He will also gain success in Venus-related matters. The person will have a large social circle in both their personal and professional lives. They may benefit from the females they have in their lives, but they have a disturbed married life. A person loves to dress well and likes to be the center of attention in any gathering.

Venus in the 11th house provides clues as to what kind of social faction this person belongs to. Kind and gracious people are born with Venus in the 11th house. They are extremely open to their innate talent for instant friendships. Usually, most of their friends will be of the opposite sex. Their busy social schedules and charisma help people with Venus in the 11th house achieve financial success. Such people are at their best when they are surrounded by a group of friends. But when Venus in the 11th house is affected, these people should be careful when socializing, as it can lead to undesirable consequences.

The 11th house of the horoscope shows your gains, sometimes huge sums of money, and your excess wealth. And Venus is the planet of wealth, luck, lust, sex, and emotions. Therefore, the position of Venus in the 11th House is a perfect combination for getting rich and living in luxury. Venus in the 11th House is an ideal location or house for Venus because Venus in the 11th House Bhava signifies the attainment of worldly joy and prosperity.

Venus aspected or conjunct with malefic planets in the 11th house can give you an extremely longing, and sometimes selfish, attitude towards worldly interests and pleasures. It can make you hoard things and seek out mundane pleasures. You may become possessive about your wealth and dislike sharing or helping others, even with friends or loved ones. You may associate with negative, toxic, and cunning people who can influence and deceive you for their selfish motives. You can create an unhealthy relationship and home environment and end up with discord and emotional stress.

12th House: This person will love traveling and will be very extravagant as well. He will also be very creative in fields related to the arts and entertainment. They may have weak eyesight. They tend to lead a long and healthy life with lots of wealth. These people are extravagant. They are inclined toward the opposite sex. They seem to have good bedtime pleasures.

Venus in the 12th house gives you tremendous powers of imagination, which can be used to become a successful artist. You will have great desires and aspirations that will surpass your limits. This position also makes you daydream about your sex drive, and you will find the life partner of your dreams. You will have high expectations of your partner. But your reality and fantasy will not match, so you will never have a fulfilling relationship because you will always judge your partner's appearance. You will be flirty and unreliable when it comes to love and married life. You will never be satisfied in a relationship.

Venus brings you passion and compassion. The 12th house is the house of loss, moksha (liberation), expenses, foreign lands, and the subconscious. Venus in the 12th house brings the greatest joy and happiness in bed through closeness and sex from an early age. Your spouse will be loving and caring, but infidelity can lead to a breakup. Your spouse will bring you happiness and good luck.

Venus in the 12th house means Venus is located in the spiritual house, making the native an inner loner. They may even have some secret backstory hidden from the public eye. Such people are usually shy and reserved. They are admirers of all things mystery and art. People with Venus in the 12th house are natural artists and creative geniuses, but unfortunately, they even hide it from the public. They are so humble that they ignore their charisma, charm, and charisma. When Venus in the 12th house is afflicted, it causes isolation, heavy costs, and ultimately death.

(vii) Shani : Represents planet Saturn

Rules: Capricorn & Aquarius

Exalted: Libra

Debilitated: Aries

Exalted / Debilitated Degree: 20°

Mahadasha Period: 19 years

Principle: Discipline, Effort.

Urges represented: Urge to defend self's structure and Integrity; Urge toward safety and security though tangible achievement.

Positive expression: Disciplined effort, Acceptance of duties and responsibilities, Patience, Organisation, and Reliability.

Negative Expression: Self- restriction through too much reliance on self and lack of faith, rigidity, coldness, defensiveness, grappling inhibition, fearfulness and negativity.

Shani is among the nine main celestial deities of Hindu astrology, which is part of the Vedic system of astrology. He is also known as the Lord of Saturdays. Shani's Tattva, or element, is air. His direction is west, and his nature is Tamas. Shani represents learning the difficult path. The word Shani is derived from the Sanskrit word Shanaye kramati Sa, which means 'one who moves slowly'. This is due to the fact that Saturn's rotation around the Sun takes around 30 years, which is slower than other planets in the solar system, hence the Sanskrit name Shani.

In Hindu astrology, Shani is referred to as the 'Demi-God'. He is the son of 'Surya', the Hindu Sun God, and Chhaya is his wife. When Shani opened his eyes for the first time as a baby, the sun went into an eclipse.

Saturn, also known as Shani, is considered a servant in the Vedic astrological system. He is associated with hard work, sadness, old men, servants, and lower-class workers, such as those in the iron and steel industry, the municipality, and the drainage works. Saturn can bring you great power, prestige, name, and fame if placed correctly. However, if badly placed, it can harm you big time. Saturn's metal is iron; its color is blue; its gem is blue sapphire or Neelam; its direction is west; and its speed is the slowest of all the nine planets. It takes about two-and-a-half years for a sign to pass through a sign, and it takes about thirty years for a Zodiac round to be completed. He is represented as dark-skinned, black-cloaked, with a sword in his hand, arrows in his hand, two daggers in his hand, and mounted on a black crow or a black raven. At other times, he is depicted as ugly, an old man, a cripple, with long hair and nails. He presides over 'shani-war' or Saturday.

Friendly planets of Saturn: Mercury, Venus

Neutral planets: Jupiter

Enemy planets of Saturn: Sun, Moon, Mars, Rahu, Ketu

Effect of Saturn in different Houses: There are many things to evaluate while giving predictions about placement of Saturn in horoscope like sign of the house, conjunction of other planet(s), aspects of other planet(s), degree of Saturn, the condition of house lord etc. However, the general predictions about placement of Saturn in different Houses of a horoscope are as below:

1st **House:** Saturn is known to be the planet of karma, discipline, responsibility, and hard work. When Shani is placed in the first house of one's birth chart, it is seen as a challenge, not an advantageous position. Saturn gives the result of the house in which it is located and the 3 aspects of the house, the 3rd, 7th, and 10th. Saturn affects the 1st house, representing a person's self, personality, physical appearance, and overall health. When placed in the first house, it can complicate a person's life by creating obstacles to their personal and professional growth. Natives can feel weak, and this position of Saturn can affect their self-esteem. It can also create feelings of distance from loved ones and their social circle. Shani's position in this house can cause health problems related to bones, teeth, and nerves. When placed in the first house, it can cause a person to struggle to establish a career and achieve success. Saturn's position in the 1st house can make a person feel isolated and alone. It can also make it difficult to form meaningful relationships with others. Some renowned celebrities with Saturn in the 1st house are Taylor Swift, Katy Perry, Salman Khan, and Sathya Sai Baba.

2nd House: Saturn in the 2nd house of astrology can influence an individual's finances, values, and self-worth. It often brings a sense of responsibility and discipline to matters related to money and possessions. This placement might lead to a cautious approach towards spending and a strong focus on saving and financial stability. However, it can also indicate challenges or delays in achieving financial goals, which may require patience and perseverance to overcome. People with Saturn in the 2nd house may be born into poverty or quickly learn to survive with very few resources. The financial situation of these natives can motivate them to be great survivors. They can start life with near-zero financial status but can reach remarkable heights. Some renowned celebrities with Saturn in the 2nd house are Rafael Nadal, Rajnikanth, Jayalalithaa, and Mukesh Ambani.

Saturn is a slow, malefic planet that respects hard work, a serious approach, and slow but sure moves. And when the Sun is in the financial house, the natives will go to great lengths to increase their income and establish a safety net, as Saturn says in Vedic 2nd house astrology. The presence of Saturn in the 2nd house implies that it will be difficult for natives to acquire material possessions such as houses, cars, etc. There may be numerous reasons preventing them from buying these goods, as Saturn is a slow-moving planet and blesses the natives according to their karmas after due diligence.

In addition, those with Saturn in the 2nd house may be overly cautious when investing money in financial instruments. In fact, natives may prefer debt funds to equity funds. They may be afraid of the risks associated with equity funds. Although safety is good, you should not attach too much importance to it; otherwise, it may affect their development. It is good to avoid risks, but at the same time, it is not necessary to become completely averse to even the most convenient forms of adventure. Overall, Saturn in the 2nd house encourages a practical and prudent attitude towards material matters.

3rd House: In Vedic astrology, Saturn in the 3rd house can bring a serious and disciplined approach to communication, learning, and siblings. It may indicate challenges in relationships with siblings, but also the potential for gaining wisdom through them. There might be a focus on hard work and perseverance in education or skill development. However, Saturn's influence here could lead to a reserved or cautious communication style. The presence of Saturn in the 3rd house of the horoscope influences communication, career, professional life, mental state, and esoteric life. However, the presence of Saturn in the 3rd house of the horoscope can create both favorable and unfavorable situations in the life of the native. People with Saturn in the 3rd house of their horoscopes are very quiet. Their sentences are flexible, and they avoids being the first in any case. They try to be very careful and sure of what they say. This quality can be especially helpful for people whose jobs or careers require a discerning attitude. People with Saturn in the 3rd house are very good at matters involving confidential information and paperwork. Residents of Saturn in the 3rd house are generally serious and methodical. But they may encounter problems due to inadequate or inappropriate communication. They are likely to remain quite isolated in life. So sometimes they can be pessimistic and prone to depression. These natives may find it difficult to maintain close relationships with their siblings and loved ones. Some renowned celebrities with Saturn in the 3rd house are Tom Hanks, Brad Pitt, Neetu Singh, Steve Jobs, and Bruce Wills.

4th House: In astrology, Saturn in the 4th house is often associated with themes of home, family, and roots. It may indicate a sense of responsibility or restriction in these areas, potentially leading to a focus on establishing stability and structure within one's personal life. The position of Saturn in the 4th house is considered lucky for natives and helps them achieve unforeseen gains in terms of business results. It also has a positive influence on the lifestyle of the natives by providing them with all the luxury amenities, wealth, wisdom, and a high-class lifestyle. People with this aspect respect their relationships and are capable of living a happy married life. They appreciate the simple joys of life, expressing their faith in their religion and traditions. These people have their own homes and rarely move to different places. According to Vedic knowledge, these individuals are wealthy and have good real estate business ability. Keep in mind that astrology interpretations can vary, and it's important to consider the entire birth chart for a comprehensive analysis. People with Saturn in the 4th house experience an unbalanced financial relationship and loss of wealth due to Saturn's karmic effects. As Vedic astrology points out, these people struggle a lot and, in some cases, even have to sell their home to stabilize their finances or pay off debt. The natives lack affection for their mothers and wives and have unsurprisingly severed their ties. These people can suffer financial crises and big losses in the real estate business. In addition, indigenous people often migrate to different places and have a distant relationship with their partner. Some renowned celebrities with Saturn in the 4th house are Ratan Tata, Priyanka Gandhi, Tom Cruise, and Madonna.

5th House: When Saturn is placed in the 5th house, natives can find it very difficult to be happy. They have to understand that life is not always about work, duties, goals, and objectives.

The 5th house is the house of play and self-expression. It is also a question of spontaneity. Saturn's influence on this house can interfere with spontaneity. Natives can be seen as asocial because they have a dark attitude towards life. They despise festivals and some social gatherings. Their preoccupation with work and serious things in life can make them unpopular.

While such people are dating, Saturn allows their dating to start a little earlier. If their date has Saturn in the 5th house, they don't need to worry. They can talk about issues like global warming and climate change in their first meeting. If their date doesn't have Saturn in the 5th house, he or she may have other ideas on how to have a good time. Furthermore, for couples, the presence of Saturn in the 5th house can also cause fertility problems.

They have to be careful not to get into one of those situations where they can't have a good time because of guilt or regret. They can sometimes let their guard down and give in to desires to avoid boredom or restlessness. Otherwise, they will have a harder time finding joy in anything, and that's never a good thing, especially if Saturn is weak in the 5th house. They don't want to increase their risk of becoming anxious or depressed, so they need to make sure they aren't overworked. The only good thing about Saturn transiting through the 5th house is that the natives will succeed when they are too loud or vocal. When they become overly emotional, they will realize the situation and calm down immediately. Those who see them from afar may not understand their worth, but those close to them know the greatness of their character and their inherent kindness. Some renowned celebrities with Saturn in the 5th house are Bill Gates, Winston Churchill, Emma Stone, and Alfred Hitchcock.

6th House: The 6th house is related to the health, food, debt, enemies, and occupation of the natives. In Vedic astrology, it is known as 'Ari Bhava' or 'Shatru Bhava'. In the zodiac circle, it belongs to the sign of Virgo. If Saturn is present in this house, you are probably a workaholic. Saturn here will bring you various results in life. Natives with a strong Saturn in the 6th house can triumph over their hidden enemies.

Individuals with Saturn in the 6th house can have a steadfast attitude. You can show more dedication to your work. Moreover, you can become a well-disciplined employee because you may have different views and ideas. You will do your best to achieve your goal. The qualities that you have can make others jealous of you. It is suggested that you should avoid high expectations of others.

If Saturn turns retrograde in your 6th house, it can negatively impact your lifestyle and health. If Saturn is present in the 6th house, things may not go as you would like. And so, you must limit your worries about things that are not in your control. Saturn transit in the 6th house can damage your reputation in society. You can have a happy and harmonious married life. You can expect a long-term relationship with your spouse. You can also expect good support from your partner. However, the presence of Saturn in the 6th house can delay childbirth. You may feel emotionally attached to your partner.

People with Saturn in the 6th house can achieve their desired career success after overcoming some obstacles in their path. Your determination at work can help you establish the career of your choice. Moreover, you can work alone to grow your own business. You may have the opportunity to complete your studies far from your place of origin. Some renowned celebrities with Saturn in the 6th house are N. Chandrababu Naidu, Lady Gaga, Isaac Newton, and Deepika Padukone.

7th House: Saturn's position in the 7th house blesses rich and famous natives. They keep their actions low and don't let others notice their actions. These natives display virtues of faith, trust, and loyalty to others. They don't talk much, but they never back down from injustice. These people can achieve remarkable achievements in business. They can also be a game changer when it comes to business growth. Saturn reflects the influence of karma, which means "whatever happens," and this greatly affects the lives of earthly people. If natives do good deeds, they will be rewarded or punished by Saturn, depending on their behavior.

Natives are endowed with strength, wisdom, knowledge, and leadership qualities. They can have a fulfilling and happy married life. In fact, people in this position get the life partner of their choice. They share values and support each other to overcome difficulties. When Saturn enters the 7th house of marriage, mutual understanding between partners becomes the backbone of their relationship. Saturn's presence also increases the divinity of the partners, which ultimately strengthens their relationship. Such natives are ambitious and passionate in their love lives.

However, under certain circumstances, Saturn in the 7th house can negatively affect the marital life of a person. The position of Saturn in the 7th house can negatively affect the relationships of natives. These natives may face a dilemma in choosing their mate. The negative impact of Saturn retrograde in the 7th house can damage the relationship between natives and their mates. In such a situation, the native can experience immense pain and suffering. There may be arguments between partners; they may become impatient, not listening to the opinions of others. They may lose their sense of responsibility and not care about their partner. Most likely, the age gap between them is more than 5 years. Some renowned celebrities with Saturn in the 7th house are Shahrukh Khan, Stephen Hawking, Sridevi, and Bruce Lee.

8th House: Saturn in the 8th house represents higher awareness, longevity, ambition, willpower, discipline, courage, determination, patience, and hard work. With Saturn in the 8th House, you can be fearless, determined, and determined.

You work very hard to achieve your goals. Once you have decided on something, there is a high probability that you will achieve it. In addition, you have serious responsibilities towards others and may interfere in their financial affairs, especially in matters relating to taxes, debt, and inheritance. You are good at managing other people's money and have a knack for running a business. However, because Saturn is the planet of limitations and restrictions, you may find yourself limited in your sexual attraction and ability to express yourself.

According to Saravali, if Saturn occupies the 8th house, the native will suffer from leprosy and anal fistula, or pudendum, will have a short life and will fail at work. However, according to Phala Deepika, if Saturn occupies the 8th house at birth, it will make the natives unclean, pious, wealthless, cruel, hungry, and shunned by friends.

If your Saturn is in the 8th house, you have a heightened awareness of the unseen. But there can be a lot of fear going there. The hot spot on Saturn usually means you will face difficulties. These things open up new ways of life for us while tearing down structures that are familiar to us. For some people with this Saturn, there can be great fear of encounters involving the unknown. Some renowned celebrities with

Saturn in the 8th house are Kristen Stewart, Martin Luther King, and Osho Rajneesh.

9th House: Saturn in the 9th house brings spiritual awakening to natives. These people have traditional ideas and religious personalities. They work very hard in life to achieve their defined goals. These natives may face a slow process in their work but gradually reach their intended destination. These people may find it difficult to open up to their loved ones, but they care about them and maintain stable relationships with their family, friends, and loved ones. These people have considerable opportunities to meet their soul mates at a young age, but they should patiently progress in the relationship. The love life of the natives will be faithful, cooperative, and productive—not too hectic but decent and stable. Such people will have a good married life; their spouses will be supportive, cooperative, and faithful.

These people have been dedicated and hardworking from a young age. They are very focused on their lives and have a fixed path in life through which they make a great career. These natives will have successful career development. According to their career reports, these natives have in-depth knowledge of their field and are always finding new insights in their respective fields, helping them thrive in the workplace.

In general, indigenous people have a spiritual, religious, and traditional character, thanks to which they have achieved a certain goal in life. They may have an emotional imbalance in their lives, but by overcoming and dealing with it, they have formed good relationships with family, friends, and loved ones in their lives. Some renowned celebrities with Saturn in the 9th house are Mary Kom, Kylie Jenner, and Julia Roberts.

10th House: When Saturn is placed in the 10th house of career, fame, and ambition, it achieves massive success only after hard work and procrastination. These natives have tremendous organizational and management skills. These people have good business sense. Success will come late, but it can take a lot of effort and hard work to achieve their goals and dreams. An unaffected positive Saturn in the 10th house can make you disciplined and virtuous by the age of 35. You will have a harmonious relationship with everyone in your life. Sasa Yoga is a typical planetary conjunction that can occur with Saturn in the 10th Bhava in Libra, Capricorn, or Aquarius, which will lead you to live a life of luxury. Saturn in the 10th House, together with Venus and Mercury, form Raja Yoga, which blesses you with luck, happiness, and wealth.

Saturn retrograde in the 10th house can bring sluggish results and slow down your ambitions and growth. But this Saturn position can make you nervous, energetic, and impulsive, going against your destiny and creating chaos in your personal and professional lives. You will fight hard for your success and finally achieve it. However, Saturn in the 10th House can create impatience and restlessness, creating problems of panic and anxiety.

Natives will gain through perseverance but will lose by being too smart and by adapting to shortcuts. However, if these people are not serious and dedicated to their tasks, priorities, work, or relationships, life can turn into a series of trials and tribulations, one after another.

Natives can also be quite ambitious but sometimes reckless and over-ambitious, which can sometimes turn out to be quite dangerous. In their quest for power, these people may break some hearts, relationships, or ties. However, certain situations can arise when these people need to get back together with their old friends for help, support, or advice. Some renowned celebrities with Saturn in the 10th house are Leonardo DiCaprio, Mohammad Ali, and Oprah Winfrey.

11th House: Saturn in the 11th house helps people with Kim's destiny to be rich, healthy, and lucky. Youth can be full of difficulties and discouragement, but the natives will never lose hope and energy. Positive, helpful, and powerful Saturn in the 11th house gives natives good results after hard work. These people are never alone, even on difficult days, but they lack true friends in life.

Natives win through business, financial institutions, speculative trading, networking, and all kinds of resources. You don't like to flaunt your wealth in front of others, and your social circle will consist of mature people. Once you've worked hard and put in personal effort, Saturn in the 11th house will make your hopes and wishes come true. Saturn in this house gives results faster than any other house.

This position gives you manipulative skills, and you can become a successful politician or businessman who can conquer the world. You will have a long and healthy life. You will have a very distinctive and clear personality with a diplomatic attitude. You will be good to your friends, family, and loved ones. People will admire you, and you will influence the masses with your work, attitude, lifestyle, and achievements. Saturn in the 11th house helps you to have lifelong friends who will always be by your side as solid pillars.

Positive Saturn in the 11th Bhava makes you work hard and make persistent efforts to achieve your goals. Saturn in the 11th House, combined with Venus, Mars, or Mercury, brings you wealth and luck. Success through politics and business is guaranteed. Self-employment can bring them high status in life.

Saturn retrograde in the 11th house can introduce you to bad companies. You may be humiliated by your own social circle. You can get involved in criminal cases and be punished for wrongdoing or illegality. This position of Saturn can give you a tough time putting off your hopes and dreams. The struggles of youth can lead to depression.

Saturn combust in the 11th house may not allow you to shine or succeed in life. It can bring you a lot of difficult times in life. You may be betrayed by friends and family members. You may struggle for a long time before having a prosperous life. There will be discord and chaos in your personal and professional lives. Some renowned celebrities with Saturn in the 11th house are Kim Kardashian, Pamela Anderson, Jeff Bezos, and Anil Kapoor.

12th House: Saturn in the 12th house influences your subconscious and causes you to accumulate wealth and success. Positive Saturn in this house will help you work hard towards your goals. Saturn in the 12th house activates your subconscious and connects you to different areas. It limits your peace of mind and increases your spiritual search. At the ages of 28 and 30, you will gradually become enlightened and progress in life. It will force you to go abroad and support the less fortunate. This position can make you work in an embassy, become a foreign minister, and go out and maintain foreign relations with other countries. You will be rich and earn money abroad. You can become one of the most powerful people by getting involved in politics. If Saturn is favorable, it will bring you the support of your partner after marriage, and you will both have a harmonious life. You will have enough time to get to know each other and take advantage of the opportunities to enjoy married life. You will be dedicated and focused on your career goals and succeed after the age of 30. Success can be delayed, but it cannot be denied. Saturn will bring you results for your hard work and personal efforts. It may take you longer than others your age to be successful, but you will achieve your desired goals.

If Saturn is retrograde, it will cause you to deal with heartbreak and loneliness in your love life. You will have temporary and non-permanent relationships. Saturn in the 12th house will strengthen your limits and create anxiety, depression, and other psychological problems in you. You will go around daydreaming and fantasizing about the future. You will be unrealistic and disciplined regarding your goals. You want to be detached and be a lone ranger. You will be serious and drown in grief. You may break a bone or lose a limb; you will always be unhappy. You will enjoy doing evil deeds. You will be lazy, distrustful, wordy, and absorbed in sinful deeds. Some renowned celebrities with Saturn in the 12th house are Donald Trump, Demi Moore, and George Clooney.

(viii) Rahu :

Rules: Virgo & Aquarius.

Exalted: Gemini & Taurus.

Debilitated: Sagittarius & Scorpio

Mahadasha Period: 18 Years

In astrology, Rahu is considered one of the nine celestial bodies known as the Navagrahas. It is often associated with mystery, illusion, and worldly desires. The effects of Rahu in different houses of an individual's birth chart can vary. Here's a general overview, but keep in mind that the interpretation may vary depending on the entire birth chart and the astrologer's approach. Rahu is the god of the ascension or north lunar node. In Hindu mythology, Rahu is considered a demon snake that devours the sun or the moon, causing an eclipse. In art, Rahu is depicted as a dragon without a body on a chariot driven by eight black horses. It is said that Rahu is a "Tamas Asura" who does everything in his power to plunge anyone's part of life into chaos. Rahu is considered to be an unlucky deity because of his bad luck.

 According to Hindu mythology, during Samudra manthan, the Asura Rahu took a sip of divine nectar, but before it could go down his throat, his head was cut off by Mohini (Vishnu's female avatar). The head remained immortal and was called Rahu. The rest of his body turned into Ketu. It is believed that Rahu's immortal head sometimes devours a sun or a moon, causing an eclipse. After the sun or moon passes through the opening at the neck, the eclipse comes to an end.

Rahu, or dragon's head, symbolizes foreigners, foreign lands, foreign travels, engineering and technical trades, smoking, elderly people, grandparents, stealing, gambling, alcohol, non-conformity, the underworld, and the evil forces of society. Rahu's color is black, his metal is mixed metal, and his gemstone is the Gomedh. For Rahu traveling, a sign takes about 1.5 years, thus completing the Zodiac round in 18 years.

Friendly planets of Rahu: Venus, Saturn

Neutral planets: Jupiter, Mercury

Enemy planets of Rahu: Sun, Moon, Mars

Effect of Rahu in different Houses: There are many things to evaluate while giving predictions about placement of Rahu in horoscope like sign of the house, conjunction of other planet(s), aspects of other planet(s), degree of Rahu, the condition of house lord etc. However, the general predictions about placement of Rahu in different Houses of a horoscope are as below:

1st House: The 1st house is the house of self. It is the physical manifestation of the personality, including physical characteristics, temperament, and personality, as well as childhood, health, and the ego and sense of self. This affects life decisions, the ability to recognize one's strengths and weaknesses, as well as one's likes and dislikes, and how they would like others to view them through their opinions, attitudes, and opinions. The main parts of the first house include the head and face, as well as the complexion, forehead, and hair, and the brain. People with Rahu in the first house are usually very brave and have a brave soul. They are driven by the desire to succeed and accomplish whatever comes their way. Rahu in the first house, his own home, inspires the natives to take risks in life. And in doing so, they have the potential to succeed in every field.

These people are very creative. They come up with innovative ideas and are therefore commended for the same in their personal and professional spaces. They are the right people for anyone looking for inspiration about anything. Also, these people can be very competitive. Their competitiveness is not limited to strangers or colleagues, but also to those close to them.

These natives have strong analytical skills. They have a strong enthusiasm for debates. These people are also a bit greedy and not really ready to share this pleasure with anyone. These people are also somewhat introverted and don't hesitate to spend time alone.

Sexually, those with Rahu in the first house are very erotic. Their sex drive is unusual, and a wonderful intimate encounter with them is guaranteed. Also, another great thing about these sexual encounters is that they are not usually inspired by flirting or momentary cravings. People native to Rahu in the first house seek to establish a real relationship with someone before undressing in front of them. Rahu in the 1st house and Ketu in the 7th house are a great combination for compatibility in love.

The negative effect of Rahu in the first house is that it makes the natives really controversial. Strongly self-confident, these people often want their views to be accepted by the masses. This behavior can be upsetting to those around.

Furthermore, although Rahu inspires people to achieve greater things in life, he does the same to create a sense of material lust in you. Rahu attracts you to get more and more and pushes you towards immoral and illegal acts. So, one really needs to master oneself in terms of financial and intellectual spending, especially in Rahu Mahadasha. In addition, the presence of Rahu can quickly make the natives susceptible to bad habits such as drinking and smoking. Rahu rules over obsessions, desires, and illusions. This affected his ability to appreciate his immature steps and run after worldly fame. In the process of achieving all these pleasures, Rahu tends to become callous to the people in his life. This behavior can lead to alienation, lack of intimacy, property and money problems, infidelity, and a lack of mental development for children in the family.

In a nutshell, Rahu, as a planet, is a snowball of negative energy. It pushes us into illusions and then accumulates bad karma. Rahu can derail anyone from the path of goodness, and so we must be very careful with the demon planet. Some famous personalities with Rahu in the 1st house are Raj Kapoor, Laloo Prasad Yadav, Michael Jordan, Nicola Tesla, Charles Dickens, Martin Luther King, and Glenn Maxwell.

2nd House: The 2nd house of Vedic astrology, also known as the house of property, is the house of income. It refers to your income, which includes your money, your possessions such as your car, your furniture, your investments, etc. The 2nd house governs your body organs like your tongue, your teeth, your eyes, your mouth, your nose, and more. The 2nd house not only restricts your physical possessions but also your intangible possessions, like your voice and your speech. Rahu in the 2nd house can influence a person's speech, family, and finances. It may indicate a desire for material wealth, but it can also create challenges in managing money and lead to impulsive spending habits. Rahu in your 2nd house is good for you. You will become rich in life. You will get a rich life partner. You will also get some property from your relatives. You will always have royal comfort and wealth to enjoy. You have a taste for delicious food, alcohol, and non-vegetarian food. You have a strong voice and can influence people with your voice. Your sexual appetite is uncontrollable. Many politicians use this Rahu position in their horoscopes. You will live a long life.

If a person is born with a Rahu in the 2nd house, it can create an unusual and unorthodox environment at the beginning of their life. This can bring parents and siblings, who will be very different from others. If Rahu is affected, it will separate you from his lineage. You will find yourself surrounded by mystical people, or you may have had past relationships with these types of people.

Your family will have astrologers, occultists, surgeons, or a life-and-death scenario. It may also bring about the experience of dealing with the strange death of a father or grandfather. Or you may be attracted to the occult, extra-terrestrials, or UFOs.

Rahu here will give you a speech such that you can easily capture the crowd with your performing arts or your knowledge, as Rahu has mystical energy, so when you speak, everyone is bewildered. Rahu is in the 2nd house, or even when he appears in the 2nd house, Rahu holds mystical energy in the house of language, so he can make you an excellent astrologer. You can also become a good banker because here you will be completely focused on material things, so you are always hungry for money and status.

So, Rahu, in the 2nd house, you will find that there is no one to help you make money, or even no one to help you. When Rahu is in the 2nd house, Ketu will be in the 8th house, so here Ketu blocks this area; it's like a blood clot, which means you don't have access to another people's money. Some famous personalities with Rahu in the 2nd house are Priyanka Chopra, Vicky Kaushal, Ravi Shanker, Stefi Graf, and Salman Khan.

3rd House: Rahu in the 3rd house can enhance communication skills and curiosity. It may bring success in endeavors related to communication, writing, or media. However, it can also indicate a tendency to manipulate others or engage in deceitful behavior. It is a good position to earn money, plan the future, and learn special skills. All cybercriminals and hackers will have Rahu's influence in the 3rd house. I would like to reiterate once again whether Rahu works at a higher or lower level. Thus, a higher level of Rahu can turn the same person into a computer genius. When Rahu gives you something, it has a hidden price, like the old slogan: Think twice before making a deal with the devil. So now that you have free will, either you can make the most of this position and make your journey to excellence, or you can take the illegal route and one day get caught stuck in the devil's game. Rahu in the 3rd house is your spouse's Bhagya Sthan (9th house), so the Rahu here will force your partner to follow different traditions and religious rules. She won't be from your caste or might be from a foreign country. Some famous personalities with Rahu in the 3rd house are Dr. Babasaheb Ambedkar, Dhirubhai Ambani, Michael Jackson, S.D. Burman, Dr. Homi Bhabha, Virat Kohli, and Leonardo da Vinci.

4th House: Rahu in the 4th house can influence domestic life, property, and emotional stability. It may create restlessness in the family environment and a desire for change. There can be challenges in maintaining harmony at home, but it can also indicate a person's inclination towards real estate or property-related ventures. Rahu in the 4th house will strongly affect your financial condition. In addition to stabilizing your relationship with your spouse, Rahu in the 4th house will also impact your relationship with your mother.

You can feel powerful, gain fame and recognition, and have great control over your business. Furthermore, you will achieve wealth befitting a king within a few years of your life. From wisdom to personal stability, the 4th house, Rahu, will bring you benefits that you may not have thought of. In addition, natives can expect their mothers' involvement in establishing a stable life. Talking about personal life, people can have a happy married life with boundless loyalty. They will seek the loving support of their spouse and have a lasting relationship. Moreover, modern conveniences such as houses, cars, and the like will also be there. People with Rahu in the 4th house will seek full support from their family and partner in times of need and adversity. Such people can also suffer the consequences of their sin. You can become greedy and have a strong need for high status through unfair means. Not only may you lack empathy, but you may also lack emotional connection with those around you. Furthermore, by nature, you will be overly possessive and sublime. In addition, you will lose the tendency to judge people accurately and rationally. With Rahu in the 4th house, the native might face a big loss in his business and great ups and downs in his professional life. They must keep an eye on their connection to their spouse and mother, as these areas could be the target of this planet. Anger problems and greedy behavior will be everywhere. People will believe in injustice and perpetuate inequality. Some famous personalities with Rahu in the 4th house are Vladimir Putin and Karishma Kapoor. Aamir Khan, Himesh Reshammiya, Serena Williams, and Ariana Grande

5th House: Rahu in the 5th house can influence creativity, education, and children. It may bring intense desires for recognition and achievement in artistic or speculative fields. There can be a tendency towards risk-taking behavior, and caution is advised in matters of romance and speculation. Such natives seek recognition and privilege in roles that allow them to be central. They are passionate about culture, politics, literature, performing arts, gaming, and celebrity betting. However, this position of Rahu disturbs his relationship with the father or the children. However, natives are usually in favor of adoption. It is a good location for literary people, theatre artists, and politicians. This film is also popular for its creative expression. They tend to take on as many roles in their lives as necessary to succeed.

Their children can be eccentric and extraordinary, likely to be adopted or out of wedlock. This position of Rahu makes married life a roller coaster, full of drama, with the possibility of marital loss and the survival of more than one marriage. These people are often involved in trades related to oil, gas, fuel, petroleum, chemicals, and explosives. As a positive trait, the native Rahu in the 5th house seeks center stage. These people are passionate about culture, politics, literature, performing arts, gaming, and celebrity betting. However, this position of Rahu has a negative impact on the relationship of the natives with their father or children. At the same time, it supports adoption. Rahu's position in the 5th House is good for literati, theatre artists, and politicians. Their creative expression is equally dramatic. The Rahu in the 5th house tends to take on as many necessary roles in life as possible in order to achieve success. Rahu's position in the 5th house is very helpful in becoming a successful actor, politician, or athlete.

As a negative trait, Rahu is a master of dishonesty, deception, and immorality. It represents swindlers, pleasure seekers, foreign lands, and drug trafficking. Rahu's bad traits are suicidal tendencies, fear and obsession, poison bites, murder, theft, and imprisonment. In short, these people crave fame and glory, but they may go too far in their quest. They can be deceived by Rahu, so they can use nefarious means and methods to achieve their goals. As we know, injustice will eventually fall, so these natives have to be very careful in this regard. Some famous personalities with Rahu in the 5th house are Narendra Modi, Mary Kom, Rajnath Singh, Pele, Steve Jobs, and Jim Karey.

6th House: Rahu in the 6th house can enhance the individual's drive for success in the workplace and the ability to overcome obstacles. It may indicate a desire to dominate others, and there can be a propensity for health issues or conflicts with colleagues. This position is known as the positive position for Rahu in the horoscope. These people desired the privileges associated with slavery. They are experts in conflict and association management. After many trials and tribulations in life that are often unaware of others, those with the 6th house of Rahu have succeeded in their endeavors through serving others. These people have a strong desire to serve those who face opposition and discord. Indigenous people tend to indulge in arguments beyond their comprehension.

As a positive trait, the native Rahu in the 6th house aspires to gain the privileges associated with bondage. They know very well how to manage the activities of associations. They can also resolve conflicts very effectively. Experiencing the hardships of daily life, these natives are aware of many ways and methods that are not known to most others. As a negative trait, people with the Moon in the 2nd house can experience serious difficulties, which can arise from poverty, bondage, divorce, drugs, war, illness, and oppression. Moreover, this location can bring unexpected benefits to the natives. It is also possible that natives invest in financial instruments that put them at risk. As a result, they can make big profits or suffer big losses. The difficulties in their lives can be solved by using the appropriate remedies for Rahu in the 6th house. To sum up, Rahu is a harmful planet that is largely considered negative. Its placement in the 6th house will produce mixed results for natives. They are very good at resolving conflicts and difficult situations and helping those in need. However, in certain provocative situations, they may exhibit disruptive behavior. Some famous personalities with Rahu in the 6th house are Yogi Adityanath, Arnab Goswami, Mel Gibson, Angelina Jolie, Akshay Kumar, and Hardik Pandya.

7th House: Rahu in the 7th house can affect partnerships, relationships, and marriage. It may bring intense desires for relationships and a fascination with unconventional partnerships. There can be challenges to maintaining harmony and stability in relationships. Such people are intentional, proud, and independent. They reduce the number of opponents and increase profits while trading with others. The Rooster in the 7th house affects all kinds of relationships you can have, especially marital relationships. This placement shows how the couple will live their lives. Rahu in this house brings blessings to couples; it makes them share deep feelings for each other, love and care for each other, and be deeply attached—making their married life peaceful and harmonious.

The 7th house is the house of marriage and your relationship with your spouse. This house regulates partnerships as well as the coordination and connection that you can have with your partner. It controls the nature of social norms and aligns with a larger pattern; it gives an idea of possible conflicts in partnership and marital relations. Contracts and agreements and their legality, etc. are also covered by this house, and this includes the legal aspects related to marriage.

This position of Rahu will also bring you good opportunities in business, especially if you have a partnership. This position also indicates that it is more likely that your spouse is from a different and distant place, even from abroad. Even so, the relationship can be good, and even different customs, traditions, and cultures will not pose a threat to the relationship or the relationship in general.

A positive Rahu in the 7th house will bring happiness to your business; you will see your business grow and expand, especially when it comes to partnerships. Here, Rahu also brings wealth, a good income, and a stable financial situation. It ensures love and affection in a couple, as well as respect and attention to the spouse's suggestions. Spouse-owned businesses will also have a good chance of success. A negative Rahu in the 7th house can bring you many obstacles in your career, especially in businesses created by people who are jealous of you or your enemies. There may be some misunderstandings with your spouse. Some famous personalities with Rahu in the 7th house are Amitabh Bachchan, Deepika Padukone, David Beckham, Prince William, Neeta Ambani, and Huma Quereshi.

8th House: Rahu in the 8th house can influence transformation, occult sciences, and longevity. It may bring intense desires for hidden knowledge and a fascination with mystical or esoteric subjects. There can be sudden changes in life and a need to navigate financial matters carefully. When Rahu is placed in the 8th house, it is generally not a good situation for the Rahu natives in the 8th house. Indigenous people may have to depend on others to maintain their finances. Surname. They can also engage in wrong ways and methods of making money that can get them in trouble.

Rahu's position in the 8th house can bring financial returns. Rahu can also provide the ability to think outside the box, which can make natives quite creative. This innovation can help Natives excel in research-related tasks.

Since the 8th house also deals with latent energies, it is difficult to understand what influence Rahu will have in the 8th house. Let us remember that as ghost planets, Rahu and Ketu bring about the results of other planets with which they are placed. However, in general, Rahu's position in the 8th house can bring more problems than benefits. Such people may develop hostility toward some people. They may argue with others, which can damage their peace of mind and that of others. Sometimes it can also lead to legal troubles such as defamation and other serious forms of humiliation.

Natives may spend money unnecessarily on cases or litigation. These people may even witness disturbances in their married lives. In fact, this is not a good planetary position for marital happiness. The Rahu in the 8th house may not be mysterious, but they can solve complex mysteries. Such people have the potential to grow in professions like intelligence agencies, detectives, etc. They can also do a good job of research. However, they should avoid unnecessary disputes and litigation. They can build on their strengths and address their weaknesses. Some famous personalities with Rahu in the 8th house are Smriti Irani, Anushka Sharma, George Foreman, Ranveer Singh, Bradley Cooper, Winston Churchill, and Lady Diana.

9th House: Rahu in the 9th house can influence spirituality, higher education, and long-distance travel. It may create a thirst for knowledge and experiences beyond the ordinary. However, there can be a tendency to challenge traditional beliefs and dogmas. The 9th house in Vedic astrology signifies knowledge, spirituality, guruhood, and fatherhood. Rahu in the 9th house can make the natives very skilled and erudite. However, they may have some element of dishonesty, as they may not practice everything they preach. The difference between preaching and practice may be a flaw in their character. Whoever Rahu has placed in the ninth house of the horoscope can be blessed under its influence with good results regarding finance, marriage, career, fame, power, health, children, spiritual growth, and many other kinds of good results. Such people will possess special or creative abilities under his influence. It can help such people enter some creative or special career fields, and they can achieve success through them, as shown in their general horoscope. Some of these people may also be creatively gifted and become professionals as actors, singers, writers, dancers, musicians, and many other types of creative professionals.

Natives are blessed with abundant and quality clothing, a large number of servants, and jewellery, and are generally always in a happy mood. The person becomes independent, in control of his own thoughts, and is a very complacent person. Not only that, he will also expect those around him to accept his thought process, adopt his plan of things, and be generally satisfied with their lives. Rahu in the 9th house can cause delays and problems in obtaining any kind of inheritance. Natives may face situations where they won't agree with their father. Furthermore, this placement will not suit your father's health, as he may have health problems. In addition, he may incur a monetary loss. Some famous personalities with Rahu in the 9th house are Charlie Chaplin, Dilip Kumar, Dr. APJ Abdul Kalam, Manoj Bajpayee, Agatha Christie, and Varun Dhawan.

10th House: Rahu in the 10th house can affect a career, reputation, and public image. It may indicate a strong drive for success and recognition in one's profession. However, there can be a constant search for new opportunities and a tendency towards restlessness in career matters. It provides the person with all the worldly fame, strong will, great wealth, and good relations with very famous people. People who have a Rahu in the 10th house will become rich and famous and achieve great success in the fields of media, entertainment, and software.

Rahu's presence in the 10th house can make the natives cunning and intelligent. They can defeat their enemies. They may have a cousin problem. Also, according to ancient texts, both men and women are able to achieve high rank and position in the government or private sector. They will earn their name and fame through their hard work and initiatives.

They are always looking for a higher position in the hierarchy, but the path to getting there is often murky. They may apply illegal and immoral means and methods to enhance themselves in life. Even the marriages of these indigenous people can be threatened. It is said that their intense desire to thrive in life can be a compensation for their childhood, where the natives lacked the basic requirements of life, such as parental care.

The harmful presence of Rahu in the 10th house will bring about many difficulties in the career and financial path and can also lead to disrepute. These people will also have enemies around. This type of position will cause poor health for the native and the mother of the native. Some famous personalities with Rahu in the 10th house are Amit Shah, Dr. Rajendra Prasad, Chris Gayle, Shahid Kapoor, John Abraham, Matthew McConaughey, Neha Kakkar, and Sourav Ganguly.

11th House: Rahu in the 11th house can influence social networks, aspirations, and gains. It may bring a desire for material success and association with influential or unconventional groups. However, caution is advised in financial matters and when avoiding risky investments. The 11th house of Rahu creates the ideal circumstances to reap great returns on your investments. You will get lucky, and your efforts will be rewarded with success and the realization of your dreams. Your overseas relationships and interactions with high-ranking government officials will benefit you. You may have strong public speaking skills, which will help improve your negotiation and persuasion skills.

Such a person has a lot of "win-win friends", especially financially. This location in Rahu suggests a high income for the natives. This type of person earns profits in the market and through social networks and receives a lot of praise and rewards for completing his or her work.

The potential danger associated with this position of Rahu is their tendency to adopt delicate means to use their social circle for economic gain. These people also ignore social and community norms. Rahu provides many friends and supporters in the 11th House who will help the person progress. This position also suggests increased wealth for the mother or wife, which will benefit the native and her children. This Rahu brings success after the age of 31 or 34. In the 11th house, Rahu benefits from the opposite sex and associates with people with integrity problems or even poor health.

This house is influenced by both Saturn and Jupiter. That person can be rich as long as his father is alive. This group of people has bad friends. After his father's death, he had to wear gold around his neck. Some famous personalities with Rahu in the 11th house are Baba Ramdev, Abraham Lincoln, Lata Mangeshkar, Neil Armstrong, Asha Bhosle, Arvind Kejriwal, Sharad Pawar, and Sanjay Dutt.

12th House: The 12th house symbolizes loss, misfortune, and deliverance. Rahu in the 12th house will attract a lot of appreciation for your work and efforts, admiration from people, and a good image in society. Your career will be benefitted, and your prosperity will improve, through your relationships abroad and if you pursue your goals there. This position will bring you a good reputation and popularity; however, if you do not protect your image, chances are some unfortunate events or circumstances may get in the way of the good work you do and the respect you get in society.

You may suffer from various health problems. You have a tendency to keep secrets and may commit improper acts. You can accumulate great wealth, but your friends may not be the best. This home also reflects your expenses in general and your specific expenses for the hospital. This house displays your connections with past lives and the habits you have retained in this life. Your spiritual orientation can also be analyzed in this house. The way you progress is tied to this house, as is the hard work you put into every activity.

You will enjoy a beautiful love life with Rahu in the 12th house. You will share a good relationship with your lover and indulge in pleasure-related activities in bed. On the other hand, married life can go through ups and downs due to misunderstandings between husband and wife because of petty issues. Some famous personalities with Rahu in the 12th house are Mukesh Ambani, Swami Vivekanand, Steven Spielberg, Harrison Ford, and Lady Gaga.

(ix) Ketu :

Rules: Pisces & Scorpio

Exalted: Sagittarius & Scorpion

Debilitated: Gemini & Taurus

Mahadasha Period: 7 Years

Ketu is the lord of the descending or south moon node. Ketu is often referred to as the "shadow" planet. It is considered the tail of the demon snake. It is said to have a huge impact on people's lives and all things. In some special cases, it helps someone reach their peak of popularity. He is essentially Tamas in nature and represents supernatural influences.

Astronomically, Ketu and Rahu denote the intersections of the Sun and Moon's orbits as they move across the celestial sphere. Therefore, Rahu and Ketu are called the north and south nodes of the moon, respectively. The fact that a solar eclipse occurs when the sun and moon are at one of these points gives rise to the story of swallowing the sun and moon.

Ketu, or Dragon's Tail, represents grandparents, technical professions, spiritual inclinations, superstition, and electronics. Its color is brown, and the gem is a cat's eye. Ketu is always opposite to Rahu, which is exactly 180 degrees. Ketu also takes about 1.5 years to go through a sign and thus completes the zodiac cycle in 18 years.

Friendly planets of Ketu: Venus, Saturn

Neutral planets: Jupiter, Mercury

Enemy planets of Ketu: Sun, Moon, Mars

Effect of Ketu in different Houses: There are many things to evaluate while giving predictions about placement of Ketu in horoscope like sign of the house, conjunction of other planet(s), aspects of other planet(s), degree of Ketu, the condition of house lord etc. However, the general predictions about placement of Ketu in different Houses of a horoscope are as below:

1st **House**: The native's personality will be very mysterious and enigmatic as well. He should always try to keep himself away from bad company. The first house speaks about your inner personality as well as your physical appearance. The placement of ketu in this house provides quite an attractive persona, so much so that it may even get hard for the people around you to ignore you or not pay attention to you.

These people may also have some kind of mark, be it a mole or a patch on their face. Some kinds of disturbances may also be present in their minds, but on the other hand, these people are inclined towards spirituality as well. Straightforwardness, aggression, and courage are a few of their characteristics. These people are also blessed with good height.

2nd **House**: This makes the native a scholar. Since the 2nd house is also the house for speech, it can also bring forth speech disorders if ketu is negatively affected. This is the house representing the family, your accumulated wealth, your way of speaking, your eating and drinking habits, and your primary education, which is called "Sanskaar". These people don't hesitate before sharing their thoughts or opinions. These people may suffer from any kind of oral disease at least once in their lifetime. It can be ulcers, fungal infections, tooth problems, etc. There may be certain facial problems as well; they may include your face, skin, eyes, or any other part of the face. Negative ketu causes disputes in the family and the loss of accumulated wealth. If well handled, it makes one happy and blessed with wealth and family life.

3rd House: This native will have a good build and an impressive physical constitution. Since Ketu is said to be a planet of separation, care should be taken as misunderstandings in relationships can occur. It is the house of communication, be it print media, electronic media, or social media. Ketu in this house gives you a courageous and adventurous nature. They have hardships in life. They have good wealth, good health, and a long age. The loss of brothers is suspected in this house. Issues in the right arm, shoulder, or ear are also seen. They usually win over their enemies. Positive ketu gives the person a position of authority in their career.

4th House: Matters related to motherhood will arise. Her health can deteriorate over time, and there is a huge chance that the native will go to a foreign land and settle there. This house represents matra-sukh, the means of happiness, peace at home, and home entertainment. Some of these people can be adopted as well. These people may also face a few problems related to their chest area (lungs, heart, and liver). This person will be far away from family happiness as they tend to live far away from their family, for example, in some other country.

5th House: This is the house regarding the knowledge of mantras, romance, affairs, and speculations. Pregnancies are also seen in this house. Such a native might get into research on spiritual topics and have a good understanding of the dark spiritual arts. Children-wise, this position is also not favorable. These people tend to know either a foreign language or are keen on mantras. They have a very spiritual mindset, but mentally, they are not satisfied. They might face some obstacles in their education. They might also face a few reproductive issues during conception. Most of them suffer from digestive problems as well.

6th House: This is the house of Disease(Rog), Enemies(Ripu), and Debt(Rin). This placement can cause mishaps in life in the form of accidents, thefts, or even unnecessary fights. But they have strong willpower. They also achieve victory over enemies. When it comes to relatives, they have issues with their maternal uncle. Calm-mindedness and strong intuitive power are few of their characteristics. They always stay away from diseases, as they tend to have a strong immune system. They are very fortunate. They will get whatever they want or wish for.

7th House: Marriage-wise, this is not a favorable position. Arguments will be there with the spouse, and there is a huge chance of them separating early. These natives are also short-tempered. Generally, a spouse's health is not good. The native can face urine problems as well as sexual problems. Internal reproductive organs and lower spine problems can also be seen in these people. Some of them may also have a few illegal relationships if they are not well regarded by Jupiter.

8th House: These natives can expect sudden wealth gains. They are likely to find themselves in the mystical realms of life, and their knowledge of occult science will be very good. They may face a lot of difficulties in matters related to finance. Ketu in this house gives you an unhealthy life or a long-lasting disease. They have a very spiritual mind-set and a deep knowledge of tantra-mantras of occult science. Usually, these people do not have any friends.

9th House: It's a good placement and will encourage the natives to go on various pilgrimage tours and even expand their knowledge on spiritual matters. In matters related to their father, they may not find themselves in favorable situations. They are quite worried when it comes to their children. They have issues with their calves and thighs. There are obstacles to receiving their family property.

10th House: This is the house of karma sthan, the karmas of this life. Profession and livelihood are also seen in this house. This will lead to a very successful career path. The natives can become powerful and even wealthy as well. People will recognize him, and he will gain respect from his society. These people become famous in their work fields. Ketu in the 10th house has a fearless and bold personality. Also have high social status and are dignified individuals. They tend to do something for their society, but they also always face some kind of obstacle to achieving their goals. In terms of their health status, they have knee or back problems, like pain or any other form of discomfort.

11th House: This is the house of aya-labh, gains, elder siblings, friends, and mother's longevity. The native will have many sources of income and will lead a good spiritual life. His personality will be strong, and he will be able to deal with tough situations in life. Ketu in this house makes a person fortunate, multitalented, educated, and gives a good personality as well. They will achieve all types of success. Ketu has issues with their elder siblings and friends. This person, as written above, is fortunate, so he will receive lots of wealth and fame.

12th House: This is the house of moksha, death, hospital, jail, and ashram. This person's whole life will be spent in pursuit of Moksha. They like to be aloof, which makes sense since their mind is completely focused on achieving the ultimate. There is also a likely chance that this native will go abroad. This person tends to travel a lot in life. They tend to have overseas trips. These people are highly spiritual, very religious, lead a high-class lifestyle, and have very strong intuitive powers as well. These people have a direct or indirect link with the hospital. In the dasha of ketu, a person usually leaves their motherland and shifts to a foreign country.

Houses

Each house in the Vedic birth chart, or Kundli, is divided into 12 equal pieces. The zodiac runs counter-clockwise from the first house to the last, i.e., the 12th, making a 360° angle. Houses represent the environment, circumstances, and situations of human life. Each house has its own distinct specialty. Each sign contains information, and each house is a transparent receptacle. When this content is added to the house, it takes on a unique quality. The "cut" of the home refers to the beginning of the house. The house stretches from the house's cusp to the following house's cusp. However, "Bhava Madhya" is the Indian term for the cusp.

Houses are used by Vedic astrologers to forecast the future and guide our present in the best way possible. Each of these houses represents or reigns over a variety of aspects of a person's life. The precise time and day of your birth might give significant insight into your life by studying your planetary positions in various astrological houses.

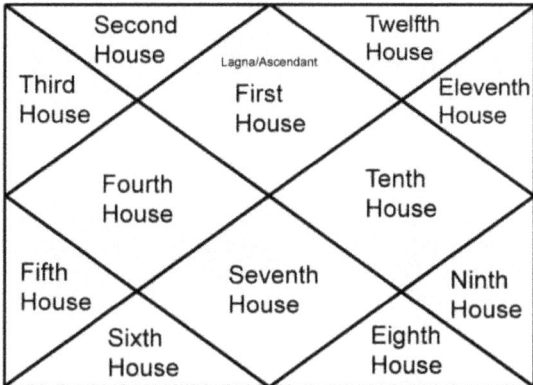

The 12 houses known as "Bhavas" in Vedic astrology are analogous to the 12 zodiac signs that form the foundation of one's life. Different signs govern each of these astrological houses.

The rashis will rise on the eastern horizon of the earth and fall on the western horizon due to the rotation of the earth on its axis, making them invisible with regard to any given place on the earth. When someone is born, a rashi will rise at the place where the individual was born. The rising rashi is known as the ascendant or lagna, and it represents the first house.

The next rashi to emerge makes the 2nd house, and so on until the 12 homes, or "Bhavas," are formed. The "equal sign" house system is the most prevalent type of house system utilized in Vedic astrology. Other house systems exist in Vedic astrology as well.

Each house begins at 0 degrees of the sign and ends at the 30th degree of the sign. The enumeration of these homes differs from chart to chart, i.e., which sign is the first house, which is the 2nd, and so on. The location of the lagna (the ascendant, or the longitudinal point of the zodiac rising in the east at birth) determines this. The house in which the Lagna falls is normally the first house in the chart, with the remaining houses following it anticlockwise in the zodiac pattern.

Each zodiac house represents an area of interest in life, and the identity of the sign in that house determines what one wants from life. The 12 houses represent the entire life cycle and the experiences a person will have throughout their lifetime.

Types of Houses:

Kendra Houses:

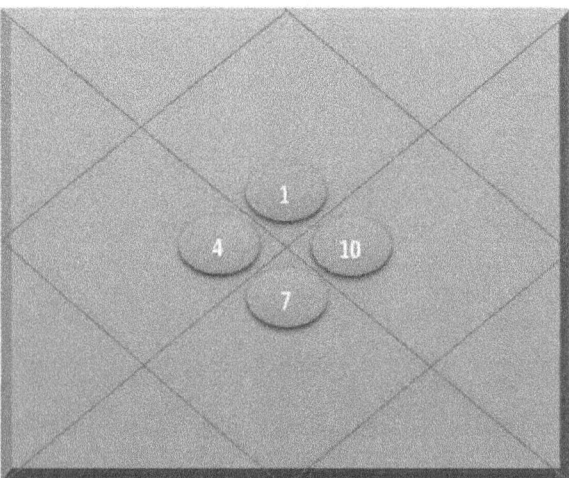

These are the best houses in Vedic Astrology and also known as Lakshmi Sthana. Houses 1, 4, 7 and 10 are considered auspicious houses and also deal with the important part of our lives. These houses are extremely powerful, especially the 10th house, representing career or profession, including images in the outside world or society. The order of ascending power of these houses is 10th, 7th, 4th and 1st. If you have a strong Kendra, then you will be able to accomplish all your goals in the current life.

Trine Houses:

In Vedic Astrology, trine houses are also known as the House of Dharma. The 1st, 5th and 9th houses are its representative. It can be marked as Individual First Class, Creative 5th and Collective 9th. They strengthen the natal chart and bestow the benefits of life. The Trine house is not as efficient as the Kendra house, but it can be said to be an encouraging house. These houses are spiritual in the form of the 5th and 9th houses.

Upachaya Houses:

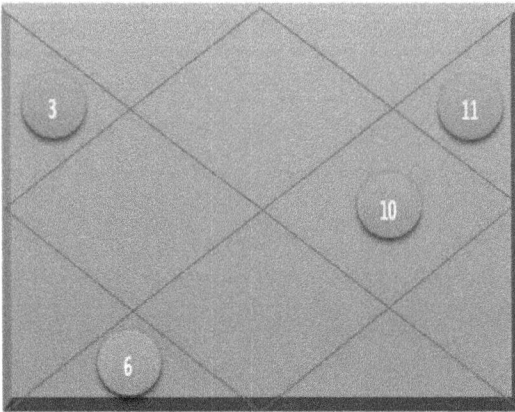

These houses are 3rd, 6th, 10th and 11th. They give multiplying effect to the houses. All planets placed in these houses will give more over time. The position of any malefic planets like Mars, Saturn, Rahu, Sun is considered good in these houses as placement here try to lessen the negative influence of these planets.

Moksha Houses:

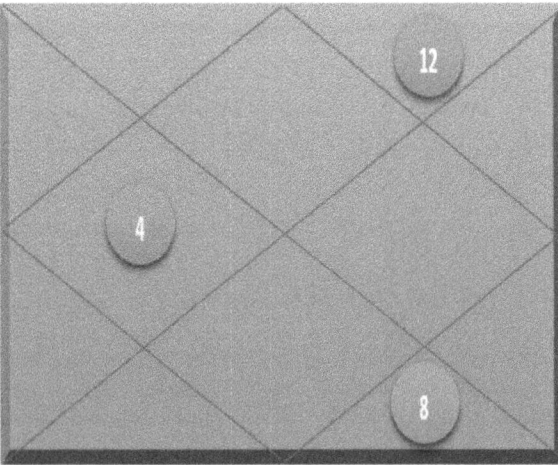

The 4th, 8th and 12th houses are called Moksha houses. These houses are associated with spirituality. These are the houses that play an important role while achieving enlightenment or salvation in one's life.

Significance of Houses in Horoscope

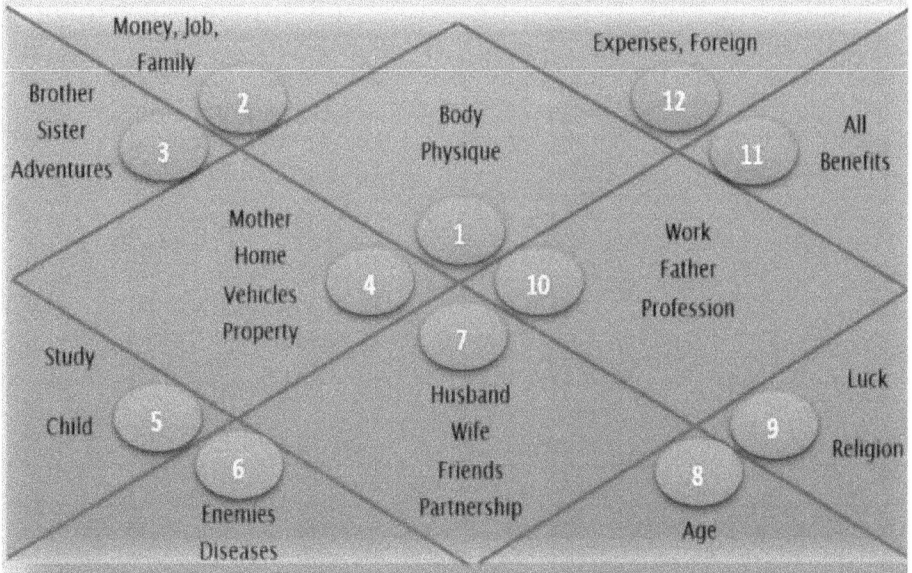

All the processes involving living and non-living organisms are represented by 12 houses. The astrologer should analyze a particular house or several houses to predict any area of life or to solve specific problems. For example, for marriage, the 7th house is the first house to be analyzed. But the 2nd and 11th houses are also considered and should be evaluated for the purposes of marriage. This is because the 2nd house denotes family, and the 11th house denotes achievement, fulfillment of desires, and joyful social occasions. Each house works according to its individual will, but the same house can be used to collect various information regarding its close relationships and even friends. This process of extending the work of a certain house is called a derivative house.

A house can bring good luck to an individual, but at the same time, it may not be good and be disastrous to relatives or friends, e.g. Lagna, or the 1st house denotes the advantages gained, and the benefit of the younger brother as a brother or sister as a younger brother is signified by the 3rd house. And the 1st house is the 11th house, counting from the 3rd house. The 1st house also shows the reputation and prestige of the mother because it is the 10th house from the 4th house. Higher education and a long journey for her children, especially the first child, are also judged by the ascendant.

The 1ˢᵗ house

Vedic name: Tanu Bhava

Lord of the House: Mars

Associated with: Aries

Good for: Jupiter, Sun, Moon, Mars, and Mercury

Weak for: Venus and Saturn

The 1ˢᵗ house, also known as Lagna or Ascendant, represents the native's nature, appearance, health, character, life purpose, behavior, date of birth, limbs, and head. It also describes a person's personality, natural behavior toward the outside world, and physical appearance. It is an essential element for the interpretation of the natal chart, and it is one of the four corners of the natal chart. It is located on the left side of the natal chart and corresponds to where the sun rises.

The 2ⁿᵈ house:

Vedic Name: Dhana Bhava or Kutumba Bhava

Lord of the House: Venus

Associated with: Taurus

Good for: Moon, Mercury, Venus, and Saturn

The 2ⁿᵈ house, also known as Dhana or Kutumba bhava, represents wealth, family, home comforts, early education, inheritance, and movable property. It also describes material possessions, how they are managed, and how money is earned. The 2nd house has a significant influence on the things a person owns during their lifetime. This property goes beyond material possessions and properties to include thoughts, feelings, and self-esteem.

As a result, this house has a significant impact on the most valuable asset an individual owns, which is his or her life. The 2nd house rules over wealth and material possessions, but it also raises questions of value.

The search for the true meaning of these and all other possessed objects that will lead an individual to a happy life is also governed by the 2nd house. In short, it covers all financial matters but also represents greed and all kinds of possessions.

The 3rd house:

Vedic name: Buddhi Bhava

Lord of the House: Mercury

Associated with: Gemini

Good for: Moon, Mars, Venus, and Saturn.

Weak for: Mercury

The 3rd house is also known as Buddhi Bhava, Parakrama Bhava, or the "House of Valorous Courage" or "Bhrathrusthana". It represents young siblings, communication (speaking, writing, and business documents), intelligence, fine arts, small journeys, "great strength (physical and mental), hands, and arms. It also deals with communication: the close human environment, primary and secondary education, learning, as well as short trips, means of transport, modern means of communication, and all those practical things.

It involves our communication skills and efforts to achieve the meaning or purpose of something. Our determination to complete any kind of daily chore is shown by the 3rd house of the horoscope. He also represents our brothers and sisters. The 3rd house has been described in various ways:

Dhairya (patience), Duschikya (bad thoughts), Uras (breasts), Karna (ears), especially the right ear; Vikrama (strength); Parakrama; Bhratru; Sahodhara (brother or sister); Virya (heroism); Pourusham (mental strength).

According to "Satyacharya", one's mental stability, determination, and words are also seen through the 3rd house of the horoscope. According to 'Sarvarth Chintamani', it represents medicine, friends, education, and short trips in an individual's horoscope. Rishi Parashara designates this house as the house of courage and effort. This house represents our mental inclinations and abilities, the instability of our mind, our memory, and the inherent inclinations of our mind. This house basically represents our interest in learning or our efforts to acquire knowledge. The sign ruled by the 3rd House in Kaal Purush Kundali is "Gemini". The natural ruler of this sign is "mercy."

The 4th house

Vedic Name: Bandhu Bhava

Lord of the House: Moon

Associated with: Cancer

Good for: Mercury and Venus.

Weak for: Mars and Saturn

The 4th house, also known as Bandhu bhava or Suhrda bhava, represents mother, emotions, education, house, property, land, surroundings in old age, vehicles, and the chest. It represents the family, ancestors, roots, and homeland of the native, both the home he originally came from and the home he will eventually set up.

The 4th house of Kundli is an important Kendra sthaan and is primarily considered the house that connects you to your roots. The 4th house has a lot to represent and holds an important place while predicting the level of peace, material gain, and happiness in one's life. This house also depicts real estate heritage, childhood, and emotions. Like the ascendant, it is an angular house.

It is the 4th house that represents your level of education and the closeness you share with your family members and your hometown. An afflicted 4th house could interfere with your college admission and may also send you abroad. People whose 4th house is afflicted often do not find happiness at home and often find themselves settling away from home. The influence of the planets in the 4th house determines what the native thinks when he or she grows up. For example. If Saturn has influence over the 4th house, natives will be disciplined, hard-working, but slow at work. It also shows your home environment and is influenced by the meanings of the planets placed in or aspecting the 4th house. The presence of the sun can provide a regal and influential family environment. enjoy while Venus can offer a luxurious and comfortable lifestyle, etc. Thus, the tone changes according to the planetary influence in the 4th house.

The 5th house:

Vedic Name: Putra Bhava

Lord of the House: Sun

Associated with: Leo sign

Good for: Jupiter, Sun, Moon, Mars, Mercury

Weak for: Saturn

5th house of astrology, where the tapestry of creativity, passion, and self-expression is woven. The 5th house, also known as Putra bhava or Suta bhava, represents children, lovers, hobbies, devotion, speculation and gambling, belly, and accumulated karma. The realm of joyful pursuits and the works of the heart, the 5th house, offers a glimpse into the depths of our inner child, lighting the fires of romance and artistic endeavors. Here, the planets align to give us the gift of a rich imagination that inspires endeavors in the arts, hobbies, and entertainment. It is also called the house of love; it reveals secrets about our romantic inclinations and the nature of our relationships with our children. Unlocking the mysteries of the 5th House, we begin a journey of self-discovery, understanding the essence of what makes our hearts dance and our souls glow with enthusiasm.

It describes a person's creative and recreational activities, his hobbies, as well as his love affairs, luck in gambling, and relations with children in general, including his own. This house includes all the pleasant things of native life.

The 5th house is also called 'Purva Punya Sthana' in Vedic astrology, which means fortune of past births. The 5th house occupies an important place among the houses of dharma in Hinduism. In this context, dharma includes the maintenance of universal law and order, including one's obligations, virtues, conduct, and observance of the law.

Accepting the dharma means trying to do the right thing, be virtuous, gain religious merit, and serve others. The location of the dhammas is the result of past karmic actions, where good deeds performed in previous lives will manifest results in the present life.

The 6th house:

Vedic name: Ari Bhava or Shatru Bhava

Lord of the House: Mercury

Associated with: Virgo

Good for: Mercury

Weak for: Jupiter, Sun, Moon, Venus, and Saturn

The 6th house, also known as Ari Bhava, Shatru Bhava, or Ripu/Rog/Rin Bhava(Enemies/Diseases/Debts), represents illness, aunts and uncles from the maternal side, disputes, servants, mental worries, enemies, strangers, and small intestines. It describes the daily life of the native, his behavior at work, his petty obligations, his slaves, his subordinate colleagues, and his pets. It is also related to health, medicine, and minor illnesses.

The 6th house includes all rivals, debt, disputes, illness, and the ability to heal and serve others. We must work hard to support our happiness. The different zodiac signs placed in different houses act as filters that add another color to the specifications of the house they are placed in.

The 6th house of the horoscope governs your work or what you do. It does not strictly deal with social situations at work or in your profession, as this belongs to the 10th House. The only two houses that matter here are the 6th and 10th houses. 6th and 10th rules career/employment

The 6th house is about what you do and how it works for you. The houses 6, 8, and 12 are called Trik Bhav in astrology. These are the unhappy Bhavas. Whenever a planet is associated with these houses, the planet loses its positivity.

The 6th house also represents sickness with Arth bhav in the elements Kaam, Moksha, and Artha; in 2, 6, and 10 bhav.

Aspects of Jupiter on the 6th house will fulfill the natives supervisory requirements. Therefore, the role of this house in maintaining the lifestyle should not be overlooked. It also signifies self-discipline, service, seriousness of action, selfless service, and the ability to work towards a better economic position.

The hard-working workers should also be analyzed in this house. Auspicious planets, if placed in the 6th house, make a person service-oriented and full of love. This person's ability to work hard and physical strength are also governed by the 6th house.

The 7th house:

Vedic Name: Yuvati Bhava

Significator: Venus

Associated with: Libra

Good for: Moon, Mars, Mercury, Venus, and Saturn

Weak for: Jupiter and the Sun

The 7th house, also known as Yuvati Bhava or Kam Bhava, represents spouse, business partner, death, respect, passion, and groin. It is opposite to the first house and thus represents other people, the native's manners towards others, and his partner. The 7th house is also known as Kalatra Bhava in Vedic astrology and is ruled by Libra. The planet Venus is the natural sign of this house. The 7th house is a weak house for Jupiter and the Sun. But it is the best house for the Moon, Mars, Mercury, Venus, and Saturn. It deals with contracts, associations, marriages, and claims to be enemies. The 7th house represents husband and wife, marriage, urinary organs, marital happiness, reproductive diseases, trade and speculation, lust, diplomacy and honor, travel, commercial tactics, and latent energy. It is thanks to the 7th house that the natives perceive other people.

The 7th house is also about collaboration and adjustment. Because that is what we need most when dealing with partners. The success of our professional and commercial partnerships also depends on the prevailing situation in the 7th House. In summary, the 7th House indicates all the situations that natives deal with every day in any way.

These may involve professionals like engineers, contractors, etc. The person who builds a home for a native or the native himself is an engineer or contractor, doctor, patient, physician, money lender or borrower of the natives, etc., as indicated by the 7th house. This house depicts the ease with which the natives integrate into society. The 7th house symbolizes an interruption in the journey. It concerns the natives' visits to various places, his reputation in society, or unfamiliar places. He is also known as one of the "Maraka Stanas." It describes union, engagement, love story, date, path, path traveled, path ahead, people or audience, flowers, sensual pleasures, number of marriages, trade, aliens, diplomacy, gifts, destruction of power, controversies, etc. According to Uttara Kalamrita, the 7th House symbolizes the adopted children of the natives.

The 8th house:

Vedic Name: Ayu Bhava

Lord of the House: Saturn

Associated with: Scorpio

Good for: Jupiter and the Sun

Weak for: Moon, Mars, and Mercury

The 8th house, also known as Ayu Bhava or Mrityu Bhava, represents death and longevity, obstacles, suffering, sexual organs and attraction, the occult, dowry, inheritance, pawns, prison, excretory organs, and accidents. It is related to the birth and death of native people. However, this does not necessarily mean actual physical death. It can be a symbolic death and is therefore synonymous with evolution and transformation. This house also represents inheritance, money earned from others, as well as sex, power, all things hidden, and an interest in the occult. The 8th house in astrology is a complex and significant area that represents transformation, regeneration, and shared resources. This house delves into the psyche, exposing hidden fears, traumas, and psychological patterns that need healing. It also explores mystical and occult issues connected with the world beyond the physical. In partnerships, the 8th house emphasizes intense emotional connections and transformative experiences. As a house of inheritance and other people's money, it means joint ventures and the possibility of financial gain or loss through investments or inheritance. The 8th House challenges individuals to accept change, face their deepest desires, and engage in personal growth by letting go and surrendering to life's mysteries.

The 8th house is a significant house as the 2nd house in the "moksha trikona," or spiritual triangle, next to the 4th and 12th houses. This spiritual triad incorporates the triad energy and provides a path to liberation. For those driven by materialistic pursuits, these three houses represent a difficult journey. However, for a soul seeking spiritual growth, they become the gateway to liberation. In these houses lies great potential, often squandered in pursuit of sensory pleasures. However, when harnessed for uplifting, they open the door to higher consciousness.

In astrology, the 8th house represents transformation, mainly because it deals with the themes of death and rebirth. This house governs the profound changes and metamorphoses that individuals experience in their lives. It delves into the process of letting go of the old and embracing the new. It often involves experiences of crisis, loss, and profound changes in life circumstances. It could indicate important life events such as the loss of a loved one, the end of a relationship, or major financial changes. Through these empowering experiences, individuals are forced to confront their deepest fears, desires, and unresolved problems, which often leads to personal growth and inner growth.

In addition, the 8th house is closely associated with emotional and psychological depth, encouraging individuals to explore their subconscious and accept the hidden aspects of themselves. In doing so, they can heal past wounds and transform their understanding of themselves and others.

The 9th house:

Vedic Name: Dharma Bhava

Lord of the House: Jupiter

Associated with: Sagittarius

Good for: Jupiter, Sun, Moon, Mars

Weak for: Mercury and Venus

The ninth house, also known as Dharma Bhava or Bhagya Bhava, represents father, luck, higher education, philosophy and religion, mentor or guru, prosperity, travel, and virtuous action. It is the realm of spirituality and philosophy, of higher ideals, of distant, material, and inward journeys. The strength of the 9th house determines whether a person has a religious mind or not. It determines the transition from conservative to modern, from orthodox to superstitious, and so on. Unlike the 3rd house, this house represents higher education and universities, as well as the understanding of abstract matters. It also deals with law, legitimacy, and religion.

Whether a person is generous or not is also determined by the 9th house. Thus, the 9th house determines the direction and flow of our thoughts, attitudes, and approaches in life. The 9th house is related to Sagittarius. In addition, Jupiter is the natural significator of the 9th house and relates to luck, wealth, fortune, higher education, wisdom, and spirituality.

In Vedic astrology, the 9th house is the best house for Jupiter, the Sun, the Moon, and Mars, and the weak house for Mercury and Venus. In addition, the 9th house is the strongest trine, and when it is combined with the 10th house, it is considered the strongest angular house; it constitutes a mighty Raj Yoga, bestowing native wealth, name, and fame in abundance according to Vedic astrology of the 9th house.

Invention, research, and exploration are under the jurisdiction of the 9th House of Kundli. The 9th House also deals with law, judgment, religious matters, education, immigration, etc. Body parts associated with the 9th house include the buttocks and thighs. In addition, the strength of your teachings and belief systems will be determined by the positions of the planets in the 9th house. Other things related to the 9th house include that you will learn many things. Higher truths and whether you are inclined towards godliness and spirituality.

The 10th house:

Vedic Name: Karma Bhava

Lord of the House: Saturn

Associated with: Capricorn

Good for: Saturn and Mars

Weak for: Jupiter, Sun, and Moon

The 10th house, also known as Karma Bhava, represents occupation, status, fame, power, father, mother-in-law, power, clothing, trade, and knees. It faces the 4th house and corresponds to the native's professional career as well as his social advancement in relation to his environment of origin. It symbolizes his ambitions and achievements in society. This also involves advertising, potential notoriety, and maternal influence. Your sector of life is determined by the positions of the planets in this house. It is basically the home of a career. An in-depth analysis of the 10th house of Vedic astrology answers some key questions like: what is your job, will you be successful, what career mistakes you might make, will you be the boss or the employee, etc. Whether you are in a position of power or serving others is within the 10th house. Your relationships with people of high rank and power are also governed by the 10th House. It also governs your earning ability.

The 10th house in astrology is the highest degree of the zodiac at the time and place of birth. And that's what it represents: your highest achievements and your desire to reach higher heights. It is about power, prestige, social status, financial strength, achievement, recognition, respect, and position. Whether you become a popular and famous face is also governed by the 10th house of the horoscope. It represents the big picture, your ultimate career goals, and the career efforts you are making to achieve them.

The 10th house is the most important angular house. When it combines with the 9th house, it forms the greatest Raj Yoga, leading people to success. It is also the "Artha" house, which means economy. Therefore, your financial prosperity and material strength are also under the 10th house. It also defines your career vision, whether you are a hard worker, an ambitious and determined person, or a lazy boy who doesn't care about career matters.

The 11th house:

Vedic Name: Labha Bhava

Significator: Sun

Associated with: Aquarius

Good for: Rahu

Weak for: Moon

The 11th house, also known as Labha bhava or Aya bhava, represents friends, hopes, income, clubs or social activities, siblings, daughter-in-law, cain-lawshins, and ankles. It represents the projects of the native, his friends, and his defenders. The 11th house in astrology is the house of wishes. It describes his friend's nature, group activities, and place in the group, unlike the more personal 5th house. The 11th House deals with all kinds of humanitarian issues. The amount of material and spiritual benefit received in the present life can be measured through the 11th house. The horoscope, or kundli, contains all the information about a person related to different aspects of his life. Most of us are interested in the material side of life and are curious about the amount of wealth gained in this life. The position of the 11th house can reveal all the secrets related to your financial and spiritual interests.

The 11th house is also known as "kama siddhi house", which also means sexual desires and their satisfaction. Kama not only expresses passion but also expresses one's hopes, wishes, and desires. Siddhi means achievement. Therefore, it represents the fulfillment or attainment of your hopes, wishes, and desires. It is a house of name and fame that one must also earn. However, it is also considered a bad house in astrology as it shows material income and profit, and if a native has a prominent 11th house, he or she will gain There are many benefits to this life, and with so many benefits, it is not possible for indigenous people to achieve spiritual progress, which is the ultimate goal of human life.

In the fixed zodiac sign, or kaalpurush kundli, the 11th house is Aquarius, ruled by Saturn. Therefore, the 11th house is closely associated with the properties of the planet Saturn. If a native has a strong 11th house, he will have a successful life with great satisfaction.

The 11th house represents multiple modes of achievement, social circles, friends, brothers and sisters, recognition, rewards, and freedom from life's pains and obstacles. It is about one's wishes, desires, aspirations, and fulfillment. It also represents income from a profession or business, higher education or foreign relations, elections, health, litigation, speculation, writing, and hard work.

The Vedic scriptures describe the 11th house as the house of elephant rides, riding (elephants, horses, and vehicles), precious clothes, jewellery, crops, wisdom, and wealth. Astrology books say that one must infer all information about these aspects of the 11th house.

The 12th house:

Vedic name: Vairagya Bhava

Lord of the House: Jupiter

Associated with: Pisces

Good for: Jupiter, Sun, Mars, Venus, and Ketu

Weak for: Moon and Mercury

The 12th house in astrology is often referred to as the "house of spending or loss". It is also the house of isolation and spirituality. The 12th House, also known as Vairagya Bhava or Vyay Bhava, represents spending, sleep (and convalescence), sexual pleasures, spirituality, long travel and pilgrimage, secret enemies, imprisonment, hospital, asylum, release, loss, residence abroad, and footstep. It corresponds to the inner self of the native: trials that last his life, hidden enemies, and deadly diseases. It is associated with places of confinement such as hospitals, prisons, monasteries, etc., and also includes loneliness and great inner crises. It represents dark and lonely places where we fear or feel isolated. Everything related to isolation is represented by the 12th house, such as hospitals, prisons, unfamiliar places, etc. The 12th house can be described in different ways:

Anthyabha (the last house); Rippa; Lopasthana (the house of disappearance); Bandha (the slave); Vigama Vyaya (loss, negation); Sayana (bed), Papa (sin), Daridrya (poverty, scarcity), Suchaha (storyteller, gossip), Kshaya (loss, decline), Dukkha (suffering), Vama Nayana (left eye), and Anghri (foot)

This house is part of the Moksha houses. It signifies suffering, loss, expense, waste, luxury, sympathy, piety, divine knowledge, worship, Moksha (final deliverance), and the state after death. The house that rules this house in the Kaal Purush Kundali is Pisces, and the natural ruler of this sign is Jupiter.

The 12th house shows loss and obstacles, restraint and limitation, wastefulness and luxury, expenses, excess income, toil, and deception. Hindu sages claim that the ownership of the 6th, 8th, and 12th lords is considered Dusthana.

In the Uttara Kalamritam, it is mentioned that the 12th house speaks of debt repayment and also deals with the connection with the father's wealth. The author of Phaladeepika called this house "Leenasthana", which means hidden house. It is the home of "True Legend". Mantreswar says that this house rules "Sayana", which means if a person is sleepy or insomniac, they can be detected by this house.

Vaidyanatha Dikshitar also states in his work "Jataka Parijatham" that visits to distant or foreign places are predicted through the 12th house of the horoscope. Ramdayalu mentions in the Sanketa Nidhi that the 12th house rules the feet in our body. It also denotes "Vyaya" or "loss" and issues a check. The 12th house represents distinctions such as prisons, refugee camps, and other institutions. It denotes an association with a hospital, sanatorium, nursing home, metallurgical institute, etc. It indicates an unfamiliar place, a change of place, or a profound change of the environment and surroundings. It is not necessary to assume remote places for foreign lands and the very idea of settling there. Places far from the birthplace of natives are also considered foreign.

Zodiac

The 12 Signs of the Zodiac

Namita Sharma was born on October 25, 1986. That makes her, according to the western zodiac system, a Scorpio—a Sun sign she likes because astrologer and bestselling author Linda Goodman says such women have "a deep, mysterious beauty, are magnetic, proud, and totally confident."

When Namita approaches a Vedic astrologer, he tells her that her sun sign is Libra. It is to be noted here that Vedic astrology principles are based on lunar and planetary movements, whereas Western astrology primarily considers only the date of birth to predict various events in a person's life.

According to the Indian astrological point of view, for the purpose of making a horoscope, fixing the planetary positions, calculating, etc., 360 degrees of zodiac signs are divided into 12 equal parts, called Rashi or signs, each 30 degree section. That is the first basic division. As read earlier, in Vedic astrology, there are nine grahas, or planets, that influence our lives. Of these seven planets—the Sun, Moon, Mars, Mercury, Jupiter, Venus, and Saturn—the real ones have mass. The other two planets, namely Rahu and Ketu, are shadow planets whose positions are calculated mathematically. Vedic astrology ignores Neptune, Uranus, and Pluto.

List of Sun Signs	
Aries	March 21 - April 19
Taurus	April 20 – May 20
Gemini	May 21 – June 21
Cancer	June 22 – July 22
Leo	July 23 – August 22
Virgo	August 23 – September 22
Libra	September 23 – October 23
Scorpio	October 24 – November 22
Sagittarius	November 23 – December 21
Capricorn	December 22 – January 19
Aquarius	January 20 – February 18
Pisces	February 19 – March 20

These nine planets do have ownership over certain rashis, represent certain things in our lives, have certain inherent qualities, and influence certain aspects of our lives. It all depends on how these planets are placed and where they are. Let's understand these basics first.

There are twelve specific constellations, or "signs," that divide the 360° orbit along the ecliptic into twelve segments of 30° each. Collectively, these twelve signs are called the zodiac. Each person is born in or under one of the twelve signs of the zodiac and is therefore more or less affected throughout their life by the planetary conditions at the time of their birth.

Each sign has a unique symbolism and a set of characteristics that give it its own kind of personality. Think of each sign as a different kind of environment in which the planets move. Furthermore, each sign belongs to a particular planet. This means that when the planet passes through this sign, it is in its original house or environment.

The names of the 12 Rasis (zodiac signs in astrology) are:

1. Aries, or Mesha, is ruled by Mars. It extends from 00:00 degrees to 30:00' in the zodiac.
2. Taurus, or Vrishabha, is ruled by Venus. It extends from 30:00 degrees to 60:00'.
3. Gemini, or Mithuna, is ruled by Mercury. It extends from 60:00 degrees to 90:00'.
4. Cancer, or Karka, is ruled by the Moon. It extends from 90:00 degrees to 120:00'.
5. Leo, or Simha, is ruled by the sun. It extends from 120:00 degrees to 150:00'.
6. Virgo, or Kanya, is ruled by Mercury. It extends from 150:00 degrees to 180:00'.
7. Libra, or Tula, is ruled by Venus. It extends from 180:00 degrees to 210:00'.
8. Scorpio, or Vrischika, is ruled by Mars. It extends from 210:00 degrees to 240:00'.
9. Sagittarius, or Dhanu, is ruled by Jupiter. It extends from 240:00 degrees to 270:00'.
10. Capricorn, or Makara, is ruled by Saturn. It extends from 270:00 degrees to 300:00'.
11. Aquarius, or Kumbha, is ruled by Saturn. It extends from 300:00 degrees to 330:00'.
12. Pisces, or Meena, is ruled by Jupiter. It extends from 330:00 degrees to 360:00'.

The Sun and the Moon own one house each, namely the 5th and 4th houses and all the other 5 planets own two houses each. Rahu and Ketu do not own any houses.

Now we'll take a look at each sign one by one:

Aries

Planetary Ruler: Mars.

Symbol: The Ram

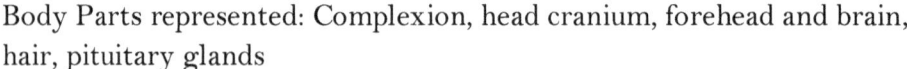

Chief domains: Leadership, playfulness, competition, self-confidence, and sense of purpose.

Body Parts represented: Complexion, head cranium, forehead and brain, hair, pituitary glands

Aries is the first sign, and it's the beginning of something energetic and chaotic. Mars is the ruling planet and includes the element of fire. It is considered the most active zodiac sign in astrology. Regardless of age, Aries has youthful energy. Therefore, Aries people have the ability to get things done quickly. In general, they are optimistic and have a strong cause. They are often looking for challenging new adventures that can push their limits. They are enthusiastic, active, and curious.

Such natives possess strong conviction and excellent physical strength. Boldness underlies their entire personality; they are very ambitious and very enterprising. A necessary complement to their traits is a propensity for recklessness and extravagance in ideas and actions. They tend to express their frustration too freely to people who are slower than them, and they become irritated at the slightest provocation. They are clearly selfish and tend to brag about their abilities at times. They possess plenty of self-confidence and assertiveness and are very successful in leadership roles where their independent perspective is a great advantage. They are generally at their best when competing against others. Physical dangers are concentrated in the head, and natives risk contracting ailments such as neuralgia, insomnia, and eye problems. As a general rule, their employment must include some form of fire use or food. Engineering or mechanical work that requires the use of tools (which may include surgery) excels. But they are also pioneering in areas such as retail store organizing. Mars is the ancient god of war and aggression. Being under the influence of Mars promotes tension and accidents. It controls fire and danger.

Taurus

Planetary Ruler: Venus

Symbol: The Bull.

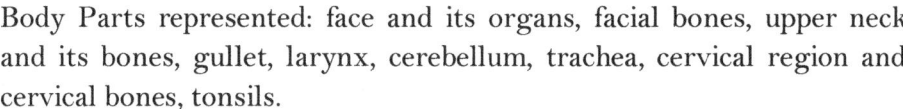

Chief domains: Loyalty, determination, thoughtfulness, sensuality, and the arts.

Body Parts represented: face and its organs, facial bones, upper neck and its bones, gullet, larynx, cerebellum, trachea, cervical region and cervical bones, tonsils.

Taurus is an earth sign like Virgo and Capricorn. Venus is the ruler, and earth is the element of Taurus. It helps to find safety and to get a good job. Gemini is the 3rd zodiac sign in the constellation. In general, people born under this sign are able to achieve a greater amount of correspondence and socialization. Stability and constructiveness are dominant personality traits. Highly methodical and tenacious, members of this group can be trusted a lot and are often characterized by honorable dealings, especially when money is involved. The danger is that stability can drift into stagnation, and strength of character only becomes stubbornness. The love of conservative ideas tends to spoil their vision and prevent initiative. Thoroughness is a prominent feature in all of their work, but there may be some lack of insight and a serious, undeveloped flaw. There is great danger in estimating on material grounds alone, but where stubbornness and toughness are desired, such people prevail. Physically, there is a tendency to gain excessive weight, and they may also have problems related to the throat. In professional matters, their constructive capacity should be freely controlled. They are successful in all types of construction and also in businesses related to clothing, confectionery, or jewelry. Not surprisingly, farming also often offers them great prospects for success.

Gemini

Planetary Ruler: Mercury

Symbol: The Twins

Chief domains: Charm, communication, logic, imagination, and curiosity.

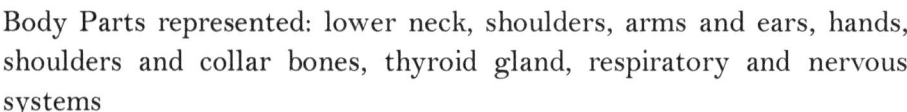

Body Parts represented: lower neck, shoulders, arms and ears, hands, shoulders and collar bones, thyroid gland, respiratory and nervous systems

Mercury is the ruler, and air is the element of the zodiac sign Gemini. People born under this sign are fun and interesting talkers.

Flexibility and cognitive agility are the hallmarks of these talented and resourceful people. They have a highly developed critical capacity and are firmly grounded in a sense of proportion. Both mentally and physically, they are notable for their sensitivity to external phenomena, and their easy understanding of people's ideas gives them an attraction in a way that makes them close with everyone they come in contact with. However, it is their flexibility and intelligence that make them a bit conflicted and unstable, and they lack the more solid virtues of focus and determination. Their diversity of interests can lead them to be accused of disloyalty, and they are certainly rarely fixed in a single agreement. Their adaptability promises success in a variety of interests, and if they seek to avoid the deadly tendency to superficiality that surrounds them, they can develop a highly selective and analytical mind. Lung disorders and diseases of the muscles and bones seem to be their main physical dangers. In professional matters, they are clearly the happiest in a career that allows them to showcase their versatility. Literature can bring them success. They are very gifted with languages; teaching, tourism, and the less pedestrian-oriented merchandising art form offer the imagination and the opportunity to exercise their ingenious minds.

Cancer

Planetary Ruler: The Moon

Symbol: The Crab

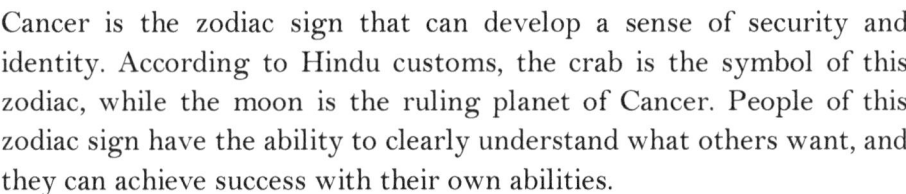

Chief domains: Creativity, compassion, emotions, sensitivity, and motherhood.

Body Parts represented: rib cage, heart, chest, lungs and breasts.

Cancer is the zodiac sign that can develop a sense of security and identity. According to Hindu customs, the crab is the symbol of this zodiac, while the moon is the ruling planet of Cancer. People of this zodiac sign have the ability to clearly understand what others want, and they can achieve success with their own abilities.

Sensitive imagination and understanding lead to widespread empathy in the lives of these people, who often become social reformers in the chariot of humanitarian progress. Generous and patient in their dealings with others, they are distinguished by their total dedication to their ideals. The danger is that idealism will only be a beautiful dream if it is not supported by an active effort in the realism of real problems. Excessive sensitivity can create in them a disease that leads to procrastination and timidity in the face of reality. Despite their empathy and willingness to make sacrifices for the common good, their attitudes can be tainted by a rather negative outlook based on an aversion to radical change. Although they persist in pursuing their ideals, they tend to prefer a rather conservative course of action and innovations often do not interest them. Physically quite delicate, they tend to suffer from nervous breakdowns, but specific disorders are often localized at the gastric or renal level. The sea has a huge attraction for them and any profession related to it will naturally have a deep attraction to them. Many people find career success based on handling liquids in one form or another. However, their main area is probably social activity in the form of leisure or institutional work, to contact others as a vital need in all their work.

Leo

Planetary Ruler: The Sun

Symbol: The Lion

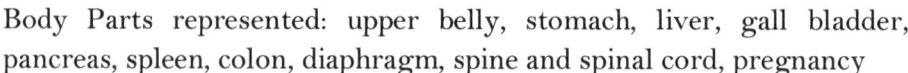

Chief domains: Power, nobility, ambition, authority, and dignity.

Body Parts represented: upper belly, stomach, liver, gall bladder, pancreas, spleen, colon, diaphragm, spine and spinal cord, pregnancy

Leo is the 5th zodiac sign, and the lion is a representative of this zodiac sign. The sun is the ruling planet of Leo, and those born in this sign have pride and leadership. People born under this zodiac sign ignore everyone. They have command and ambition for power. But most of them are innocent and bring joy to people around them. In general, they are generous, protective, warm, and courageous.

Leo is under the rule of the Sun. The ambitions of this zodiac sign are justified by their natural abilities. Sound and practical in their ideas, they have supreme governance. Their general optimism and the greatness of their whole personality lead them to a tolerant and humane vision of everything. Their own innate ability can create in them the desire to dominate others, and autocracy becomes deadly easy for them. Love of status leads to love of status pitfalls, and showiness is often one of their weaknesses. Sometimes pompous, they cling to ideas already received and tend to worship the past to the detriment of the present. However bold and magnanimous, they are characterized primarily by a generous vision and tolerance for the ideas of others. Straightforwardness is the lifeblood of their being, and they abhor conspiracies, always fighting openly. The strength of their character always makes those around them respect them. The heart is often at the heart of any physical disability they may have, and they tend to suffer when unwell due to palpitations or fever. Clearly incapable of leadership, they do best in management positions, especially in the civil service. The world of finance attracts many people, and here it is. In addition, they are likely to succeed. The law is another valuable area for their efforts.

Virgo

Planetary Ruler: Mercury

Symbol: The Virgin (Unmarried girl)

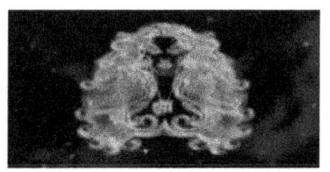

Chief domains: Intelligence, resourcefulness, courtesy, modesty, and service.

Body Parts represented: waist, navel, lower abdomen, kidneys, small intestine, upper part of large intestine, intestinal function, and appendix.

Virgo is the 6th sign of the zodiac. People born under the sign of Virgo are dedicated, responsible, and organized. Mercury is the ruling planet, and Earth is the sign element of Virgo. They are shy by nature, but they have a generous personality. They like to create something on their own. By helping others, they become happy.

Mercury is the ruling planet of this zodiac sign. Virgo natives shine with their sharp distinctions and insight. Their intellectual ingenuity and versatility of the whole personality, in which the powers of intuition are not insignificant, give them the ability to do well in almost any field of activity. The speed of their mental and physical reactions gives them an advantage, and in their case, the speed of the brain is combined with the skill of the hand. Selfishness is their main danger, and selfishness can cut them off from empathy for others and cool their emotions. If they are not controlled by high principles, their ability to judge their judgment can degenerate into only overly critical power, and there is always the danger that their wealth may not be as productive. An intense love of detail and a healthy skepticism are hallmarks of the type of mind that prefers to focus on the world of ideas rather than actions. To a certain extent, this concern is necessitated by the physical fragility that characterizes them and the constant need for analysis to which it is so well-suited. Digestive and neurological disorders may require attention and are closely related to the general characteristics of the entire personality. Science, literature, psychology, and all activities that depend on the ability to discriminate—from manual work to statistical analysis—are suitable for these people, but in general, despite magnificient machine skills, they still do better in intellectual activities.

Libra

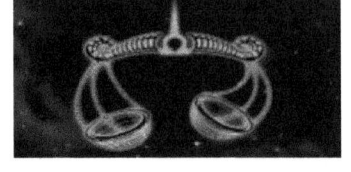

Planetary Ruler: Venus

Symbol: The Scales

Chief domains: Balance, justice, aesthetics, optimism, and ethics.

Body Parts represented: pelvic girdle, lumbar region, bladder, lower part of large intestine, inner sexual organs such as ovaries, uterus, cervix, testicles and prostate gland

Libra is the 7th zodiac sign, and Venus is the ruling planet of Libra. People under this sign are superficial and aggressive. But at the same time, they are also graceful and harmonious. Air is the element of Libra.

A judicial spirit supported by a lively and curious intelligence is the first characteristic of these people, and they are distinguished by their impartiality and love of justice. Essentially, truth seekers are constantly trying to bring order to chaos. While strongly loyal to their ideals, there is nothing rigid about their views, although they insist on methodically handling events. Fairness and judgment can cause hesitation, which sometimes closely resembles true cowardice, and this is their main weakness. Faced with a big problem, they tend to procrastinate, and inaction often becomes their biggest vice. This is added to a dose of sensuality that manifests itself in ostentatious or excessive affection. Ingenuity is fundamentally appreciated by these people, and they are very persuasive, able to present multiple facets of an issue in all their complexity. However, obsession with the material elements of a situation can blind them to larger issues, and they suffer from limitations often associated with the judicial-minded type. Physically, their weakness is probably some form of kidney disorder or diabetic disorder, but they respond very quickly to proper treatment.

Scorpio

Planetary Ruler: Mars

Symbol: The Scorpion

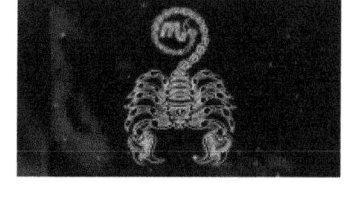

Chief domains: Intensity, mystery, criticism, harshness, and secrets.

Body Parts represented: scrotum and anus, outer sexual organs, excretory organs, pelvic bones

Mars is the ruling planet of the zodiac sign Scorpio. The scorpion is the symbol of this sign. The majority of people born under this sign have a mysterious darkness around them. They have the ability to keep secrets and feel emotions very strongly.

Scorpio is under the rule of the planet Mars. Their fixed purpose combined with thorough execution makes them highly effective individuals capable of solving the most difficult problems. Thankfully, their courageous intensity, tempered by prudent measures, saved them from the extremes to which their rigid determination could lead them. Great responsibility can be safely assigned to them, as they are fully responsible for all their work. It is the strengths of their personalities that make up certain weaknesses, chief among them being a certain degree of insensitivity to the feelings of others. There can be a corresponding tendency towards distrust in most relationships, and they tend to be quite indifferent to normal human emotions and reactions. Their thoroughness gives them a rather scientific mind; however, they are easily fooled by misjudgments. Instead of being reserved, they are vulnerable to secrecy, while their inherent caution tends to significantly limit their initiative. As part of their health, they must guard against ulcers and rhinitis. In terms of temperament, they are particularly well-suited to investigative work, from research work to police discovery. Surgery, chemistry, statistical work, and even military careers are all suitable.

Sagittarius

Planetary Ruler: Jupiter

Symbol: The Archer

Chief domains: Virtue, wisdom, spirituality, good fortune, and religion.

Body Parts represented: thighs, left leg, thigh bones, bone marrow, hips, hip joints and the arterial system.

Sagittarius is the ninth sign of the zodiac. The archer is a symbol of this sign. Sagittarius is ruled by the planet Jupiter. Through spirituality, they find peace and harmony. People born under this sign are very intelligent and driven. During the trip, they gather a group of friends from many different regions. They are optimistic and open-minded.

Vitality is the hallmark of these people, who are often found in the ranks of athletes. Independent thinking based on steadfast honesty makes them popular with others, while their own mental strength and outspoken enthusiasm instill an unshakable optimism. Overconfidence is their main danger, and they tend to be too easily fooled by overzealous enthusiasm. Their fickle minds make them somewhat unreliable, and they tend to constantly rebel against accepted ideas and practices. The abuse of sporting interests is possible and has the risk of creating a rather belligerent, often offensive spirit. To balance these flaws, they can use their unwavering good nature and common benevolence in their intentions. The colorful and vibrant notes of their personalities are aided by keen intelligence, often fueled by ambition. Any outside job suits them perfectly, but their rather philosophical way of thinking also promises them success in teaching, judicial, pastoral, and all related professions. Banking is another suitable career because, oddly enough, it is financially viable.

Capricorn

Planetary Ruler: Saturn

Symbol: The Goat

Chief domains: Deliberation, philosophy, discipline, stubbornness, and skepticism.

Body Parts represented: knee and kneecaps, joints and bones

Capricorn is one of the most disciplined zodiac signs, and the goat is its symbol. In general, they are capable of achieving anything. They are mostly disciplined and silent characters. They value life, but they are very sensitive by nature. Most of them will fight fiercely for what they believe is right. Some of them have rigid and pessimistic personalities.

Capricorn is under the rule of the planet Saturn. Ambition is often the driving force behind the personalities of these people, whose lives often unfold along disciplined lines. They possess the power of concentration to a definite degree and often achieve their goals through perseverance and persistent diligence. Thrifty, skilled, and loyal, they possess stable basic personalities. Introspection, with its sadness and possible fanaticism, is their greatest danger. Strong in their beliefs, they tend to be intolerant of opposition and utterly ruthless when human needs conflict with the achievement of a particular goal. They may be narrow-minded and particularly unsympathetic to anything outside their limited range of interests.

The power of focus gives them tremendous momentum along fixed lines and they have the ability to pay close attention to detail. They are excellent organizers even if their caution tends to limit the scope of their work. Intensely selfish, they tend to build their lives on a fateful conception of the order of things. Cramps, especially rheumatism, toothache, skin or hair diseases are common forms where physical troubles strike them. All kinds of routine and organizational work allow them to exercise their talents. They do well in all kinds of jobs that require discipline and also in fields such as agriculture, mining, and government.

Aquarius

Planetary Ruler: Saturn

Symbol: The Water Bearer

Chief domains: Altruism, social justice, patience, idealism, and renunciation.

Body Parts represented: lower portion of legs, pain in legs, problems of low productivity of blood, cancer of leg.

Saturn is the ruling planet of Aquarius. Intelligence, spontaneity, and independence are some of the traits of people born into this sign. They are open and creative. At the same time, they have a stubborn and unpredictable personality. The water bearer is the symbol of Sagittarius. Humanism in its fullest sense animates these people, and the stability of their character is based on a scientific and tolerant view of people and things. Complete sincerity, patient understanding, and easy friendliness ensure harmonious relationships and help them maintain peace of mind in the face of the most unfavorable circumstances. However, their composure sometimes sinks into mere daydreaming, and spirituality can rob them of their assertiveness and ability to realistically deal with a coordinated situation. Excessive wakefulness can lead to worry about trifles and also overstress the energy in the effort to deal with pervasive concern. Emotionally, they tend to alternate between skepticism and sentimentality and thus destroy the stability that is the foundation of their personality. They are highly creative with excellent reasoning skills, and, in fact, they represent scientific thinking at its best. Their tolerance and benevolent outlook allow them to adopt an extremely optimistic perspective, and a harmonious relationship has always been their goal. Their speed of decision-making and impulsive activities are the complete opposite of their temperament, so they do best when operating in a quiet atmosphere. Hypersensitivity is often their main physical weakness, and they tend to have neurological or blood disorders due to poor circulation. Complex scientific work or humanitarian endeavors have great appeal to them, but all activities based on the use of electricity and things like aviation and radio are within their grasp, and they often find maximum satisfaction in one area or another.

Pisces

Planetary Ruler: Jupiter

Symbol: The Fishes

Chief domains: Shyness, depth, beauty, mysticism, and knowledge.

Body Parts represented: left eye, lymphatic system and feet

Pisces is the 12th and final sign of the zodiac. Jupiter is the ruling planet of this sign. Water is the element of Pisces. Most of the time, they are talented people, and they do their best. Those who come under this sign have better emotional connections with other beings. They are also known to be the most tolerant of all the zodiac signs.

People born under this sign are usually driven by the power of their imagination. Their warm hearts and supreme nobility extend their sympathy, and noble principles have a special appeal to them. They like to live on a romantic scale and are particularly sensitive to color and movement. Inspiration and intuition play an important role in guiding their actions, with the result that they tend to live at a slightly higher level than the rest of humanity.

The price they pay for their idealism is a certain insensitivity to conventional value standards that tend to make them hopelessly unrealistic in ordinary business. Their ideas are often incoherent, and they have a strong aversion to specific actions that in reality seem like sheer laziness. Their hypersensitivity tends to make them worry unnecessarily, leading to shyness and distrust of contact. However, their imagination and sensibilities make them a basic art form, and they have not only great creative gifts but also the ability to set others on fire. They are romantics constantly trying to escape the dirty reality of their lucky dreamland. They are especially addicted to heart or liver disorders and may be more worried about colds and flu than usual. They will certainly do their best in occupations that leave room for the imagination, such as literature, philosophy, and religion. Maritime activities also interest them, and many find expressions of romanticism in the entertainment world.

Vimshottari Dasha System

In Vedic astrology, the Dasha system is quite unique in terms of prediction. To predict the timing of events, knowledge of dasa and bhukti (sub-period) is essential. There are more than 40 types of dasha systems in Vedic astrology, like Yogini Dasha, Jaiminis Chara Dasha, Chaturseeti Sama Dasha, Panchottari Dasha, Kaalachakra, etc. But a very popular and widely accepted dasa system is the "Vimshottari Dasha System".

According to the Vimshottari Dasha system, the life expectancy of a native is estimated to be 120 years. If we see it in reality, then we will understand that in Kaliyuga, the normal human lifespan is generally estimated to be 120 years. And we know that Vedic astrology considers nine planets (Sun, Moon, Mars, Mercury, Jupiter, Venus, Saturn, Rahu, and Ketu). Thus, these nine planets take 120 years to complete a cycle.

The basic basis of the Vimshottari Dasha system is that it is calculated based on the position of the moon in different constellations. There are 27 nakshatras, or stars, in a 360° zodiac, and all the planets will move along these constellations. So at any time, the planets will be placed in one of the 27 nakshatras. The jurisdiction of each nakshatra extends to 13°20'. Each nakshatra is divided into 4 parts called padas, or quarters, and each pada will have a 3°20' arc. To calculate the Vimshottari dasha system, knowledge of the moon's position is required.

The unique feature of Vimshottari Dasha is that not all planets have the same number of years. There is only one 120-year dasha cycle that spans nine planets. Each of the nine planets is assigned three nakshatras.

Period of the Mahadasha Cycle of Planets

The period and order of all the mahadashas of nine planets in a native's life are as follows:

- Ketu: 07 Years

- Venus: 20 Years
- Sun - 06 Year
- Moon: 10 Years
- Mars: 07 Years
- Rahu, 18 years
- Jupiter: 16 Years
- Saturn: 19 Years
- Mercury, 17 Years

The order of subdivision of the Vimshottari Dasha System is in the following order:

1. Maha Dasha: In this dasha, the full results of the planets can be seen according to their placement in your kundli. The first Mahadasha depends on the degree of the moon at the time of birth and the nakshatra in which the moon was traveling.

2. Antardasha: This is a sub-period of Mahadahsa. A planet's Mahadasha includes the Antardasha of all nine planets. The first Antardasha is always the same as that of the planet Mahadasha; for example, if the moon is in Mahadasha, then the Antardasha will start with the moon. Antardasha is also known as the "Subperiod" or "Bhukti".

3. Pratyantar Dasha: This is further a subset of Antardasha. Mahadasha includes 9 Antardashas, and 1 Antardasha includes 9 Pratyantar Dashas. Pratyantar Dasha plays quite an important role in everyone's life. Major events in one's life can be seen from this dasha.

4. Sookshma Dasha: This is the 2nd-last subset in the series. Here, 1 Antardasha includes 9 Sookshama Dashas. Usually, Sooksma Dasha for each planet lasts for a few days or weeks.

5. Praanadasha-Prana Dasha is the last in the Dasha series. Usually, Praanadasha dasha for each planet lasts for a few hours or days.

In the absence of accurate birth time (in 2nds), an astrologer should not analyze the Sookshma and Praandasha.

A few guidelines were mentioned to predict the effects of the mahadasha.

- If a planet occupies Vargottamamsa, it will produce very favorable effects during its dasha period.
- The mixed effects are observed in the mahadasha of a planet that is Vargottama in its sign of debilitation or is combusted by the Sun.
- Adverse results arise during the mahadasha of any of the lords of the 6th, 8th, or 12th houses or the mahadasha/antardasha of planets posted in the 6th, 8th, or 12th houses.
- The mahadasha of a planet that is the lord of a kendra (1, 4, 7, 10) will be unfavorable if it becomes naturally benefic and will be good and favorable if it is a natural malefic (due to Kendradhipati dosh).
- The Dasha of all planets ruling trikona (1, 5, 9) will be favorable.
- The lords of the 3rd, 6th, and 11th houses, however benefic, will also produce negative influences in their dasha.
- If the lord of the 8th house also rules over Lagna (1st house), it will be auspicious and produce good effects in his dasha.
- The Sun and Moon, even if they are in the 8th house, only bring good effects during their dasha.
- If the lord of trikona is in kendra and the lord of kendra is in trikona, dashas and antardashas of both such planets will be auspicious. The effect will be very favorable (Raja Yog effect).
- The lord of a trikona house in Maha dasha and Antar dasha of Kendra Lord will produce good effects. Even if the two planets are not connected, the dasha of one planet and the Antar dasha of the other will produce good effects.
- If Rahu and Ketu are not connected to any planet and are located in an auspicious house (Kendra or Trikona), then they will produce good effects during their respective dashas.
- Results are likely to be favorable if Dasha Lord is placed on a good axis with each other (1:7, 3:11, 4:10).

Analyzing dashas in the horoscope

To get started, you need to fully analyze your birth chart. Each house in the chart and the position of each planet should be analyzed as much as possible. Don't put too much pressure on yourself; it's important that you enjoy studying. If you start feeling bored, close your book and go out for a walk or with friends! No one is born an astrologer; we have all learned and are still learning.

Now for analyzing your Dasha planets, the starting point of the planetary cycle in your life is calculated using Nakshatra when you were born. You have 2 planets defined here: one that is the ruler of the Mahadasha period/major (let's assume its Venus) and the ruler of the minor/antardasha period (let's assume it's Saturn).

Now you have to go back to your basic horoscope chart and check the following to find out more about Venus and Saturn, which will give you the physical context in which they manifest. You'll also need to count from your moon sign's date of birth to get the emotional context.

1. See the houses where signs owned by the Mahadasha planet, namely Venus, are placed in the horoscope. What aspects of life are covered by these houses? Are these houses auspicious? Are the planets placed in these houses benefic or malefic?

   In our example, if Venus owned Libra, it was in the 2nd house, and Taurus was in the 9th house. The Mahadasha/main period of Venus will be more focused on the aspects of life indicated by the 2nd and 9th houses. The 2nd and 9th houses are auspicious houses indicating family, treasures, joy of life, etc., and philosophies, patrons or colleagues, religious inclinations, etc. So 20-year-old Venus Mahadasha will mostly be a pleasant time where these aspects of life will be in focus.

   Now, if the Saturn antardasha or sub-period is activated in the mahadasha of Venus, we need to analyze Saturn in a similar way. As we know, Saturn owns Capricorn and Aquarius, and if Capricorn is in the 5th house and Aquarius is in the 6th house, we need to analyze the 5th and 6th house properties. The 5th house is for creativity, luck, fame, and activities that will make you stand out, but the 6th house is the position of illness, suffering, enemies, debt, etc. Therefore, this sub-period of Saturn will be a combination of these two aspects.

2. We need to see where the planet is located and whether it is comfortable in that position. Is it a sign of a friendly, neutral, or enemy planet? Is it exalted, debilitated, combustible, retrograde, conjoint, or aspected by a malefic or benefic planet, etc.?

In our example, if Venus is placed alone in his own house in Libra in the 2nd house and aspected by Jupiter, It is in a very good position because it is in its own Libra sign. Venus is also in the 2nd house (he is the natural owner of Taurus, the 2nd sign of the zodiac) and is therefore very comfortable. Being aspected by benefic Jupiter will allow him to expand, deepen his understanding of philosophies, etc., so the results will be very beneficial. Now, Venus from the 2nd house will also aspect the 8th house, Aries, from its position here, thus balancing any accidents or traumatic changes indicated by the 8th house. So Venus, in its Mahadasha, will give good results.

We now turn to Saturn's Antardasha analysis. Suppose Saturn is placed in Pisces in the 7th house. Saturn in Jupiter-owned Pisces is good enough. But Saturn on the 7th will limit partnerships and make you work hard on alliances, deals, marriages, and more. As the owner of the 5th house, his placement in the 7th will yield good results. But as the owner of 6th place in 7th place, it can create issues. This shows a mixed result.

Now finally analyze how the main and sub-planets interact in the birth chart. So in our example, check out how Venus and Saturn interact to get the final result of how the mahadasha of Venus and Saturn will be for you.

In our example, Venus is in the 2nd house, and Saturn is in the 7th. Therefore, they are in the uncomfortable aspect of 6/8. So expect some mischief regarding broken trust and some traumatic transformation related to all those keywords we've seen this time around.

3. An important point is the last antardasha of the main mahadasha period, which is called the chidra-dasha, or closure of the mahadasha.

This is extremely important as it gradually reduces attention to the aspects of life indicated by the planet Mahadasha; it closes open questions one way or another and prepares you for a Mahadasha of the upcoming Mahadasha of a new planet. In our example of the 20-year Venus Mahadasha, the final chidra-dasha phase will be Ketu for 26 months, during which you will gradually separate yourself from the objects indicated by Venus and prepare for the Mahadasha of the next Sun. Again, this analysis may seem tedious, but you only have to do it a few times in your life for the planet Mahadasha and for the planet Antardasha for a few months or years.

General results of the mahadasha of 9 planets

Though there are many things that are required to check the results of the mahadasha of planets, things like:

- The nature of the Dasha Lord (whether natural benefic or malefic)
- Its functional abilities (functionally beneficial or malefic)
- Location in the house
- Location/Placement in the sign
- Its involvement in good or bad yoga
- Which are the houses of rulership of Dasha Lord?
- Position and conjunction with planets and aspects
- Other dignities, such as Dig Bala (directional strength), etc.

However, if we want to know the broad results of mahadasha on nine planets, they can be as follows:

Sun Mahadasha:

The Mahadasha of Sun is for 6 years. If the sun is benefic for the ascendant or lagna and is placed in Kendra or in the 11th house, then the native is likely to obtain wealth through the government. He will enjoy much happiness, prosperity, and comfort. Sun-related items or objects will bring benefits. This is the time for promotion, power, and authority. The paternal relationship, i.e., the relationship from the native's father's side, will be helpful. If the sun is associated with the 5th lord, then the person is blessed with kids. If the sun is associated with the 2nd Lord, the native may have big savings. And if the sun is associated with the 4th Lord, a native is blessed with lots of property and vehicles in his life. On the other hand, if the sun is malefic, there will be a loss of wealth and property, demotion, and loss of reputation. The person is usually away from his motherland, or, in other words, the person is settled abroad. The person may also have low self-esteem and lack confidence. He may suffer from bone fractures, high blood pressure, hair fall, itching in his eyes, and cardiovascular problems. The person may also suffer from gastrointestinal or dental diseases. The relationship with the father will decline. One can perform Surya Dosh Nivaran puja to alleviate the evil effects of weak Sun Mahadasha.

Moon Mahadasha:

The mahadasha of the moon lasts for 10 years. A benefic moon is likely to bring prosperity to the natives. The moon is considered strong when it is in Kendra, or the 11th house. The moon is a feminine character, and that person has the ability to get rich with feminine or moon-related items. Individuals can hold any auspicious ceremony and purchase vehicles; they can see the birth of a son, and Goddess Laxmi will bless them. The person will have mental peace, and the relationship on the maternal or mother's side will be good. During the time of Dasha, the person travels a lot. The person gets promoted in his job, or if he is a businessman, then his business expands. He is blessed with properties, vehicles, ornaments, and accomplishments. He tends to receive favors from the government. A north-west direction is usually good for this person. He attracts wealth.

However, a malefic moon can give opposite results. It will lead to mental fatigue, depression, and the loss of wealth and property. The relationship on the maternal or mother's side also deteriorates. Natives may be disturbed mentally, causing depression. It may also lead the person to have BP-related issues or respiratory-related issues like asthma, cough, fever, insomnia, etc. He may face troubles due to females. If there is a conjunction of Rahu and Moon, it will increase the misfortunes for the natives, and the situation will get worse. To lessen the effects of Moon Mahadasha, one should chant Chandra mantra 108 times a day; wear a silver ring with a 5-carat pearl on Mondays; or offer bilva patra and milk to Lord Shiva on Mondays.

Mars Mahadasha:

The lifespan of Mars Mahadasha is 7 years. Strong Mars placed in Kendra or in the 3rd, 6th, 10th, or 11th houses will bring favorable results. That person has the ability to acquire land and wealth and rise to a high position. The person is courageous and has the strength to face any problems or challenges in their professional or personal lives. The native's physical strength is quite strong. This person is quite stubborn and strict. The person has the capability of becoming a minister or of working in an administrative field. The south direction will be good. Relationships with siblings will improve, and an increase in jewelry may be seen. The enemy will not be able to defeat you.

However, weak or malefic Mars can lead to accidents, physical injury, and an increase in blood-related illnesses. There will be conflicts with the woman. He may have wounds on his body. Native people may also suffer from high blood pressure. They may face a lot of art cases due to their tetoency of fightingtonfight arguhave. Mars Mahadasha's influence on airy signs will likely pose a risk from hurricanes and plane crashes. In the earthly signs, this might cause damage from collapsed buildings, earthquakes, and accidents in the mines. In a firey sign, it may signify fire, electric shock, and bshock to the dancers, while in a watery sign, there may be a drowning. There will be ego conflicts between siblings. One can wear red coral on Tuesdays or wear Trimukhi rudraksha around the neck to lessen the malefic effects of Mars Mahadasha.

Rahu Mahadasha:

The mahadasha of Rahu lasts for 18 years. Rahu placed in the 3rd, 10th, or 11th house in exaltation, along with the beneficial lord in Kendra, will bring success and advantage to the natives. He is capable of acquiring wealth, a new home, royal recognition, jewelry, and contacts with diplomats and foreigners. As Rahu symbolizes foreigners, foreign land, and travel, natives might go abroad, and there's a high chance of their settlement as well. It also represents the technical field of aircraft, and therefore the person may become a pilot only if he or she has a keen interest in this field. Along with it, this planet also represents the share market, speculation, gambling, and betting. They may earn this as their 2nd source of income, or these people would also like to earn from a short-cut method.

If Rahu is malefic, it affects people negatively. That person will have mental problems and break up with his wife and children. He will probably move to an unhygienic place and may have health problems, business failures, and a loss of wealth. There will be debt, epidemics, and diseases that will appear unexpectedly. Native thinks and plans a lot, but does not execute things. A person may face some trouble or a break in his studies. During the dasha of the planet, the person is likely to change his stream as well. Rahu may involve the person in court cases or debts. He may also get stuck in any kind of conspiracy. Most likely, he might be bitten by a snake. Donating urad dal and sesame seeds will help limit the influence of the malefic Rahu.

Jupiter Mahadasha:

Jupiter is the largest planet, and its Mahadahsa lasts for 16 years. Jupiter is the god of knowledge, and it will direct people to spirituality. One can see the birth of children; there will be benefits with yellow items. The person may take pilgrimage; he may go to holy places during the Dasha of Jupiter. He tends to live in a big house. He has a well-known face in his work as well as in his social area. This person will be socially active in the religious place or be the head of that place as well. He will have a good knowledge of the Vedas and Vedic culture and scriptures. He will also have good relations with his relatives, friends, and neighbors. He or she is likely to become a teacher, judge, yogi, professor, philosopher, etc.

Malefic Jupiter may use defamation. This also happens when Jupiter is in the 6th house of the natal chart. This will bring unhappiness and anxiety to the natives. He will deviate from spirituality and be more likely to have a break between his studies, which may cause obstacles to their earnings. People can doubt this person's character, and even this person can have certain bad moral qualities as well. He may have bad luck when it comes to property or gold. Possible loss of wealth, children, or mental fatigue Liver diseases like jaundice and cancer may also occur. To limit the evil effects of Jupiter Mahadasha, one can fast on Thursdays and pray to Lord Brihaspati, give jaggery to crows, and make offerings to saints.

Saturn Mahadasha:

Saturn Mahadasha lasted for 19 years. A strong Saturn is likely to be placed in the 11th house or in the Kendra of natives birth chart. There is an opportunity to get rich from business related to Saturn. Natives will succeed through hard work and become rich through farming, education, government, jobs, and in a western direction. He may be a union leader or the head of society. He may have a lot of workers who work under him. This person can be an industrialist or work in the fields of oil, chemicals, gas, machinery, agriculture, iron, and steel. The west direction is usually profitable for them. These people can be involved in public services and receive accomplishments.

When Saturn is weak or in conjunction with Rahu, Ketu, or Mars, it leads people to unethical activities. The person is likely to become addicted to alcohol and turn to criminal activity. There will be loss of property, divorce, theft, grief over children, and emotional anxiety. He will suffer from stomach ailments, paralysis, and chronic diseases. It can cause family tension as well as mental tension, insomnia, hardship in working life, poor health status, etc. This person's mental peace can be disturbed when it comes to their relationships. This person is usually a loner and doesn't like to meet or interact with anyone. This person may have problems with his lower extremities. Pouring cow's milk with sesame on Shivlinga on Saturday or performing the pooja of Lord Shiva on Saturday can help limit the influence of malefic Saturn.

Mercury Mahadasha:

Mercury Mahadasha lasts for 17 years. Strong and favorable Mercury in lagna occurs when it is placed in the Kendra or 11th house of the chart. That person has the ability to become rich through business, education, and sports. Mercury is the god of communication, so anything that involves communication will be rewarded. There will be an increase in wisdom, and people will experience mental peace and happiness. This person always looks younger than their age. His correspondence is very strong and effective. He talks in a logical manner. He is likely to become a writer, philosopher, poet, or good orator. He can benefit from printing presses, publishing-related work, advertisements, book releases, etc. He also benefits from his friends and relatives. This person has a good sense of humor and has the ability to talk wisely and sweetly in any situation. The north direction suits them best.

Malefic mercury will lead to mental illnesses, restlessness, and skin problems. Fortune will be lost, as will diseases related to the urinary tract. Native may suffer from nerve problems, venous-related issues, skin disease, digestion issues, low immunity, and rheumatoid arthritis. They don't seem to have good relationships with their relatives or friends. They have a lot of arguments with them and may not get any help from them. Dasha brings bad results if Mercury is located in the 6th, 8th, or 12th house. Feeding cows with green vegetables or giving green clothes to loved ones can reduce Mercury's harmful effects.

Ketu Mahadasha:

The mahadasha of Ketu lasts for 7 years. A powerful Ketu is likely to bring Moksha. Ketu placed in the 11th house is considered auspicious. There will be favors from the monarchy; children and citizens will likely have access to transportation and will have to travel a lot. The person is very fond of mantras and foreign languages. He may receive a sudden financial gain. The people also take pilgrimages, usually during this mahadasha.

The weak Ketu can cause discord between family and loved ones; there will be suffering, secret plots, backstabbing, and evil tendencies. The risk of cardiac arrest increases. Diseases similar to Rahu and Mars are likely. He may injure himself frequently and have wounds all over his body. He may face trouble with people, or he may be associated with bad moral activities like gambling, due to which he may lose everything. He gets detached from his friends, relatives, and neighbors. He also loses accumulated wealth as well as properties. Worshiping Lord Ganesha or lighting the diya with ghee will help.

Venus Mahadasha:

The mahadasha of Venus is the longest mahadasha among the nine planets and lasts for 20 years. Venus is strong, particularly when placed in Kendra or in the 11th house of the chart. This period is beneficial for marriage. A person is likely to become rich from business related to Venus. There will be an affection for poetry, music, and entertainment. The natives may get all they want. He may become a good artist, singer, dancer, painter, or sculptor. He can also do well in the fields of mass communication or can also become an actor or actress. They have a blessed marital life, and the bond with their partners is very strong. Marriages usually take place during the Dasha of Venus, and they are likely to be blessed with a baby girl. The love life of the native is blessed. He may get all types of ornaments, luxurious houses, and vehicles, and he may become very fond of scents and perfumes. Natives will be attracted to love, jewellery, perfume, and vehicles and will also be obsessed with their physical appearance. They earn a lot and spend a lot.

Malefic Venus will result in increased costs for unethical activities such as alcoholism. Perhaps there will be opposition and separation from loved ones. Problems with occupational status, sexually transmitted diseases, and women's suffering are all possible. Natives become unhappy and uncomfortable in life. Their relationships with their opposite-sex friends are also not very good. Even though they'll have a good amount of money, they become reluctant to spend it on themselves. To remove the ill effects of Venus, one must wear silver jewelry or have a silver coin in their wallet. He can also donate white clothes to girls.

Dashaswami and Transit of Planets:

If the planet of the mahadasha or dashaswami is in Aries, Taurus, Cancer, Sagittarius, or Capricorn during transit at the beginning of its dasha, the native will receive the result at the end of the dasha.

If the planet of the mahadasha or dashaswami is in Pisces during transit at the beginning of its dasha, the native will get the result in the middle of the dasha.

If the planet of the mahadasha or dashaswami is in Gemini, Leo, Virgo, Libra, Scorpio, or Aquarius during transit at the beginning of its dasha, a native will get the result at the beginning of the dasha.

Nakshatras

In English, nakshatras are called "lunar mansions". In Vedic Astrology, Nakshatra refers to the stars/constellations. The 360° zodiac system is divided into 12 zodiac signs. There are a total of 27 Nakshatras in astrology, and therefore the value of each star is 13° 20'. Nakshatras are considered a means of divine worship. These 27 constellations are based on the motion of the Moon, which moves about 27.3 days around its orbit. Thus, an individual's birth star is calculated based on the position of the Moon in one of these stars. A Vedic astrologer examines the nakshatras with the zodiac signs to determine additional details about a person's innate characteristics.

A Vedic astrologer examines the nakshatras with the zodiac signs to determine additional details about a person's innate characteristics. In ancient times - 28 nakshatras were considered in contrast to modern times when only 27 Nakshatras are counted - there was a 28th Nakshatra called Abhijit, located at 6°40' to 10°53' in Capricorn in the Sidereal zodiac. This overlaps with the last stage of the 21st Nakshatra Uttarashada and the first stage of the 22nd Nakshatra, Shravan. Traditionally, the 27 Nakshatras are the spouses of the Moon. But Lord Krishna explicitly mentioned in the Bhagavad Gita that Abhijit was his personal Nakshatra, making him the 28th. Abhijit Nakshatra is ruled by the god Brahma.

Story of Nakshatras

According to Hindu mythology, King Daksha had 27 daughters and Moon married all the 27 daughters of the king. Based on the names of 27 daughters of the King there are name of 27 Nakshatras. After his marriage, Moon was fond of spending time only with one of his queens, named Rohini, which is also considered the Moon's 'exaltation point'. All the 26 other Nakshatras complained to the King regarding this, and the King repeatedly asked the Moon to change his behaviour, but the Moon did not alter his character. The King was very angry at this and he cursed the Moon, which caused it to shrink.

The curse caused the Moon to start waning in size, and the consequences were not good. All the deities intervened, requesting the King to take back the curse. The Devtas assured the King that the Moon would equally visit and spend the same time with all his wives. However, since the curse could not be taken back completely, the King said that the Moon would restore the strength for half of the month only. This is the main reason why Moon completes the zodiac covering all 27 nakshatras in one month and the change of size moon causes 'Purnima' and 'Amavasya'.

Characteristics of Nakshatras

The concept of Nakshatra system in Vedic astrology is really rich. Nakshatra corresponds closely to the planets, the divine and the purpose of life, the guna and the divine. Furthermore, it is related to caste, gender, dosha, element, temperament, animal, wind direction, etc. When interpreting the Nakshatras, all these indicators are considered in detail.

1. Sex

According to Vedic Astrology, Nakshatras are divided into two types or genders, male Nakshatras and female Nakshatras. In general, men are more enthusiastic and active than women.

Ashwini, Bharani, Pushya, Ashlesha, Magha, Uttara Phalguni, Swati, Jyeshta, Mula, Purvashadha, Uttarashadha, Shravana and Purva Bhadrapada are considered as male constellations.

On the other hand, female Nakshatras are:

Krittika, Rohini, Mrigashirsha, Ardra, Punarvasu, Purva Phalguni, Hasta, Chitra, Vishakha, Anuradha, Dhanistha, Shatabhishak, Uttara Bhadrapada and Revati are considered as female nakshatras.

2. Temperament

When we look at the Nakshatra, there are three different sub-categories: deva, manushya, and rakshasa. Deva is made up of ashwini, mangashirsha, punalvasu, pushya, hasta, swati, anuradha, revati. Manushya is made up of bharani, rohini, ardra, shravana, purva, and udara. Rakshasa is made up of krittika, ashlesha, magha, chitra, vishakha, jyestha, mula, dhanishka, and shatabhishaka. People who have more planets in the rakshasa nakshatras are known to be cruel, while those who have more planets in the deva nakshatras are usually gentle.

3. Animal

Vedic astrology constellations or Nakshatras are closely linked to the animals. By determining the ascendant to which you belong, you can determine the totem animal of your astrological sign. Additionally, you can meditate upon your particular animal and observe its characteristics, as this will help you to gain a deeper understanding of yourself in the future. Thus, according to the science of Nakshatra, each astrological sign belongs to a distinct animal, which provides a detailed representation of the type of person you will become.

4. Guna

There are three types of guna in the Nakshatra of Vedic astrology: the Rajas, the Sattva, and the Tamas. The Rajas represent the spark of energy that possesses the ability to manifest the world. The Sattva, on the other hand, represents the liberation of the individual and the concept of going beyond materialism and the roots of materialism. Tamas guna are usually related to materialism or materialistic things.

All these Gunas have 9 Nakshatras each and 4 zodiac signs are covered for each guna. The 9 lunar mansions of astrology under the Rajas guna are represented by the first 4 Zodiac signs of Aries, Taurus, Gemini, and Cancer. Sattva Guna also has 9 Nakshatras covered under the Zodiac signs of Sagittarius, Capricorn, Aquarius, and Pisces. Tamas Guna also has 9 Nakshatras, and covers 4 zodiac signs namely Leo, Virgo, Libra, and Scorpio Sagittarius.

How to determine your Nakshatra?

To determine which constellation or Nakshatra you belong to, it is necessary to provide accurate birth information such as date of birth along with year, place and time. With this information, the astrologer can check the exact position of the Moon on the date of birth details and tell you which Nakshatra you belong to. Therefore, at birth, your Moon position will determine your Nakshatra. Also, the importance of your horoscope will be paramount. It will give you more information about the position of the Sun, the Moon and the positions of the other planets in the time of birth. Taking this perspective is essential as it provides a comprehensive understanding of your health, personality, etc. Now a days there are many sites available at internet where you can know your nakshatra by filling in basic details like, time, date and place of your birth.

Nakshatra Syllable Chart

The name of a newborn baby can give an indication of his/her personality and help in selecting the name for the baby. This is the reason many Indian parents consult an astrologer soon after birth to know the starting syllable of the baby's name. It is thought that naming your child based on their nakshatra plays an important part in shaping their character, life, and fate.

Depepnding upon your baby's Nakshatra, there are certain syllables that are considered as lucky to start your baby's name. These syllables are said to bring good luck and good fortune in life. The Nakshatra only provides you with a syllable or sound for your baby's name to begin with. Then, you can choose any name that starts with this syllable. A lot of parents consult the Nakshatra for their baby's name.

In the table below, you will find the syllables that you can begin your baby's name with.

Birth star	Suggested letters
Ashwini (Awasthi, Aswini)	Chu, Che, Cho, Choo, La, Laa
Bharani	Li, Lu, Le, Lo, Lee
Krittika (Karthikai, Krithika)	Aa, Ae, E, Ee, Ai, A, I, Oo, U
Rohini	O, Va, Vaa, Vi, Vee, Wa, Wu
Mrigashira (Makayiram, Mrigasira)	Ve, Vo, Ka, Kaa, Ki, Kee, We, Wo
Ardra (Arudra, Thiruvadhirai)	Ku, Kam, Ja, Cha, Gha, Da, Na, Jha
Punarvasu (Punartham, Punarpoosam)	Ke, Kay, Ko, Ha, Hi, Hee
Pushya (Pooyam, Pushyami)	Hu, He, Ho, Da
Aslesha (Aayilyam)	Di, Du, De, Do, Dee, Me, Da
Magha (Makha, Makam)	Ma, Maa, Mi, Mee, Mu, Me
Purva Phalguni (Pooram, Pubba)	Mo, Ta, Taa, Ti, Tee, Tu
Uttara Phalguni (Uthiram, Utram)	Te, Ta, Taa, To, Pa, Paa, Pi, Pee
Hastha (Atham, Hastam)	Pu, Sha, Shaa, Na, Poo, Tha
Chitra (Chitta Chithira)	Pe, Po, Ra, Raa, Ri, Ree
Swathi (Chothy, Chothi)	Ru, Re, Ro, Roo, Ta, Taa

Vishakha (Vishakam)	Ti, Tee, Too, Te, Tu, Tae, To
Anuradha (Anizham, Anusham)	Na, Naa, Ni, Nu, Ne, Nee, Noo, Nae
Jyeshta (Triketta)	No, Ya, Yaa, Yi, Yu
Moola (Moolam, Mula)	Ye, Yu, Ba, Bi, Yo, Bhi, Bha, Bhaa, Bhee
Poorvashada (Pooradham, Purvashada)	Bu, Da, Bhoo, Pha, Dha, Fa
Utharashada (Utharadam)	Be, Bo, Ja, Ji, Bha, Bhe, Bho, Jaa, Jee
Sravana (Shravana, Thiruvonam)	Ju, Je, Jo, Khi, So, Khu, Khe, Kho
Dhanishta (Avittam)	Ga, Gi, Gu, Ge, Gee
Satabhisha (Shatabhisham, Chathayam)	Go, Sa, Saa, Si, Su, Soo, See, Gau
Poorva bhadra pada (Purvabhadra, Pururuttathy)	Se, So, Dha, Dhi, Di, Da, Daa, Dee
Uttara bhadra pada (Uthrittathy)	Du, Tha, Jha, Na, Gna, Jna, Da, Gy
Revathi	De, Do, Cha, Chaa, Chi, Chee

The brief characteristics of all these Naskhatras are:

ASHWINI

The gold horse-headed nakshatra is called "Ashwini nakshatra". The god's belonging to this nakshatra are known as "Ashwin kumars". This is the first nakshatra in the astrological system. Ashwin kumars are sons of the god Surya, and his wife Sanjana, and by worshipping these gods, you will get the best educational, health and medical results. This nakshatra is covered under Dev Gana and symbolizes feminine energy. The people in this constellation are honest and cheerful. The Ashwini kumars are always willing to take risks and try new things. This nakshatra is considered 'the star of transport' and under its influence, the people are more adventurous and energetic. They are restless and impatient, always moving, always doing something. They are irresponsible in their actions and act immaturely. The nakshatra controls all forms of transports.

Symbol- Horse head

Ruling planet- Ketu

Gender- Male

Gana- Deva

Guna- Rajas/rajas/rajas

Presiding Deity- Ashwini Kumaras, the horse headed twins

Animal- Male Horse

Indian Zodiac- 0° – 13°20' Mesha

Favourable Activity: Commence a journey, trade, and transactions, involve in sports activities, and also starting sales, business or repaying loan/debts

Ashwini Nakshatra Padas

1st Pada: The first pada is located in the constellation of Aries, and is ruled by Mars. This pada is characterized by courage, energetic activity and independent spirit. It is a quarter of energy, movement and initiative.

2nd Pada: The 2nd pada is in the constellation of Taurus, ruled by Venus, and is associated with resourcefulness and practicality. It is associated with all the graceful and brilliant aspects of the Ashvati Kumaras.

3rd Pada: The 3rd pada falls in the constellation of Gemini, ruled by Mercury. This pada has a communicative and humorous aspect of the Ashvati Nakshatra, and it is associated with the aspect of rapid decision-making.

4th Pada: The 4th pada, in the constellation of Cancer, is ruled by the Moon, and is the center of mental and physical healing. It is characterized by compassion.

Characteristics of People Born in Ashwini Nakshatra:

Male	Female
Such males are known to have a handsome face, bright and big eyes, a broad forehead, and a big nose. He will always be grateful to the people who love him and will do anything for them, no matter what it takes. He is the best friend that you can get when you are in need. His patience, even in the face of great danger, makes him unique. However, it will be difficult to manage him when he goes crazy. Because of his strength, he is able to give you the best advice, but he is afraid of criticism to the extent of paranoia. He believes that people are conspiring against him.	The women of the Ashwini Nakshatra have a knack of seducing everyone with their sweet talk. She is very patient. Her heart is pure, but she is oversexed and wants to indulge in sex constantly. Although she lives in the modern world, she also lives in the old world and respects all old people by touching their feet at all auspicious moments.
He is a jack of all trades and a master of none. Ashwini Nakshatra natives are best suited for this because they are good at nearly all kinds of jobs but are not masters of any of them. They love music and nurture their literary aspirations. However, they will have to struggle until the age of 30. After that, they will make steady progress until 55. He is very frugal, and yet he keeps running out of money.	She's likely to work in an administrative position. She'll work full-time until she's 50, but then she'll leave. This is mostly because she'll be financially stable and because she wants to do a bit of social work. She'll also spend more time with her family.

He loves his family very much, but he may be humiliated by them because he is very stubborn. He does not get love and affection from his father. He can get help from his maternal uncles. His friends will help him more. He gets married between 26 and 30 years of age and will have many sons instead of daughters.	For the native Ashwini, the marriage generally takes place between 23 and 26 years of age. However, if the marriage takes place outside of this period, one can observe that there are a lot of issues. In the love life of Ashwini, both partners have to struggle, as such marriages either lead to divorce, separation, or even the death of the spouse.
Most of the time, the male of the Ashwini Nakshatra has good health. Except for seasonal changes like cough, cold or viral infections, he has normal health. In his later years, he should be cautious about bone pain, digestive problems, or chest pain, as these may be signs of something serious.	On the health side, not many issues are expected, but avoid mental stress and anxiety. If these things get out of hand, it can affect brain function. She should also be cautious while cooking and avoid getting too close to a fire. Driving also requires caution and safety.

BHARANI

Bharani literally translates to 'The Bearer'. There are 27 nakshatras in astrology, and Bharani is the 2nd nakshatra in astrology. This nakshatra's astrological mate is Venus, which translates to 'Shukra'. Bharani is associated with women's attributes such as flexibility, power, and creativity. It also has qualities like adaptability, transformation, and commitment to change. It is considered 'the Star of Restraint'. Under its influence, people undergo various struggles for personal development and transformation. People under the influence of Bharani tend to be jealous, self-doubtful, honest, and disciplined. They place more importance on their own opinions.

Symbol- Yoni

Ruling planet- Venus

Gender- Female

Gana- Manusha

Guna- rajas/rajas/tamas

Presiding Deity- Yama

Animal- Elephant

Indian Zodiac- 13° 20′ – 26°40′ Mesha

Favourable Activity: Performing destructive deeds such as demolishing, poisoning, setting fire, and confronting enemies

Bharani Nakshatra Padas

1st Pada: The first pada is located in the sign of Leo, which is ruled by the sun. This pada is associated with creativity and high artistic talent. However, it is also associated with selfishness and the ability to hurt others without thinking.

2nd Pada: The 2nd pada is in the sign of Virgo, ruled by Mercury. This pada focuses on hard work and determination. It is associated with altruism and the individual knows exactly what they are doing in the face of chaos.

3rd Pada: The 3rd pada falls in the sign of Libra, ruled by Venus. This is associated with the individual's ability to balance the opposite sides of their body. However, they are likely to engage in excessive sex, and whether or not it is beneficial for them depends on their maturity.

4th Pada: The 4th pada of the first born person in the Bharani nakshatra falls under the Scorpio sun sign Navamsa, which is ruled by Mars. The first born person will be full of energy, and they will be very productive, and they may even discover something new. However, the first born person must make sure that the surplus energy is used in a constructive and responsible manner.

Characteristics of People Born in Bharani Nakshatra:

Male	Female
Bharani-born men are usually not likeable. He may not be a very nice person, but he has the well-being of everyone in his heart, and he will never	The maidens born in this nakshatra have a pure and humble personality. She respects her parents and the elderly

hurt anybody. He is very honest, and if he wants to tell the truth, even if it means hurting someone, then he will tell the truth, and nothing will stop him from doing it. He never goes against his conscience, which is why he has to face a lot of issues in his life. But he is a very forgiving person, and if someone sincerely apologizes to him, he will forgive and forget everything and start interacting with them as if nothing had happened.	people in the house. But she is a free spirit and doesn't like to be told what to do or what not to do. She will do what she wants. Her personality is brave and daring.
There is no permanent good or bad luck for this native. After 33 years, his life will change for the better. He is a versatile person and can do any kind of work, be it administration, business, sport, music, performing arts and advertising, or even cars. He can also be a good doctor or judge. The tobacco business may be good for him. He will be successful if his business is located on the east side of his house.	Bharani Nakshatra women will be self-sufficient. She will earn her own living. She will be a receptionist, a tourist guide, or a shopkeeper in a big shop. She is a forward-runner. She will not wait for a chance but will go for it. She will not be afraid to do what she wants and is likely to be a good sport.
He loves his family very much but may be humiliated due to his adamant behavior. He usually fails to win his father's love and affection. If he needs help, it will probably come from his maternal uncles. Friends will help him. He usually gets married between the ages of 26 and 30 and will have more sons than daughters.	She generally gets married around the age of 23. She will be the dominant person in all household chores, but she will be completely trusted by her husband. However, with her in-laws, she is likely to face frequent problems. Females born in Bharani are somewhat aggressive, so her partner should be very patient when dealing with her.
Natives of this Nakshatra will not have major health problems, even if he does	This Nakshatra-born woman will be in good health, although

not take good care of them. Later on, he may face dental problems, diabetes, body aches, stroke, ringworm, and malaria. He doesn't eat much and believes that we eat to live, not live to eat.	she may suffer from frequent menstrual problems and uterine disorders. Tuberculosis is another thing she should watch out for.

KRITTIKA

Vedic Astrology classifies Krittika as the 3rd lunar station of the Moon. This constellation is composed of a cluster of seven stars, each representing a spear or knife, which is why the literal meaning of the constellation is "The Cutters". The name of the nakshatra has been derived from the six mothers of Lord Shiva's son, Kartikeya, whose name translates to "The Krittikas". Sun (Surya) is the Astrological companion or the Lord Planet for this naka, while Agni, the God of Fire, is the ruling deity. It is seen as a source of 'power' and 'energy'. It is also referred to as 'the star of fire'. Under its influence, individuals are known to be ambitious, passionate, and determined. They are known to be successful in all aspects of life, and are known to be great protectors and gatherers.

Symbol- Knife or razor

Ruling planet- Sun

Gender- Female

Gana- Rakshasa

Guna- rajas/rajas/sattva

Presiding Deity- Agni

Animal- Female Sheep

Indian Zodiac- 26°40' Mesha – 10° Vrishabha

Favourable Activity: Daily mundane actions, fire ceremonies and to buy furniture and electronics

Krittika Nakshatra Padas:

1st Pada: This first pada of Krittika Nakshatra falls in the constellation Sagittarius ruled by Jupiter. Here, the emphasis is on generosity. Their bravery may even make them want to pursue a career in the military. The planets bestow strength, endurance, and will.

2nd Pada: This 2nd pada of Krittika Nakshatra falls in Capricorn Navamsa ruled by Saturn. Here, morality is emphasized, although it has a physical rather than spiritual manifestation.

3rd Pada: This 3rd pada of Krittika Nakshatra falls in Aquarius Navamsa which is also ruled by Saturn. The approach will be generous and compassionate. Here, the focus is on learning and accumulating knowledge.

4th Pada: This 4th pada of Krittika Nakshatra falls in Pisces Navamsa ruled by Jupiter. The meaning of this pada is that it is acutely aware of material comforts and efforts to achieve them are encouraged.

Characteristics of People Born in Krittika Nakshatra:

Male	Female
A man with Krittika Nakshatra is very intelligent, but sometimes he loses patience to achieve his goals and therefore needs a lot of perseverance. He runs from project to project without actually advancing at all. However, he gives great advice to others, who often surpass him to achieve their own goals. This native is a warm person and the best friend one can have. However, if the friendship prevents him from doing what he wants, he will quickly abandon the friendship. He has a special ability to earn money, but he never wants to be obligated to anyone, which slows down his progress significantly. He must be determined to move forward,	Women are supposed to be sensitive and emotional, but that doesn't mean they succumb to the emotional blackmail of others. The native women of Krittika Nakshatra are all emotional and strong from within, which some people misunderstand as arrogance; therefore, she suffers. In addition, she is quarrelsome and tends to be overweight at work as well as at home.

even when he needs someone's help, because he can always return that help in some other form.	
Men born in Krittika will often go to work far away and settle down. It can even be a foreign country. If he wants to be an entrepreneur, he has to get rid of the idea of doing it in partnership with someone. The government played an important role in his career, and he benefited greatly from it. Entrepreneurs will reap maximum benefits from business activities related to exporting yarn, pharmaceuticals, and handicrafts, while specialists would do well in the fields of medicine or engineering.	Very few of these female species born in Krittika are educated enough to find work, so they end up becoming housewives. She can also earn a living as a worker in agriculture or construction. However, with her education, she can work as an administrative officer, teacher, doctor, or even engineer.
As the saying goes, "Behind every successful man, there is always a woman". This scenario is no different; the native Krittika Nakshatra is generally the lucky one in married life. His companion will skillfully handle household chores. She will also be loyal and virtuous. However, he may have to live apart due to unavoidable circumstances that may get in the way of his married life, and he may not be able to enjoy it to the fullest. This separation may be due to the ill health of their father or mother, who lives far away from them. The men are usually Mama's boys, and here the native men of Krittika Nakshatra are closer to their mother, but on the other hand, the father can be a famous figure, hence he cannot continue living with them. Striving is a part of life, and until the	Women of this Nakshatra usually are unable to enjoy the happiness of a happy married life. She may be forced to live separately due to unavoidable circumstances. She may not be able to conceive or, in some cases, be married until age 37. She cannot maintain a healthy relationship with her loved ones, even when they are very benevolent, simply because she cannot properly understand their intentions. She lives in a fantasy world, and therefore most of the time she will feel lonely.

age of 50, you will have to strive a lot, on the positive side, even though the periods of 25–35 and 50–56 years old will be very favorable.	
The natives of Krittika Nakshatra often neglect their health by not eating enough nutrients. The health problems they often face are related to teeth, malaria, tuberculosis, brain fever, accidental injuries, and poor eyesight.	The native women of Krittika Nakshatra are observed to face health problems related to their stress and tension. Sometimes they can also get tuberculosis.

ROHINI

The term Rohini is said to mean 'The Red One'. So the literal translation of Rohini Nakshatra in English is "The Red Lunar Mansion". The constellation Rohini is the 4th of the 27 Nakshatras mentioned in Hindu mythology and astronomy. People born in the zodiac sign of Taurus in the Moon position from the $10°$ to the $23° 20'$ are born in this Nakshatra. Having the Moon as the ruling planet of this Nakshatra, people born in this Nakshatra tend to seek attention and moreover can be very attractive and charming. It is considered the "star of ascension". Under his influence, people are beautiful, charming and have a certain standard. They love material things and possessions and have a high standard of living. They are critical of others and tend to look down on people. They are talented and creative people. Also, natives are known to be atheists and selfish in nature. However, they tend to give unconditional love to animals and less fortunate people.

Symbol- Ox cart or chariot

Ruling planet- Moon

Gender- Female

Gana- Manusha

Guna- rajas/tamas/rajas

Presiding Deity- Prajapati

Animal- Cobra

Indian Zodiac- 10° – 23°20′ Vrishabha

Favourable Activity: Build homes, plant trees, purchase property, lay a foundation, and buying agricultural property

Rohini Nakshatra Padas

1st Pada: Mars will rule this quarter, or pada. This position makes the natives angry. Very brave and are likely to commit atrocities. They can be wasteful spenders and waste money on unnecessary things.

2nd Pada: Venus rules this pada. The moon will be in Vargottama this quarter. They will have a great personality and be very attractive. They may be very interested in art, music, or any other creative talent. They will be knowledgeable, wealthy, and enjoy life. They will have control over the senses, or indriyas.

3rd Pada: Mercury rules this pada. They will be artistically gifted. They will have the power to communicate effectively and convey their thoughts. They will do well as writers, poets, accountants, etc.

4th Pada: The moon rules this pada. The Moon will be very strong in this position as the Moon is exalted in the appropriate rasi and amsa. They will be appreciated by those close to them, helpful to others, and intelligent. They will be rich and possess all the happiness. Even in adverse situations, they will stand their ground. They will be intuitive and very imaginative.

Characteristics of People Born in Rohini Nakshatra:

Male	Female
People of Rohini Nakshatra descent can be very short-tempered. He can become uncontrollable and very stubborn. He doesn't care about anyone's opinion but his own. This person tends to find fault and is constantly looking for something to criticize others for. He mostly follows his heart rather than his mind. However, he is a family man and can	Women of Rohini Nakshatra origin are well educated and well dressed. Although she is very weak on the inside, on the outside, she makes people believe that she is an influential person. This person is pragmatic but can be very angry and even violent when

sacrifice everything for his loved ones.	provoked.
The Rohini Nakshatra men usually face many trials and tribulations between the ages of 18 and 36. These problems can be of an economic, social, or health nature. These natives know their best period is between 38 and 50 and 65 and 75 years old. He should be wary of business partners; otherwise, people may deceive him. The native must always be careful not to entrust all his projects to anyone unless he is absolutely sure that he is fully worthy of his trust.	The native Rohini Nakshatra woman is capable of doing any task assigned to her. This native has an average education and is ideal for a career in fashion design.
It is found that the native of Rohini Nakshatra usually doesn't get any benefit from his father. He may be more attached to his mother and other maternal relatives. He cannot strictly follow religious and moral laws. As a result, it is found that his marital life is generally in disarray.	The native Rohini Nakshatra woman will enjoy her family life. She will love her husband; it will also be reciprocated, and the children will bring her great joy. However, sometimes she develops a suspicious attitude towards her husband because of jealousy. If she doesn't control this tendency, her marriage may even end in divorce.
Rohini Nakshatra males are prone to blood-related diseases, such as blood cancer or blood sugar. Jaundice and urinary disorders also trouble them.	For female natives of this nakshatra, health is generally not a cause for concern. She may have some minor ailments, including leg pain, breast pain, menstrual disorders, and a sore throat.

MRIGASHIRA

The word Mrigashira comes from a combination of two Sanskrit words. These are Mriga, which means deer, and Shira, which means head.

Therefore, when put together, the word Mrigashira means deer head. Sometimes Mrigashira nakshatra is also known as Makayiram nakshatra. This nakshatra is considered "the star of the search." Under its influence, people tend to become travelers and tourists. They are always looking for new things and new knowledge. They love to collect and increase their possessions. They are very intelligent and good at discovering things. They travel a lot to give more meaning to their lives.

Symbol- Deer's head

Ruling planet- Mars

Gender- Female

Gana- Neuter Deva

Guna- rajas/tamas/tamas

Presiding Deity- Soma

Animal- Female Serpent

Indian Zodiac- 23° 20' Vrishabha – 6° 40' Mithuna

Favourable Activity: Learn music, conducting dance, and arts and marriages. They are also ideal for the enjoyment of pleasures, making new friends, and wearing new clothes

Mrigashira Nakshatra Padas

1st **Pada:** The first pada of Mrigashira Nakshatra fell into the hands of Simha (Lion) navamsa, ruler of the Sun. They will be well-built and beautiful. The father of the natives will be in trouble. They may serve in government offices or be affiliated with the government.

2nd **Pada:** Mercury rules this pada, or district. These people are more interested in acquiring knowledge. These people are patient but active. They will have a research-oriented mind. However, they may have selfish and cunning motives in their attitude.

3rd **Pada:** This pada is ruled by Venus. The natives are generous and generally handsome. They are knowledgeable and intelligent people.

They are like dreamers and use their imagination to their advantage. Therefore, they will do well as writers, filmmakers, etc.

4th Pada: This pada is ruled by Mars. The Moon in this position is weak compared to other quarters. In this position, they may not be able to express their thoughts and feelings correctly. These people may find it difficult to communicate effectively. They may envy and hate others. But they will be brave and positive.

Characteristics of People Born in Mrigashira Nakshatra:

Male	Female
He tends to be suspicious but is also very open and honest in his dealings with others, expecting them to reciprocate the sentiment. He is susceptible to being manipulated by friends and family and should therefore be wary of them. He will not blindly trust them, as this will only lead to his heartbreak later on. When he realizes he has been deceived, he will continue to interact with them, but in a cautious manner. He believes in more than just a simple life and high-mindedness; he also upholds higher standards. He is highly intolerant of those who have preconceived notions and judgmental opinions, or those who behave dishonestly. In addition, he may have a dual personality, as what he presents to the outside world may not reflect his true self.	This female native is an intelligent and philanthropic individual. She is always aware of her surroundings and is witty, yet she is also self-centered. She has a strong temper and must be able to control it, or she may cause harm. She is educated and has an interest in the arts. She will have children and be a devoted spouse. She accumulates wealth from a variety of sources and is fond of material possessions. She enjoys a variety of cuisines and has many ornaments and branded garments. It can be said that she is greedy for the finer things in life.
The natives of Mrigashira Nakshatra will be well educated. Financially, his advice often makes a lot of sense, but the problem is that he can't implement it in his own life. This is why he always	The Women of Mrigashira Nakshatra are often not considered to be learned. They are simply not interested in the studies. With no interest in

finds himself short of money. If he is an entrepreneur, he is likely to succeed after the age of 32. Between the ages of 33 and 50, he will be full of energy and completely satisfied with his income during this period.	learning, these native speakers seem to learn over and over again. And in the end, they give up education. However, if Jupiter is favorably placed in the constellations of Magha, this person makes rapid progress in education to reach the pinnacle of her field.
He had to deal with health problems during his childhood. Frequent constipation will eventually lead to abdominal pain, cuts and wounds, and pain in the shoulder near the collarbone.	The women of Mrigashira Nakshatra are usually busy with various household chores, even after marriage. She likes to dominate her husband and may have had some love affairs in the early years of her life. However, after getting married, she changes and shows all her heart for her husband. The women of Mrigashira Nakshatra are in poor health, and as a result, they can suffer from serious diseases such as goiter, STDs, menstrual problems, and body aches.

ARDRA

The icon or symbol depicts grief. Under its influence, people tend to be destructive. They grow through destruction. They are good at overcoming and using bad things to their advantage. They tend to be emotionally distant when it comes to others and are cold and strict. They constantly endure and overcome obstacles that lead to their inner maturity.

Symbol- Tear drop

Ruling planet- Rahu

Gender- Female

Gana- Manusha

Guna- rajas/tamas/sattva

Presiding Deity- Rudra

Animal- Female dog

Indian Zodiac- 6° 40′ – 20° Mithuna

Favourable Activity: Filing a divorce, breaking a relationship, black magic, exorcism, and other brash/bold activities

Ardra Nakshatra Padas

1st Pada: Jupiter rules over this pada. The people with 1st Pada are kind-hearted and have good character. They like to live a lavish lifestyle. They will be knowledgeable but will become arrogant because of their knowledge. They like to dominate others.

2nd Pada: This Pada is ruled by Saturn. These are hardworking folks. They will have many goals in life, and they may employ hook-and-crook methods to achieve them. They may like to do many things simultaneously. But will have problems achieving them. They sometimes behave arrogantly and act without morals. They may become too selfish at times.

3rd Pada: Again, Saturn rules over this pada. These individuals need a push or inspiration to do anything. Once they are ready, they want to do everything immediately. They may become very cunning and cruel. They will be knowledgeable and scholarly figures. They may be too obsessed with material possessions.

4th Pada: Jupiter rules over this pada. In this quarter, there will be a bit of philosophy in their attitude. They like to enjoy life as it comes, yet they are very ambitious. They are liked by relatives and friends.

Characteristics of People Born in Ardra Nakshatra:

Male	Female
The native of Ardra Nakshatra is ready to do any job assigned, and he does it responsibly. In general meetings, he creates humor and becomes the center of attention. His intuition is sharp, and he is a good psychologist. With friends and family, he will behave in a friendly manner, but in rare cases, he can be ungrateful to those who serve him.	The native women of Ardra Nakshatra are well-educated and mild-mannered. Financially, she is a profligate spender and loves to spend. She is smart and helpful, but can be very picky at times and can find fault with trivial things. Some of them are likely to have parents who have divorced many times.
The native of Ardra Nakshatra has the ability to absorb a lot of general knowledge and has a good memory. He is also compassionate and calm, so even in difficult times; he is able to maintain his composure. He rarely gets attached to one type of job but prefers to multi-task. He respects the opinions of his colleagues, even if they disagree with him. In general, he sets up a career to work away from home, or maybe even abroad. In terms of work, he will reach his peak between the ages of 32 and 42.	The woman from Ardra Nakshatra will surely succeed in her studies and later in the field of research or science. She usually specializes in electronic engineering or is a pharmacist. She can also make a lot of money as an independent consultant.
Usually, in the case of a native of Ardra Nakshatra, there is a delay in marriage. But if it happens early, it is unlikely that he would have been able to live with his wife due to practical problems or even incompatibility. He will face some problems in his married life, but he won't let them show on his face. Marrying late will be good for him	Like her male counterpart, she often chooses to marry late. But she cannot enjoy reciprocal love and does not win the affection of her husband or family. Her married life usually doesn't go smoothly, and even her children cannot become a source of happiness for her. It is observed that in some cases, her husband dies or she goes

because his wife will take good care of him.	through a painful divorce.
In terms of health, he is most likely suffering from some illness, which may even be incurable. He must watch out for diseases and be careful of paralysis, heart disease, and teeth. He may also have asthma, a dry cough, or some kind of hearing loss.	The women from Nakshatra are found to have menstrual problems, asthma, and problems related to the blood, uterus, ears, nose, and throat.

PUNARVASU

Symbol- Quiver of arrows

Ruling planet- Jupiter

Gender- Male

Gana- Deva

Guna- rajas/sattva/rajas

Presiding Deity- Aditi

Animal- Female cat

Indian Zodiac- 20° Mithuna – 3°20′ Karka

Favourable Activity: Buy automobiles, vehicles, beginning a journey or procession, travel, change of residence or job, and other major changes

This Nakshatra is considered the "star of innovation". Under its influence, people are good at overcoming bad situations. They have a positive outlook on life and are inspiring and kind. They have a forgiving nature and are loved by all. They love to travel and are content with what they have.

Punarvasu Nakshatra Padas

1st Pada: This pada falls into the Aries navamsa, and Mars rules this quarter. Those born in this pada will be mentally hesitant, overly absorbed in mundane affairs, ruthless, and hungry for victory. They are useful to others and will lead an honourable life. They will be very active and aggressive. They can speak very quickly and in a harsh tone. They may be in trouble because of their communication.

2nd Pada: Venus rules this quarter. These people are famous and have charismatic personalities. They will be artistically gifted. They will have fun and help others. These people are good communicators and would do well in a mentoring role. These people are appreciated by all. They may want to taste different foods and prefer more expensive foods.

3rd Pada: Mercury rules this pada. This pada is also called Martyamsa. These people are excellent communicators; they speak politely and are liked by everyone. They are considered to be the types of people who have mastered all professions. They are also business-minded people. They like to dress well and want to show a good image in society.

4th Pada: The moon reigns over this pada. These people are rich, famous, and charismatic. They will be sensitive and emotional, but they may not show their emotional side to the outside world. They can become scholars and will have a sacrificial nature for others. They can be family-oriented people loved by all.

Characteristics of People Born in Punarvasu Nakshatra:

Male	Female
Men born in Punarvasu Nakshatra are said to be very spiritual and religious. They tend to have good nature and good manners in their youth, but as they grow older, they gradually begin to adopt a more rude and arrogant attitude. As they mature, they gradually become less and less likeable, and because of this, being friends with them can be a bit stressful. Sometimes they can long for things they can't have, but they can't be called materialistic because they're usually content with	Punarvasu females can have sharp tongues because they like to talk a lot, leading to frequent fights and arguments between friends and family. This also makes many people resent her. But deep down, she has a heart of gold and knows how to show respect to whoever she deserves. She likes to live comfortably; therefore, she will have all forms of material comforts in her home and will also have many maids and servants.

what they already have. What is non-negotiable for them are illegal activities, and they will not do them themselves and also never let their loved ones do any illegal activity. Along with that, they can be very generous and helpful to others.	
Punarvasu man cannot work in any business where he will have to cooperate with someone because he is a lone wolf; hence, he will not be able to succeed in business. In addition, they will become a teacher or a performer that suits them best. Until the age of 32, he should be more careful when making important decisions due to adverse circumstances. Due to their honesty, it is very difficult for them to succeed in business and get rich.	Women in this nakshatra can pursue a career in the show business because they have true love as well as talent in music. They will also be very interested in various folk dances and want to be certified in these art forms. Chances are, if they decide to use these talents and make it their profession, they will also earn a lot of fame and money.
Punarvasu men respect and cherish their parents and teachers, but for them, it is difficult to have a perfect marriage. For them, the possibility of marriage failure and a 2nd marriage is very high, and frustration and concern about their partner's health can lead to an unhappy life. There may also be frequent disagreements with other family members, which can ultimately lead to mental health issues.	Punarvasu women are very lucky to find their life partner because they will get a very handsome husband, and with that, they will also have a very fulfilling married life. While there may be times when they have disagreements, it's nothing too serious to worry about. The women of this nakshatra will have a very good relationship with their husband, and with him, they will have a healthy and happy married life.
These nakshatra males are among the healthiest, as they have very strong digestive systems and tend to drink lots of water and take care	The Punarvasu females will face many health problems, such as pneumonia, indigestion, earache, goitre, jaundice, or even

of themselves. Although they worry about their health with the most subtle signs of illness.	tuberculosis. This is due to the fact that they do not care about their health, leading to serious illness. To avoid this, women in this nakshatra should pay more attention to their health.

PUSHYA

Symbol- Wheel

Ruling planet- Saturn

Gender- Male

Gana- Deva

Guna- rajas/sattva/tamas

Presiding Deity- Brihaspati

Animal- Ram

Indian Zodiac- 3°20' -16°40' Karka

Favourable Activity: Activities related to Arts and Crafts, mechanical activities, decorative activities, herb collection and medicine preparation.

One of the meanings of Pushya is "one who nourishes", signifying vitality, strength, and a warm and caring nature. Pushya Nakshatra is the 8th Nakshatra in the series of Nakshatras in Vedic Astrology. Under its influence, people tend to be very religious and value their beliefs and laws. They believe they are always right and tend to be arrogant towards those who disagree with them. They are kind, help people in need, and share.

Pushya Nakshatra Padas

1st **Pada:** The lord of this pada is Sun. People born in this neighbourhood will experience suffering. But they have strong willpower. They may have spiritual inclinations. There will be heightened desires in the physical world or in the spiritual realm. They will follow the rules of the country. They command power at home and in the work environment.

2nd Pada: Mercury rules this pada. These people are smart. They are emotional but realistic. They will constantly think about useless things and waste their resources. They can be very hardworking people and do everything on purpose. They put a lot of effort into planning, but when it comes to execution, they may fail.

3rd Pada: Venus rules this pada. They can have beautiful eyes and pretty faces. They enjoy their lives. They may love a lavish lifestyle and be interested in art and carving. They will have a very balanced state of mind. When they take on a project, they think about all the pros and cons of the problem, and if problems arise, they show patience. In this pada, they can show selfish behaviour at times.

4th Pada: The ruler of this pada is Mars. When the moon reaches the 4th pada, it becomes a bit difficult for the natives. The spirit of such people will be very fragile. These people may be at risk of stress and guilt. Sometimes they can become too apathetic and carefree.

Characteristics of People Born in Pushya Nakshatra:

Male	Female
The male natives are old-school romantics with latent emotional personalities that prevent them from making difficult life decisions. These people find it difficult to leave someone and are therefore faithful lovers. These people found it difficult to take tough decisions to change difficult lives. However, the emotional nature of these people also makes them generous. This person is always in the mood for indulgence and can therefore be selfish about it. Such a person has a few select friends and doesn't pay	It can be difficult for a woman born in Pushya Nakshatra to find peace for herself due to her busy schedule throughout her life. Usually she is too sweet, and her childish behaviour is one of her qualities that people tend to use against her. As a person born in Pushya Nakshatra, she may have experienced cases where she gave her all to someone and got nothing in return or even suffered. However, despite the difficulties, the woman born in Pushya Nakshatra believes in God's plan and is a devotee. She likes to

much attention to those outside his circle. Praise inflates his ego, while criticism diminishes it. The gentle nature of these individuals makes it easy for them to fall for the wrong company. Therefore, men born in Pushya Nakshatra should be very careful with whom they attach themselves, whether personal or professional.	follow family rituals and do things wholeheartedly. Sexual nature is one of her cherished qualities, but she needs to make sure that she doesn't use it for the wrong reasons.
Men born in Pushya Nakshatra have the will to accept any job. These people want to show the world that they can do anything and everything and thus take on tasks, whether they are capable of handling them or not. However, having too much work causes them stress and disinterest in other commitments in life. Furthermore, since these men are emotional people, even a small criticism of their work can make them sad. However, these people don't want to leave a task unfinished if they've already committed to it. Aka, a boy from Pushya Nakshatra is born strong-willed and overcomes difficult obstacles to achieve his goal.	Women born in Pushya Nakshatra are smart investors. This woman has good money management skills. She can get good returns by investing in land, buildings, and properties. Also in the professional world, the woman born in Pushya Nakshatra is famous and holds important positions faster than anyone else. Many may argue that her looks are the reason for a quick promotion, but you can credit the quick wits and intelligence she has as she was born in Pushya Nakshatra.
Men born in Pushya Nakshatra are more family-oriented or dependent on the family for most of their lives. Even if you earn a lot of money, you will still get help from your family whenever you need it. Usually, the appearance of the slightest problem in life will	Women born in Pushya Nakshatra have less time for family matters and therefore may find it difficult to create good compatibility with their partner. In fact, your spouse may even suspect you of cheating in some cases. So creating space for work-life balance is something you need to do

trigger panic mode in men born in Pushya Nakshatra. Then they don't even think once before ignoring all the relationships in life until their problems are resolved.	right away. This Nakshatra-born woman also struggles with not being able to express herself. Fighting this can help you meet more compatible people.
Men born in Pushya Nakshatra can face health problems from birth until the age of 15. If you cross this age successfully, you will live a relatively disease-free life. However, try not to be lazy about everything in life.	Just like native men, women born in Pushya Nakshatra can also experience health problems until the age of 20. Skin-related problems like acne and pimples can make you uncomfortable. However, medication is not the cure for these problems, but time.

ASHLESHA

Symbol- Coiled Serpant

Ruling planet- Mercury

Gender- Female

Gana- Rakshasa

Guna- rajas/sattva/sattva

Presiding Deity- Nagas

Animal- male cat

Indian Zodiac- 16°40′ – 30° Karka

Favourable Activity: Filing a divorce, breaking a relationship, black magic, exorcism, and other brash/bold activities

This nakshatra is considered the "clinging star". One of the meanings of Ashlesha is "hug" or "tight embrace," which denotes sensuality, attachment, and a charming personality. Under its influence, people tend to become wise and intelligent. But they often use their wisdom for dark deeds. They have a tendency to be cunning and lie. In the end, they have to bear the consequences of what they did, which led to their maturity. They do not like to be humiliated or criticized. Ashlesha Nakshatra's symbol is a coiled snake or serpent. Snakes are mystical and highly spiritual beings, and a coiled snake symbolises Kundalini energy.

Ashlesha Nakshatra Padas

1st Pada: The first pada falls under Sagittarius Navamsa and is ruled by Jupiter. It means hard work, dedication, and perseverance. You may have to deal with enemies, and your health may not be optimal at certain times of the year.

2nd Pada: The 2nd pada comes in Capricorn Navamsa and is ruled by Saturn. During this quarter, you will be extremely ambitious and show all your negative traits to achieve your goals with hooks or with crooks. You also won't be able to get rid of your possessions, becoming quite possessive of the physical, materialistic world.

3rd Pada: The 3rd pada comes in the Navamsa of Aquarius and is ruled by Saturn. Secrecy will prevail in this phase, and you will be affiliated with the mystical Nakshatra faction. Planets can affect your mother's health.

4th Pada: Ashlesha Nakshatra's 4th pada comes in the Pisces Navamsa, ruled by Jupiter. Here, you may have to deal with illusions and moral struggles. It was in Pada that the last Ashlesha snake was killed. People in this stage become mentally weak and cannot control others much. On the other end, the father's health may be negatively affected.

Characteristics of People Born in Ashlesha Nakshatra:

Male	Female
Males born in Ashlesha Nakshatra are a bit confusing and are tough to understand. He is very intelligent and cunning, and he knows how to turn any situation in his favor. Therefore, the native is also a very business-minded individual. There are two sides to Ashlesha Nakshatra-born men. The outer side shows that he is a compassionate	Women born in Ashlesha Nakshatra are thoughtful but lack self-control. The latter can have an impact or slow down a person's speed when it comes to achieving goals in life. If she develops the ability to not be distracted by outside forces, she will succeed in life faster than anyone else. Moreover, the woman born in

person, and the inner side shows that he is a bit selfish. However, selfishness benefits these people because they use it to focus on themselves and improve their lives. The man here believes that if he does well in life, then he can do well to others. In general, people born in Ashlesha Nakshatra are helpful and trustworthy leaders.	Ashlesha Nakshatra has a shy nature that makes it impossible to get along with anyone and everyone. People might think it's a matter of attitude, but the woman doesn't care. Women here can also be very argumentative and don't want to lose a conversation, even if they know they're wrong. This is what you should work on, or else you risk losing the people you love.
Ashlesha Nakshatra born men excels at tasks related to creation. Streams like arts and commerce are better for you, even if you're good at science. In the future, you will definitely want something of your own, and your creative instincts will help you get it yourself. However, males born in Ashlesha Nakshatra should be cautious when starting a business, as there is a possibility of heavy loss of money until the age of 35. Thereafter, your business, if any, will grow.	The woman born in Ashlesha Nakshatra will be very effective in whatever she does. She has a good chance to be part of the administrative framework. However, if she is not well educated, she will start her own business, which will grow exponentially until she turns 40. The Ashlesha Nakshatra-born woman may want to retire early and, fortunately, will be able to do so. However, ladies should not pay attention to other people's deeds when doing business.
The Ashlesha Nakshatra-born man is a well-behaved partner. He assumes everyone's responsibilities, even if his parents or wife are capable of taking on those responsibilities. However, in the early stages of any relationship you enter into, it will be difficult for your partner or wife to understand your feelings and moods. To combat this, spending time together helps. You will have a long, happy married	The Ashlesha Nakshatra-born woman turned out to be a very family-oriented person. However, it is not limited to that. The harmony she can have with her parents-in-law and her husband depends on the freedom of choice she has in her family. A woman may not be as attached to her mother as she is to her father. Also, due to her shy nature, she needs time to fall in love with someone.

life.	
Men born in Ashlesha Nakshatra should lead an active lifestyle. Even though he doesn't have any serious illnesses, he is always mentally exhausted. Men born in Ashlesha Nakshatra should watch out for symptoms that can lead to jaundice, digestive problems, and joint pain in the legs and knees.	Women born in Ashlesha Nakshatra are more active than their male counterparts. However, she is also more likely to be under the influence of drinks or even drugs. Also, women born in Ashlesha Nakshatra face physical symptoms that can lead to problems like dropsy, jaundice, indigestion, and hysteria. She may even have frequent nervous breakdowns.

MAGHA

Symbol- Royal throne

Ruling planet- Ketu

Gender- Female

Gana- Rakshasa

Guna- tamas/rajas/rajas

Presiding Deity- Pitris

Animal- male rat

Indian Zodiac- 0° – 13°20' Simha

Favourable Activity: Performing destructive deeds such as demolishing, poisoning, setting fire, and confronting enemies

The word Magha refers to anything large, colossal, or out of bounds. It also indicates magnificence. Magha Nakshatra refers to guardian angels that protect us from adversities and guide us through difficult times. Achievement is the main theme of this Nakshatra. Under its influence, people tend to be great leaders and do things well. They love power and wealth and work for it. They need to be recognized. They are loyal to the people they care for. They have a high opinion of themselves and sometimes tend to be arrogant towards others.

Magha Nakshatra Padas

1ˢᵗ Pada: The 1ˢᵗ Pada of Magha Nakshatra falls in the Mars-ruled Aries Navamsa. It focuses on willpower. Here, the throne was secured after killing the many-headed snake, Ashlesha Nakshatra.

2ⁿᵈ Pada: The 2ⁿᵈ Pada of Magha Nakshatra falls in the sun sign of Taurus Navamsa, ruled by Venus. Pada focuses on the king's ascension to the throne. The focus here is on the task, organising the material, and creating a good image.

3ʳᵈ Pada: The 3ʳᵈ Pada of Magha Nakshatra falls in Gemini Navamsa, ruled by Mercury. The focus here is on pursuing the arts and listening to lectures by scholars. Knowledge and mental activities are paramount here.

4ᵗʰPada: The 4ᵗʰ Pada of Magha Nakshatra falls in Cancer Navamsa, ruled by the Moon. Natives love rituals, ancestor worship, and family pride.

Characteristics of People Born in Magha Nakshatra:

Male	Female
The man born in Magha Nakshatra is a multi-talented soul. These people work hard and are not afraid to try new things in life. He is affectionate by nature and treats others with patience. Although he always listens, he doesn't like people who try to create nuisances in his life. He has a very special taste in people and is not only passionate about beauty when it comes to love. Having a likeable personality and a sense of humour is what will get you on his side. The benevolent nature of the men born in Magha Nakshatra is not only for humans but also for everything around	The women born in Magha Nakshatra are as afraid of God as their male counterparts. However, they are not calm. The woman born in Magha Nakshatra is short-tempered and quarrelsome. The woman here also enjoys material comfort. However, she doesn't depend on anyone to have them for herself. The woman born in Magha Nakshatra is capable of taking on the responsibilities of her family and profession. However, she mostly devotes herself to her career goals and accomplishes them well. She is spiritually inclined and helpful, and you will never be upset

them. The natives fear God and therefore carefully consider their every move. However, as he continued to live his life, the natives ended up making many unidentified enemies.	if you go to her for advice of any kind.
A man born in Magha Nakshatra will have to wait until the age of 27 to succeed in work or business. However, these people are likely to come from wealthy families and therefore will not face problems such as lack of wealth. Natives are also very hardworking but must use their potential correctly. The man born in Magha Nakshatra will probably change careers several times in his life. This is a good thing because their next trade will always be better than the previous one. They should make sure that they don't get distracted in their lives trying to build a career, as this might be fatal.	A woman born in Magha Nakshatra will have a good professional career if she is sufficiently educated. In fact, if the planet Jupiter finds a place in this nakshatra at the time of your birth, then no one can stop you from enjoying a successful career and a lavish life. This position on Jupiter allows a woman to have a very high position in her professional life. The effect of Jupiter is that wealth is attracted from all sides. She is also likely to marry a very rich man and lead a lavish life. However, she shouldn't complain about all these luxuries.
Men born in Magha Nakshatra will have a very healthy and comfortable married life. Your wife will be faithful and will also help you with your monetary and non-monetary responsibilities. Referring to children, probably two, you will be more attached to your first child. Moreover, you will share a very lively relationship with your mother-in-law and also earn money from her. You will have 2–3 relationships in your life.	Women born in Magha Nakshatra are quarrelsome and thus can become the cause of friction in the husband's family. Such arguments, if left unchecked, can lead to tension between you and your husband. If you want to combat such traits, you have to try to love, and maybe there will be a love match. As a person, you are very intelligent and pass these qualities on to your children, ensuring that they are more attached to you than anyone else.

Males born in Magha Nakshatra must take care of themselves until the age of 15. After that, they are less likely to have serious problems until age 55. However, beware of problems that can lead to cancer, asthma, or epilepsy.	Women born in Magha Nakshatra are not usually prone to health problems. However, you should pay special attention to your eyes and head. In addition, all symptoms that can lead to problems such as hysteria, uterine disorders, blood disorders, and jaundice should not be ignored. If left untreated, they can cause serious problems in the future.

PURVA PHALGUNI

Symbol- Hammock, front legs of bed

Ruling planet- Venus

Gender- Female

Gana- Manusha

Guna- tamas/rajas/tamas

Presiding Deity- Bhaga

Animal- Female rat

Indian Zodiac- 13°20' – 26°40' Simha

Favourable Activity: Performing destructive deeds such as demolishing, poisoning, setting fire, and confronting enemies

It is a powerful nakshatra and is also known as Bhagadavaita. Wonderful feelings and perceptions such as love, sensual pleasure, prosperity, and enjoyment are all positively affected by this nakshatra. This nakshatra can signify origin, growth, or creation, while sometimes it can also symbolise closure or destruction. In fact, Purva Phalguni Nakshatra is said to be the place where the seeds of creation and further growth are held, and it also leads to disintegration, destruction, and union in the universe so that new creation may form once again.

Under its influence, people tend to be very carefree and relaxed. They like to enjoy it. They communicate well and are very social. They are loyal and kind to those they love, and they have long-lasting relationships. They are usually very lazy, but they are talented and very creative.

Purva Phalguni Nakshatra Padas

1st Pada: The 1st Pada of Purva Phalguni Nakshatra falls in the Navamsa of Leo, ruled by the Sun. It represents the self-image, or ego. Smart natives can use their knowledge to educate others in their neighborhood.

2nd Pada: The 2nd Pada of Purva Phalguni Nakshatra falls in the Virgo Navamsa, ruled by Mercury. Here, the focus is on the hardworking and commercial nature of the natives.

3rd Pada: The 3rd Pada of Purva Phalguni Nakshatra falls into the Libra Navamsa, ruled by Venus. This phase represents the creativity of Venus. Here, the focus is on peace and relaxation.

4th Pada: The 4th Pada of Purva Phalguni Nakshatra falls into the Scorpio Navamsa, ruled by Mars. The focus here is on emotions, family life, courage, and introspection.

Characteristics of People Born in Purva Phalguni Nakshatra:

Male	Female
Men born in Purva Phalguni Nakshatra usually have very successful careers in whatever field they choose. They will have a successful career in life, but there is also a chance that they will face some kind of mental disorder due to various problems. They love their independence and freedom and will not despise those who try to take away their freedom. These nakshatra males have very soft voices, and they possess powers of intuition that they will use for the benefit of others.	Purva Phalguni Nakshatra women are the ones who control everything they do. They are polite and honest, very friendly, and knowledgeable about the arts. Their pure nature makes them want to serve for the good of society and also do charitable work. Due to their honesty, it will be difficult for them to engage in any illegal activities or do anything that could harm anyone in any way. All these traits make him a very likeable person. But

They also love to travel.	what they should think about changing is their desire to rejoice with their success with missing people. It is the only thing that can prevent them from achieving social success.
Purva Phalguni men don't like working under others, so jobs where they have to answer to their superiors won't be the best career choice for them. Due to this nature, their hard work will often not be appreciated by their superiors, and they will be hated by them, which will ultimately keep them from getting promoted and delay their success. They are prone to having enemies without their knowledge, which makes it difficult for them in their careers, even if these men are very honest people and would never try to achieve success by sacrificing others. The males of these nakshatras are very intelligent, so even if someone tries to deceive or conspire against them, they will easily pass. They are more likely to take risks with different jobs until the age of 45, and then they will be quite satisfied with their position. There is a high probability that people will try to defraud them financially, so they should avoid lending money to others.	The women born under this nakshatra are very intelligent, and they will want to put this to good use by pursuing a career in the scientific field. Their curious nature will make them want to be passionate about scientific research, and they may choose to be a teacher as a career. It will be rare for her to be dissatisfied with her success, as she is sure to be financially successful.
Regarding married life, a man born in this nakshatra will be lucky enough to have loving children and a loving wife. His wife will be a good	Women born in Purva Phalguni Nakshatra usually have a loving and caring family with happy, healthy children and lovely

housewife and he will have a very good relationship with her for a healthy and happy life. Unfortunately, he may not make it to the one he loves, but that doesn't mean he will have an unhappy marriage. They are more likely to live far from their birthplace and family.	husbands. Family is the most important thing for these women, as they are willing to sacrifice everything for the family. Also, they are not among those who forget a good deed has been done to her and will surely return her for the generosity she has received.
Apart from very minor ailments like dental disease, stomach disease or in rare cases diabetes, they will lead healthy lives and rarely have to worry about their health.	Women in this nakshatra will live a healthy life without serious health problems. While they may have to deal with minor issues including menstrual problems, breathing problems or asthma, they are not too serious to cause concern or affect their lifestyle.

UTTARA PHALGUNI

Symbol- Hammock, four legs of bed

Ruling planet- Sun

Gender- Female

Gana- Manusha

Guna- tamas/rajas/sattva

Presiding Deity- Aryaman

Animal- Bull

Indian Zodiac- 26°40' Simha- 10° Kanya

Favourable Activity: Build homes, plant trees, purchase property, lay a foundation, and buying agricultural property

It is called the "star of patronage". The word Uttara means later or later, and the full word Uttara Phalguni translates tree of fig or red tree. With the combined effects of Leo and Virgo, this nakshatra is about personality and a real, down-to-earth approach to life. Under its influence, humans are kind and loving creatures. They love making friends. They are at their best when they are in a relationship. They are kind and like to help people. They don't do well on their own and tend to be insecure. But when in a relationship, they tend to be dependent and caring.

Uttara Phalguni Nakshatra Padas

1st Pada: : Falls in Sagittarius Navamsa and is ruled by Jupiter. Because of this Jupiter's influence, natives will be very virtuous and they always want to be on a bigger side.

2nd Pada: Falls in Capricorn Navamsa ruled by Saturn. These people can be very disciplined and practical.

3rd Pada: Falls in Aquarius Navamsa ruled by Saturn. These people are likely to be intelligent and goal-oriented.

4th Pada: Falls in Pisces Navamsa ruled by Jupiter. Due to the Jupiter's influence, these people tend to be very spiritual.

Characteristics of People Born in Uttara Phalguni Nakshatra:

Male	Female
One of the best personalities and characters, the men in this nakshatra will have a very prosperous life as they are very hardworking and also have a life full of luck. These men will lead a much more disciplined life and will also be somewhat orderly, as their desks or workplaces are rarely cluttered. They will maintain a hygienic and clean lifestyle. Sometimes they will do things that they may regret in the future because they tend to speak before they think. In general, they are a bit impatient and have low tolerance. Because of this, even if they have a good heart,	It is believed that the women of this nakshatra have a heart of gold and are not against anyone. Even if someone hurts them in some way, they are quick to forgive them because they believe that forgiveness is the right thing to do in life. Due to this nature, the children of this nakshatra will have practically no enemies. Along with this, they also have a very calm and cool nature that helps them stay focused and calm in difficult situations. For this reason, they are a very friendly person, and people love to be around them.

they can annoy some people. They will devote themselves to social work and lead a happy life.	
Men of this nakshatra will rarely seek help from anyone else regarding their profession, as he is said to be a self-made man. Although they are never wrong in their decisions, they are very responsible by nature. He is also a very stubborn person, as whatever he decides can never be changed. They are honest by nature and will never imagine cheating on someone and will look down on those who try to deceive them.	Uttaraphalguni nakshatra women are very good at mathematics and can play with numbers. So she will become a very good math teacher and can also pursue a career in management or administration. There is also the possibility that they will have a successful acting or modeling career.
Like everything else, the men of Uttaraphalguni Nakshatra will have a very healthy and happy married life, with almost no conflict between them and their wives. They will also have a better half who proves to be a good housewife.	Women of this nakshatra will have a happy life after marriage as their children and husband will bring them endless joy. They will be a good housekeeper and handle household chores extremely well. Their husbands will also be rich and because of this, they are more likely to want to show off their wealth to others, which can leave them vulnerable to jealousy.
Since the men in this nakshatra will maintain good hygiene and lead a disciplined life, they will not have to worry about their health but accept some minor problems like liver problems, dental problems, body aches and indigestion, but that also only happens for a short time.	Apart from some minor health problems like mild asthma, migraines or menstrual problems, the health of women in Uttaraphalguni Nakshatra will generally be stress-free and they will live a healthy life.

HASTA

Symbol- Hand or fist

Ruling planet- Moon

Gender- Male

Gana- Deva

Guna- tamas/tamas/rajas

Presiding Deity- Surya

Animal- female buffalo

Indian Zodiac- 10° – 23°20′ Kanya

Favourable Activity:

Hasta Nakshatra is known for his ability to create and manifest anything. Hasta Nakshatra represents the power of expression and creativity and is achieved through hard work and determination. It is also associated with art, creativity, and communication. Under its influence, people tend to be good with their hands. They are good healers and artists. They are very intelligent and talented people. They are good at catching things quickly. It is very difficult for them to let go of things and emotions. They love work where they can help others with their skills.

Hasta Nakshatra Padas

1st Pada: The 1st Pada of Hasta Nakshatra came in the Mars-ruled Aries Navamsa. It signifies excess energy and makes natives experts in shady activities.

2nd Pada: The 2nd pada of Hasta Nakshatra falls on Taurus Navamsa ruled by Venus. Here, the emphasis is on practicality and material pleasure. The natives here are more honest than the natives of other padas.

3rd Pada: Hasta Nakshatra's 3rd pada arrives during the Gemini Navamsa ruled by Mercury. This pada belongs to entrepreneurs and professionals. The natives of this pada are very intelligent and astute.

4th Pada: Hasta Nakshatra's 4th pada comes under the Cancer Navamsa ruled by the Moon. Here, the emphasis is on family harmony and material security. The best and worst qualities of the natives manifest in this pada.

Characteristics of People Born in Hasta Nakshatra:

Male	Female
Males born in Hasta Nakshatra are cold and humble in nature. He leans more towards the opposite sex because he gets more attention from them. However, this attribute can also work against you if you are too tempted. However, for others, once they get to know you, it's hard for them to ignore you or stay away from you. Males born in Hasta Nakshatra are also very helpful. They can be trusted for any need, and he humbly tries to help everyone. The man born in Hasta Nakshatra is a very practical person. You will never see him flaunt his wealth or disrespect others. In short, these people help make the world a better place.	Women born in Hasta Nakshatra can be very shy and therefore less talkative. Shyness is one of the qualities of an introvert. However, the shyness will naturally disappear as they get to know you better. Women born in Hasta Nakshatra also have a wild side that not everyone knows. Just like her male counterparts, the Hasta Nakshatra-born woman also descended to earth. However, she is very outspoken about the things she finds wrong. During this stage, she is less concerned with the impact her words can have on someone. It may cause others to resent him, but that is completely their downfall. These women are also known for their physical attractiveness, a quality that will improve over time for them.
Males born in Hasta Nakshatra do not like to procrastinate and are therefore much disciplined. The quality makes him a sought-after professional. However, these natives are naturally inclined towards business opportunities. Men born in Hasta Nakshatra are of average to	Native women born in Hasta Nakshatra are hardly financially tied to their families in any way. Therefore, most of the time they do not work. However, according to astrology, not working will waste the creative instinct that Hasta Nakshatra women are born

good academic standing. In addition to education, they also have the instinct to acquire special knowledge. In these people's lives, career uncertainty will prevail until the age of 30. This is due to the fact that natives will want to try a few things in life before settling down. Once you've found your place, the period between the ages of 30 and 42 will be the happiest time for you, both professionally and personally.

with. The woman can work in creative fields like interior design, wedding planning, media, etc. Your spouse will likely support you in your efforts. Moreover, even if they are not fully educated, these women will always have the skills necessary to earn a good living.

Men born in Hasta Nakshatra year have a happy married life. The man is fortunate to have a faithful and understanding wife who always supports him in personal and work decisions. Understanding between them will help avoid any friction in the marriage. Women of men born in Hasta Nakshatra desire a lot of attention, so it is important that you take care of this need. However, this couple can conceive late.

Women born in Hasta Nakshatra will find a compatible partner. However, there will be mistakes in your love life until you turn 25. Therefore, you should be very careful in who you date or stay with because the risk of heartbreak is always lurking for you. Women born in Hasta Nakshatra will be married into a middle-class to wealthy family. You will have a good relationship with your in-laws and in the family you were born into, you will be more attached to your mother.

Men born in Hasta Nakshatra will be prone to minor health problems like colds and coughs throughout their lives. As a person born in Hasta Nakshatra, you must practice breathing exercises as there is a high chance that you will develop breathing problems after 30 years have passed.

Women born in Hasta Nakshatra enjoy the luxury of good health, but minor ailments still prevail. Any symptoms that can lead to problems like high blood pressure, varicose veins and asthma should not be ignored as they can disturb your peace at the later stage of life.

CHITRA

Symbol- Pearl, gem

Ruling planet- Mars

Gender- Female

Gana- Rakshasa

Guna- tamas/tamas/tamas

Presiding Deity- Vishwakarma

Animal- female tiger

Indian Zodiac- 23°20′ Kanya – 6°40′ Tula

Favourable Activity: Learn music, conducting dance, and arts and marriages. They are also ideal for the enjoyment of pleasures, making new friends, and wearing new clothes

This is called the "star of opportunity". Chitra Nakshatra is the fourteenth and brightest Nakshatra of the zodiac visible to the naked eye in the sky. It is one of the few stars represented by a single star. The star Chitra is located in the lower part of the constellation Virgo. It is considered the abode of "Tvashtar" or Vishwakarma by ancient Vedic prophets. Under its influence, people are very charming and beautiful. They know how to express themselves well. They communicate very well with others. They are very artistic and have a good imagination. They are very good at creating new things and making great artists. In this Nakshatra, things related to roads, dams, metal expansion, chariots, ships, etc., can all be started and done auspiciously.

Chitra Nakshatra Padas

1st Pada: The 1st Pada in Leo Navamsa is ruled by the Sun. It focuses on introspection and tries to apply everything to real life. This native must try to control their pride so that self-expression is positive and free of selfishness.

2nd Pada: The 2nd pada of Virgo is ruled by Mercury, and the emphasis here is on learning to discriminate, self-discipline, and participating in group activities. It has been observed that ambition often comes true in this pada.

3rd Pada: This 3rd pada of Chitra Nakshatra falls in Libra Navamsa and is ruled by Venus. The focus of native is on music, art, and exotic science. It also has the potential to incur unnecessary costs and undo good work.

4th Pada: This 4th Pada of Nakshatra comes in Scorpio Navamsa and is ruled by Mars. Here lies an excess of energy used to pursue all kinds of ambitions and even futile goals. A conscious effort must be made to channel the energy in a positive direction.

Characteristics of People Born in Chitra Nakshatra:

Male	Female
The male born in Chitra Nakshatra is a nature lover. These people are also very intelligent and use this trait to discover things that can benefit them greatly. Males like to be ahead of others and therefore never miss an opportunity to try something new for themselves. Her suggestions and ideas are well thought out, earning her praise in both her personal and professional life. Because he is artistically gifted, he is able to make a good first impression on others, especially with the opposite sex. The native man is a good partner and cares about the smallest needs of everyone around. However, when life doesn't treat him well, he can become rude even to his loved ones. They are intelligent but at the same time very emotional. Compared to people born in other padas, they have to work a little harder to	Women born in Chitra Nakshatra love their freedom too much. She is blunt by nature and tired of being told what she should and shouldn't do. However, her desire for freedom is less genuine as she usually only enjoys the freedom she desires after the age of 25. However, once she has obtained her freedom, she must be careful not to fall prey to sinful activities, as women born in Chitra Nakshatra are more prone to fall into sinful acts. The situation can be remedied by making sure you make friends carefully. Speaking of friends, the woman here may have very few friends but they will all be very helpful.

succeed and will likely benefit greatly from their social connections.	
In terms of career, the man born in Chitra Nakshatra is very hardworking but still struggles until the age of 32 to find success on his own. However, once past this age, he will achieve success in many endeavors. In fact, people born in Chitra Nakshatra after turning 33 will be unexpectedly rewarded, and it doesn't take much effort. The best professions for a man born in Chitra Nakshatra are architect, engineer, pilot, and anything related to tourism. If he is in business, the native will make a lot of money in partnership or even if he works with his parents.	In terms of profession, a woman born in the year of Chitra Nakshatra does well in medical-related fields such as doctors or nurses. In addition, you also have a favourable opportunity to become an actress, model, or influencer. Whatever a woman does, she does it with total dedication and is capable of achieving the desired results from it. Astrologers say that a woman born in Chitra Nakshatra is also very lucky for her husband and should be part of it to achieve career prosperity.
The native male born in Chitra Nakshatra is more compatible with his siblings than anyone else. Regarding his wife, this person is quite suspicious by nature, which can become the cause of marital tension. Although the relationship is stable, there will often be friction with his wife. It is his credit to have taken on many responsibilities throughout his life and to have been criticised for those responsibilities without complaint.	The native woman born in Chitra Nakshatra should make sure that her horoscope matches the boy's before marrying him. Getting together, if not done, might lead to serious concerns for the couple in the future. Furthermore, there are risks of sexual incompatibility between you and your spouse, which can only be rectified if both of you are open about it. The woman needs to be more committed to the relationship if she wants it to work.
A male native born in the Chitra Nakshatra may have to deal with major health problems after the age	Females born in the Chitra Nakshatra, just like males, may have to deal with major health

of 25. This is because he doesn't take much care of his health. Problems in the kidney and bladder are quite common for people born in this nakshatra.	problems after the age of 25. This is because he doesn't take much care of his health. Problems in the kidney and bladder are quite common for people born in this nakshatra.

SWATI

Symbol- Sword, coral

Ruling planet- Rahu

Gender- Female

Gana- Deva

Guna- tamas/tamas/sattva

Presiding Deity- Vaya

Animal- male buffalo

Indian Zodiac- 6°40' – 20° Tula

Favourable Activity: Buy automobiles, vehicles, beginning a journey or procession, travel, change of residence or job, and other major changes

Under its influence, people tend to be good at communicating and expressing their thoughts and ideas. They make great artists. They are curious and are always ready to learn new things. They are intuitive and have great instincts. They can sometimes be shallow and egoistic.

Swati Nakshatra padas

1st Pada: Those born under the 1st pada of Swati Nakshatra are knowledgeable, intelligent, and have good grasping skills. They look attractive and have pleasant personalities. They attach great importance to family customs and rituals. They are also brave and can handle any job.

2nd Pada: The 2nd Pada falls in Capricorn Navamsa and is ruled by Saturn. The natives born under the 2nd pada of Swati Nakshatra undertake illegal, unreliable, and greedy jobs yet maintain good relations with their families. They are direct and attention-seeking in their creative pursuits.

3rd **Pada**: The natives born under the 3rd pada of Swati Nakshatra are kind, intelligent, technical, skilled, and have business connections in science. They use the latest and greatest technologies and information. The nature of these natives is arrogant and greedy. They are likely to succeed in business, especially in partnership.

4th Pada: People born under this pada are extremely flexible and creative in difficult situations. They are intelligent but, at the same time, very emotional. Compared to people born in other padas, they have to work a little harder to succeed and will likely benefit greatly from their social connections.

Characteristics of People Born in Swati Nakshatra:

Male	Female
A male born in Swati Nakshatra likes to do things on his own, i.e., he is independent. Rarely, these natives live by rules that ensure that no one is harmed by their actions. Men born in Swati Nakshatra are classically romantic and very affectionate towards you, even if you are not dating them. They know how to make you feel comfortable and are never afraid to show respect when necessary. These people also crave love and are not used to being single after a certain age. On the other hand, these men often go through a long period of bad times when they want to get people out of their lives. Furthermore, the man born in Swati Nakshatra never forgets anything and thus carries with him childhood scars into adulthood.	The woman born in Swati Nakshatra is very outgoing, sociable, and compassionate about her goals in life. However, these modern qualities in her did not prevent her from being religious, for she was also a godly, pious person. The woman, although she is sociable, finds it difficult to make new friends. The same goes for finding a mate, as she takes her time to make the right choices when it comes to relationships. But when it comes to love, she is very loyal and honest and won't hurt you, even if you are the first to do it. Swati Nakshatra-born women take everything in life as a lesson and believe in moving on. Also, she doesn't like to travel much and prefers to stay at home as much as possible.

The man born in Swati Nakshatra is intelligent but can only use the full capacity of his intelligence after the age of 25. Until then, he may suffer both financially and mentally. Astrologers advise people of this age to focus on practical skills until the age of 25 so that they can succeed in their careers after that. In terms of career, the best time for this person is between 30 and 60 years of age. The most suitable profession for people of this age is anything related to wood. Also, any business must be done in partnership to get the best benefit. Speculative investments hurt your wallet.	The Swati Nakshatra-born woman is capable of more than she can imagine when it comes to her professional life. If she works with dedication, nakshatra will support her by allowing her to have more name and fame in her profession than she could have imagined. However, this woman, born in Nakshatra, will have to work a little hard to get an education. She may also have to give up; such a scenario would only delay, not take away, her success. Any job that involves a lot of travel is suitable for a woman of Swati Nakshatra origin, although she does not like to travel much.
Men born in Swati Nakshatra year will have to work harder to have a happy married life. The reason for the incompatibility could be due to lack of finance and the controversies surrounding the situation. However, the marriage will be compatible enough that no stranger or even your respective family will be able to find out what is going on. Also, men born in Swati Nakshatra are more likely to have an arranged marriage. He also won't be very attached to his father.	The woman born in Swati Nakshatra is very attached to her family. This love can often cause her to make compromises that she doesn't want to. This may have been painful for her, but the love and affection she received from her children more than made up for it. However, part of the compromise must also be with your husband. Speaking of husbands, the two of you will have average compatibility and can create a healthy and happy marriage. With your parents, you will share a close bond with your mother.
The health of men born in Swati Nakshatra will be excellent. However, he can sometimes suffer from stomach problems, piles, and	The woman born in Swati Nakshatra is very attached to her family. This love can often cause her to make compromises that she doesn't want to. This may have

bone pain.	been painful for her, but the love and affection she received from her children more than made up for it. However, part of the compromise must also be with your husband. Talking about husbands, the two of you will have an average compatibility and can create a stable and happy marriage. You share a close bond with your mother.

VISHAKHA

Symbol- Decorated archway, potter's wheel

Ruling planet- Jupiter

Gender- Female

Gana- Rakshasa

Guna- tamas/sattva/rajas

Presiding Deity- Indragni

Animal- male tiger

Indian Zodiac- 20° Tula – 3°20′ Vrishchika

Favourable Activity: Daily mundane actions, fire ceremonies and to buy furniture and electronics

This is called the "star of purpose". The first three quarters or padas of this Nakshatra are in the zodiac sign Libra and the last quarter in Scorpio. Since this Nakshatra connects the signs of Libra and Scorpio, it signifies transitions in life as well as new initiatives and beginnings. These people born in Nakshatra have a wonderful way of life and it depends on the Moon quarter in the natal chart. On Libra's side, the native will be sociable and outgoing, while in Scorpio, intense and secretive. Under his influence, people set goals and ambitions. They are hard working, determined and very focused. They like competition and never give up easily. They can be very jealous of others and often get angry when things don't go their way.

Vishakha Nakshatra Padas

1st Pada: The 1st Pada of Vishaka Nakshatra falls in Aries Navamsa and is ruled by Mars. People born in this pada are inspirational and romantic. They work really hard for their social ambitions and can go all the way in a love affair.

2nd Pada: The 2nd Pada of Vishaka Nakshatra falls under the Taurus Navamsa and is ruled by Venus. People born in this pada will be very creative and talented. This pada makes the natives smart.

3rd Pada: The 3rd Pada of Vishaka Nakshatra falls on Gemini Navamsa and is ruled by Mercury. People born in this pada may be interested in reading, religion, etc., and they have excellent communication skills.

4th Pada: The 4th Pada of Vishaka Nakshatra falls under Cancer Navamsa and is ruled by the Moon. People born in this pada can easily become jealous. They are also very affectionate and sensitive.

Characteristics of People Born in Vishaka Nakshatra:

Male	Female
The native man born in Vishakha Nakshatra has a very optimistic nature. These people are full of energy and intelligence that they use to get the most out of whatever they do or any situation. The natives fear God and are therefore aware of their actions. Indigenous people's value system is conservative, however, they do not accept anything that goes against human rights or simply harms a human's worth in any way. Furthermore, males born in Vishakha Nakshatra hate superstition. A man who loves	The native woman born in Vishaka Nakshatra exudes charm due to her sweet and gentle nature. This woman is both friendly and a dedicated professional with the goals in life she has worked so hard to achieve. Moreover, a woman born in Vishakha Nakshatra is usually naturally beautiful. However, this trait makes her receive a lot of attention from the opposite sex, but also the envy of other women. That's why she has to be careful with who she calls her friend. In addition to her

everyone. He has a humility towards animals and nature. On the other hand, a native can be very rude to you when he needs his space. In such situations, it is better to leave them alone.	intelligence, she is also very religious and often goes on pilgrimage. On the other hand, a lady must be more open to people than to limit herself to her charms.
The native male born in Vishakha Nakshatra has the blessing of speech. So anything related to words is a good profession for him. His talent for public speaking also gives him the ability to convince anyone and anyone. Therefore, these people can even try their hand at politics if they want to. The native born in Vishakha Nakshatra is quite lax when it comes to saving money and thus can become a profligate spender. However, if one is an entrepreneur, one will eventually learn to save. Moreover, a career in banking is also good for these natives.	The native woman born in Vishakha Nakshatra has a love for all things art. Therefore, these women will have a good career if they spend their time in a profession like fashion, poetry, media, advertising and anything related to travel or become influencers. Furthermore, support, be it from parents or spouse, is a basic need for women born in Vishakha Nakshatra to succeed in life. So you should marry someone who sees your goals as his goals and this will make you independent and self-reliant in life.
The native male born in Vishakha Nakshatra is close to his mother but may not get the best of her due to some contingencies or being away from her. The native shares a casual relationship with his father. However, he will receive material benefits from his father. However, less attached to his father, the male born in Vishakha Nakshatra will become an autonomous person. Talking about the spouse, the native will share a great relationship with her. Both of you will live the life you imagine with very little getting in the way of your love and peace.	The native woman born in Vishakha Nakshatra is a family oriented person who has always supported her family both personally and professionally. A woman gets along well with her husband who loves her because of her independent and focused nature. The two of them together can only achieve so much if they delay the birth of a child a little. The woman is likely to be close to her mother. Besides, she will also have a good relationship with her father-in-law.

Talking about the health of the man born in Vishakha Nakshatra, he has to be careful while driving because he is very prone to paralysis until the age of 35. After this age, your health is still good, with few respiratory problems.	Talking about the health of the woman born in Vishakha Nakshatra, this woman is prone to kidney disorders and general weakness. However, these problems are not serious and can be avoided simply by taking good care of self. Eating junk food should be avoided.

ANURADHA

Symbol- Triumphal archway, lotus

Ruling planet- Saturn

Gender- Male

Gana- Deva

Guna- tamas/sattva/tamas

Presiding Deity- Mitra

Animal- female deer or rabbit

Indian Zodiac- 3°20′ – 16°40′ Vrishchika

Favourable Activity: Learn music, conducting dance, and arts and marriages. They are also ideal for the enjoyment of pleasures, making new friends, and wearing new clothes.

Anuradha nakshatra is the 17th nakshatra out of 27 nakshatras. There are 2 stars in this nakshatra shaped like an umbrella. According to few astrologers, there are 4 stars in this nakshatra which are shaped like lotus or umbrella. According to the Vedic sages, it is a tapasvi punishment. The deity of this nakshatra is 'mitra', one of the 12 adityas. Anuradha means welcome Radha, follow Radha or stay behind Radha.

Anuradha nakshatra is influenced by saturn and mars hence it has tamogun. This Nakshatra draws its energy from Saturn and Mars, so the natives are always ready to do something new and different. Under his influence, people become very good leaders. They are very organized in everything they do. They are good at balancing work and relationships. They know how to cooperate and adapt, whether in a relationship or as a team. They know how to share and make good friends.

Anuradha Nakshatra Padas

1st Pada: The 1st pada comes on Leo Navamsa. People born in this pada are intelligent and quick learners. They are eager to learn and gain professional qualifications.

2nd Pada: The 2nd pada comes to Virgo Navamsa. This pada-born native is a constant learner. He is also much disciplined. These qualities help him achieve success much faster than others.

3rd Pada: The 3rd pada comes from Libra Navamsa. Locals born in this neighborhood are social and can have many friends. This can be a boon for them as the larger circle makes them want more in life.

4th Pada: The 4th Pada comes on Scorpio Navamsa. People born in this pada have abundant energy to pursue all kinds of esoteric and overt goals in life.

Characteristics of People Born in Anuradha Nakshatra:

Male	Female
Males born in Anuradha Nakshatra are attractive in appearance, however, may not appeal to everyone. Their glowing eyes are the distinctive attractive feature of these natives. In essence, natives are confident and hardworking. He has a special ability to handle difficult situations easily and systematically. However, his mind wanders in fear of what would happen to him in the future. Double-mindedness not only stresses him out, but it also prevents him from enjoying his life fully or even forming	The woman born in Anuradha Nakshatra has an innocent appearance but has a confusing personality that only few people can see. This personality of hers speaks to her sexual nature, which she is afraid to talk about but is not someone who matches her feelings, aka she finds one another. The woman born in Anuradha Nakshatra has a heart of gold and is very helpful to others. She likes to live a simple life and is less influenced by what

relationships with the opposite sex. These people can also be a bit stingy, but the quality turns out to be a blessing for them.	other women are doing. However, the fact that she is not "feminine" is something that can make your mother worry a lot. The woman has a good group of friends and she naturally shines in social and political matters. You will most likely meet the person you love after turning 23.
Male born in Anuradha Nakshatra is usually advised to start his own business. You have a character who wants to lead, and so leading from the top is not only easy, but also very satisfying. It's also likely that you started making money at the age of 18-20. It will greatly improve your experience, which will help you build your own business for years to come. Career prospects until the age of 48 are very good for you. After that, poor health may cause you to lose interest in the business, but profitability will not decrease.	The woman born in Anuradha Nakshatra will have a good career if she is passionate about art. It's good to be studying hard, but a college degree won't do you any good because you might choose or be interested in a completely different career. Many professional performers of this dance art form are known to have been born in this Nakshatra and you can too.
Males born in Anuradha Nakshatra will be close to both his mother and father. He will receive monetary benefits from his father, who will also help him in business. However, if you are doing business together, there is a risk of friction between the duo. Such guys belong to old school but could end up with a woman who leans slightly towards the modern side of the world. The match may not seem compatible at first, but by being together, both of you will learn each other's ways and thus be able to live a	The woman born in Anuradha Nakshatra is born with the label of an idol mother who helps her children achieve glory. She herself is ambitious and always ready to do more and make the most of her time. Therefore, the work-life compatibility between her and her husband is amazing. In addition, the baby also takes care of the mother and is more attached to the father. Her devotion to her in-laws makes her even more desirable.

happy life together.	
Men born in Anuradha Nakshatra are in good health. However, minor health problems such as dental problems, coughs, colds, and constipation can often be on your side.	A woman born in Anuradha Nakshatra might experience menstrual problems. The chance of having irregular periods is also common for these women. Moreover, after turning 26, headaches and runny nose problems can also keep you up at night. To combat them, you will have to adopt an active lifestyle.

JYESTHA

Symbol- Umbrella, earring

Ruling planet- Mercury

Gender- Female

Gana- Rakshasa

Guna- tamas/sattva/sattva

Presiding Deity- Indra

Animal- Male deer or rabbit

Indian Zodiac- 16°40' – 30° Vrishchika

Favourable Activity: Filing a divorce, breaking a relationship, black magic, exorcism, and other brash/bold activities

Natives under its influence are wise and intelligent. They tend to be experienced and good at handling power and wealth. They protect family members and are often the rulers of their family. They face many difficulties in life. They are not very social and have few trusted friends.

Jyeshta Nakshatra Padas

1st Pada: The 1st pada of this Nakshatra falls in the Sagittarius Navamsa that's ruled by Jupiter. Financial interests will keep you going and occupied. You may think of going for higher studies. Natives are very generous during this pada.

2nd Pada: The 2nd pada of Jyeshta Nakshatra falls in the Capricorn Navamsa that is ruled by Saturn. This phase is a responsible phase, and you will do what is right, not what is convenient.

3rd Pada: The 3rd pada of this Jyeshta Nakshatra falls in the Aquarius Navamsa that is ruled by Saturn. Natives are sensitive to other peoples needs and offer them help to the maximum extent. They should be careful of getting trapped in sexual encounters.

4th Pada: The 4th pada of Jyeshta Nakshatra falls under the Pisces Navamsa that is ruled by Jupiter. It is easy for you to get carried away by emotions during this phase. Such native adore children and is interested in exploring the science.

Characteristics of People Born in Jyestha Nakshatra:

Male	Female
Men born in Jyeshtha Nakshatra are usually very practical and do not like to brag about their achievements. Due to this nature, they are often underestimated by others. These males are very stubborn and don't take anyone else's opinion into account. They like to do whatever their conscience tells them to. One thing to keep in mind when interacting with them is that they are not good at keeping secrets and will confide in others at the first opportunity. Once they discover something very important, it will be very difficult for them to carry on with their normal lives without taking it off their chest. So you have to be careful about what is shared with these men. They are also very angry. This causes them to	The women of this nakshatra are very sensitive and remember everything that is said to them. These women care a lot about how they look and how people perceive them. What people think of them means a lot to them, and they often take their opinions into account. The children of this nakshatra are very passionate lovers. They love blindly and are easily discouraged when they are betrayed in love. They easily become jealous when they are in a relationship. They are also very intelligent and thoughtful about the people and situations around them. Along with this, they can never

unintentionally hurt people.	be found in a messy environment as they are very organized and like to keep their surroundings clean and tidy.
These nakshatra males are very hardworking and passionate about making a name for themselves. Unlike their peers, they will start looking for a job or way of making money much earlier. They will follow their hearts while building their careers. This will allow them to be more successful than their peers. They are likely to leave their homes, to continue their studies or to work. While they will be successful in whatever they do, they will also be fickle about exactly what they want to do. Until the age of 50, they struggle quite a bit with this instability, especially between the ages of 18 and 26. They are advised to stay calm and stick to their decisions. After attaining age of 50 years, they will be quite comfortable with their situation.	Although they are smart and intelligent, getting a good education is not the most important concern of women in this nakshatra. Thus, their academic performance will be average and basic, and they will be satisfied with their husband's income. They are not afraid to take care of their home and family and are comfortable with their own business. It is often noticed that these women are rarely the winning members of the family, but this does not mean that they will experience financial difficulties. This means they will have a husband who earns enough for the family to have a comfortable life.
Jyestha nakshatra men usually see a difficult life with their families. The relationship with their siblings and mother won't be the best and they won't get much support from them. Due to their stubbornness, free spirit and independence, they will not be able to form close relationships with their loved ones. However, they will have a very sweet and happy married life with a loving and somewhat controlling wife who will not tolerate them getting drunk in the house.	Women in this nakshatra will have to be careful about their social environment after marriage as it is likely that they will have family members and relatives or even neighbors who often try to create tension in their lives. More often than not, these women will find themselves in the middle of a conflict because they often fail to maintain a harmonious environment. Because of all the

	constant stress in the family, they will have to struggle with mental illness.
Apart from some minor health problems like chronic pain in hands and shoulders, stomach problems, asthma, dysentery, colds and fever, the men in this nakshatra will not suffer from these problems that can seriously stress them out.	Women in this nakshatra will not have the best health during their lifetime as they will have to experience many serious health problems like uterine problems, chronic body aches in hands and shoulders, even is an enlarged prostate.

MULA

Symbol- Bunch of roots tied together

Ruling planet- Ketu

Gender- Female

Gana- Neuter Rakshasa

Guna- sattva/rajas/rajas

Presiding Deity- Nirriti

Animal- Male dog

Indian Zodiac- 0° – 13°20′ Dhanus

Favourable Activity: Filing a divorce, breaking a relationship, black magic, exorcism, and other brash/bold activities.

Mula Nakshatra is the nineteenth Nakshatra in the series of lunar constellations or Nakshatras in Vedic astrology. This is called "the root star". These four quarters or padas of this Nakshatra belong to the zodiac sign Sagittarius. It is one of the gandanta Nakshatras where transformation occurs from the physical to the spiritual realm. The symbolism of Mula Nakshatra is a group of linked roots that signify hidden things, realms and events. These Nakshatra-borns will have a strong foundation and knack for getting to the heart of things. They have the ability to dig deep and find solutions even in the most difficult situations.

Under his influence, people are good investigators and good at uncovering secrets. They face different ups and downs in life that give them feelings of pain and loss. They are often resentful in nature and always blame others for their plight.

Moola Nakshatra Padas

1st Pada: The 1st Pada of Moola Nakshatra falls on the Mars-ruled Aries Navamsa. This area is associated with all kinds of physical and mental activities, depending on the evolutionary state of this native.

2nd Pada: The 2nd Pada of Moola Nakshatra appears in the Venus-ruled Taurus Navamsa. The emphasis here is on the study of occult science. On a material level, natives will be very hardworking and will achieve all their goals.

3rd Pada: The 3rd Pada of Moola Nakshatra falls in Gemini Navamsa ruled by Mercury. Here, natives believe in word juggling that helps them communicate well.

4th Pada: The 4th Pada of Moola Nakshatra falls on Cancer Navamsa ruled by the Moon. The focus here is on the constant struggle to relate to the people around them on an emotional level.

Characteristics of People Born in Mula Nakshatra:

Male	Female
Native born in Moola Nakshatra values his time and tries to create a peaceful environment for himself and those around him. He also tends to do things on his own, which sometimes makes him vulnerable and very busy with the side things in life. The man himself is too worried about the future, which makes him unable to choose anything other than restlessness. In fact, the natives are influenced too much by the people around them. Internally, the native is	The native woman born in Moola Nakshatra is a pure hearted woman. Ladies will go to any heights for those they love. This nature sometimes messes things up because people tend to take advantage of their goodwill for personal gain. Therefore, you need to be careful with who you call friends. Apart from good, women born in Moola Nakshatra can also be very stubborn like a bull. It might show her on a bad

an individual who fears God and lives with the belief that God will take care of everything for him. However, faith did not stop him from working hard.	side, but she definitely knows how to use her stubbornness to her advantage. Her stubbornness is what allows him to achieve greater things in life, but combining it with jealousy can lead to disaster. She may have to go through several heartbreaks in her life.
Men born in Moola Nakshatra are prone to falling into debt traps as they struggle to manage their finances. Therefore, the best idea for him is to save as much as possible. In fact, when it comes to managing finances, and even other things in life, he's very good at giving advice to others but can't follow that advice for himself. Speaking of money, natives earn from many sources. In addition, he may change jobs many times in his life. After 25 years, it's best to stay away from friends who are extravagant in nature, because when you're with them, you'll likely end up spending beyond your means as well.	Native women born in Moola Nakshatra often find it difficult to study. This is because she is less focused on her studies and more focused on other artistic and social activities in her life. However, when Jupiter is in a favorable position in Moola Nakshatra, this is a good time to start anything educational; as Jupiter will help you pursue it. The Moola Nakshatra-born woman also excels in health-related jobs.
The native male born in Moola Nakshatra loves his loved ones more than anything else. However, sometimes he is unable to express these feelings or does not have the time to do so, which can make him feel disconnected from his family. Speaking of family, the native can hardly get benefits from his parents and he is a self-made man. He is very helpful in managing and raising children. Moreover, when the native	The native women born in Moola Nakshatra have the danger of separation hanging over their heads. This may be due to their husband's rebellious nature. The Moola Nakshatra-born woman is very much looking for attention from her loved ones and she can very quickly get upset if she doesn't receive it. On the positive side, benefic planets that are favorably placed in her horoscope

thinks about the future, he is a good planner.	can ease obstacles to her marriage. She should try pleasing Mars for a happy married life besides talking about problems with her husband and children.
Men born in Moola Nakshatra may face symptoms that can lead to tuberculosis, paralysis or persistent stomach problems. The ages when natives should take special care of health are 27, 31, 44, 48, 56 and 60 years old.	Native women born in Moola Nakshatra may face stomach problems. She will have to be especially careful in the later years of her age: 27, 31, 38, 56 and 60

PURVA ASHADHA

Symbol- Elephant tusk, fan, basket

Ruling planet- Venus

Gender- Male

Gana- Manusha

Guna- sattva/rajas/tamas

Presiding Deity- Apas

Animal- Male monkey

Indian Zodiac- 13°20' – 26°40' Dhanus

Favourable Activity: Performing destructive deeds such as demolishing, poisoning, setting fire, and confronting enemies.

This Nakshatra is called the "invincible star". Under its influence, the people are independent and strong. They always try to improve the situation by raising their status. They are good at manipulating and influencing others and have excellent communication skills. They have anger problems and are often aggressive.

Purvashada Nakshatra Padas

1st Pada: The 1st Pada of Purvashada Nakshatra falls under the Leo Navamsa ruled by the Sun. In this pada, the emphasis is on the pride and confidence of the natives, who love to be the center of attraction.

2nd Pada: The 2nd Pada of Purvashada Nakshatra falls in the Virgo Navamsa ruled by Mercury. In this pada the planets will ask the natives to work hard to earn money and they will be rewarded.

3rd Pada: The 3rd Pada of Purvashada Nakshatra falls under the zodiac sign Libra Navamsa ruled by Venus. The person with this pada is comfortable and loves all material comforts. It has been observed that thenative people reap the fruits of their labor during this time.

4th Pada: The 4th Pada of Purvashada Nakshatra falls on the Scorpio Navamsa ruled by Mars. In this Pada we see that the natives are arrogant, mysterious and secretive. Natives of this pada acquire a lot of occult wisdom.

Characteristics of People Born in Purva Ashadha Nakshatra:

Male	Female
Purvashada nakshatra males are very intelligent and intuitive. They call themselves brave and full of courage, but when the time comes, they often don't come forward and behave bravely. There are times when they will have no choice but to do something outside their comfort zone, to get out of a difficult situation. They are easily swayed by the persuasion of others and agree to do things that will later harm them, even though they are terrible at making big decisions. The males of this nakshatra usually have a very sharp tongue and know how to use it in an argument. Therefore, it is very difficult to win over an argument against them.	Ambitious is the right word to describe a Purvashadha nakshatra woman as she will do anything to achieve her goals. They are very intelligent and knowledgeable with a great work ethic and are also driven to achieve good results in their work. Due to this nature, they will be among the best performers in their business. In terms of personality, they are outgoing, outspoken and can make friends very easily, but sometimes they go overboard with others and end up hurting them. They also tend to make

	empty promises and end up breaking them. Women of this nakshatra are very intuitive and can find solutions in difficult situations.
The males of this nakshatra are intelligent and alert. So they can easily become doctors or even surgeons. But that doesn't mean they can't go to another area. In fact, they will find success in any profession they choose, and whatever works for them. But they must be careful if they choose to be an entrepreneur and only move forward if they are surrounded by people they trust and believe in wholeheartedly. They will also be interested in paranormal studies. Before and around the age of 32, it will be difficult for them to maintain a stable career, but when they turn 50, they will gradually build a stable and orderly life.	Due to their high achievement nature, the women of this nakshatra will want to receive a very good education and their academic performance will be better than others. Since they love to learn and acquire knowledge, careers like teaching or university professors will suit them best. They can also become bankers due to their competitive nature and will do well in this job as well. From an early age, these women will want to make a spiritual connection with nature and become attuned to them.
There is not much compatibility when it comes to their parents for these Purvashadha nakshatra males, but they will have a good relationship with their siblings. They are lucky enough to spend most of their lives abroad. Although they may marry later than their peers, they will have a happy and healthy married life with some minor disagreements here and there with their partner. Unlike their parents, they will have a very close relationship with their in-laws. They will also have a lot of luck when it comes to children because their children will be smart and successful in the family.	These nakshatra women will have a very good compatibility with their husbands and they will have a very healthy relationship. The bond between them and their husband will grow stronger throughout the marriage and their love will deepen over time. They will have a very loving husband who will keep them happy, but their children may not be helpful to them or do not meet their expectations.

The health of these males is generally good early in life, although they always feel that things are not going as they should. And as a result, they might invite an illness that takes time to heal. The disease will not affect their lifestyle and work performance.	Women born in Hasta Nakshatra are rarely financially tied to the family in any way. Therefore, most of the time they do not work. However, according to astrology, not working will damage the creative instincts that Hasta Nakshatra women are born with. The woman can work in creative fields like interior design, wedding planning, media, etc. Your spouse will likely support you in your efforts. Moreover, even if they are not fully educated, these women still have the skills to make a good living.

UTTARA ASHADHA

Symbol- Elephant tusk, small cot, planks of bed

Ruling planet- Sun

Gender- Female

Gana- Manusha

Guna- sattva/rajas/sattva

Presiding Deity- Vishwadevas

Animal- Male mongoose

Indian Zodiac- 26°40' Dhanus – 10° Makara

Favourable Activity: Build homes, plant trees, purchase property, lay a foundation, and buying agricultural property.

This is called the "universal star". Uttara Ashada Nakshatra is the 21st Nakshatra in the series of Nakshatras in Vedic astrology. The first quarter or pada of this Nakshatra is in the zodiac sign Sagittarius while the other three are in Capricorn. The word 'Uttara Ashada' is translated as 'ultimate invincibility' or 'ultimate invincibility' which means final victory.

Under his influence, people are patient, gentle and kind. They have great staying power. They are responsible people, and they do their job with great determination. They are sincere and never lie. They often become lazy when they lose interest and what they are doing.

Uttarashadha Nakshatra Padas

1st Pada: The 1st pada of Uttarashada Nakshatra falls in the Sagittarius Navmasa ruled by Jupiter. Here, the emphasis is on values and the development of self-confidence. Native will gain and acquire a lot of knowledge.

2nd Pada: The 2nd Pada of Uttarashada Nakshatra falls in the Capricorn Navamsa sign ruled by Saturn. The Sun, Jupiter, Mars and Ketu are very strong here. The focus here is on your thoughts, desires, and strategies to achieve your goals.

3rd Pada: The 3rd pada of Uttarashada Nakshatra falls into the zodiac Aquarius Navamsa ruled by Saturn. The focus here is on accumulating knowledge and creature comforts.

4th Pada: The 4th pada of Uttarashada Nakshatra falls in the astrological sign Pisces Navamsa ruled by Jupiter. Here the emphasis will continue to shift from the physical to the spiritual aspect of things.

Characteristics of People Born in Uttara Ashadha Nakshatra:

Male	Female
Uttarashada Nakshatra men are among the most famous because they are smart and talented. These males are very intelligent, hardworking and are the trump card in everything they do because they are very versatile. They also get along very well with others as	Women of Uttarashada Nakshatra are usually considered to be quite wild in nature. They often don't get along with others as they can be very aggressive at times. Care should be taken when dealing with these women as even the slightest language breakdown or any form of

they are not self-centered and like to appreciate the hard work of others. For this reason, they easily gain popularity and attention, even if they don't mean to brag or praise about themselves. Although it becomes quite difficult to understand them and establish a deeper connection with them, as they are somewhat secretive and rarely reveal their true feelings and emotions. They are God-fearing people and care about how their actions affect others. So they rarely do anything that might hurt others by following the principles of the Dharma. Since they are very intuitive about their surroundings, it is easy for them to spot malicious and people with wrong intentions.	provocation, even in a friendly manner, will upset them and may create misunderstandings and may lead even to big fight. Although they are very straightforward due to their excessive aggression, they are often judged and misunderstood by others.
The males of this nakshatra have to be careful what they stick to or intend to do. They should evaluate all sorts of possibilities before committing to any kind of business proposition, because chances are the person they want to work with doesn't have the best intentions. Such natives should also be careful if they want to get into anything controversial, as they are advised to avoid this path altogether. Although they are successful in everything they want to do, they will see significant career growth after the age of 38.	Women born in Uttarashada Nakshatra tend to achieve all kinds of fame when it comes to their profession. They will receive spiritual support from the universe to help them become successful writers. Due to their intellectual nature, they will then receive a very good education and also try their hand at banking or teaching.
Men in this nakshatra will be	Women of this nakshatra may suffer

blessed with a happy and healthy married life. The man will find a wife who will love him very much. His childhood is generally normal and healthy and he never has to witness any hardship in their family while growing up. Because of this, he will be very unprepared for certain situations and it will be extremely difficult for him to overcome these situations. Especially his wife's health will be of great concern to him. He will face major life changes between the ages of 28 and 31.	difficulties related to their married life. There may be situations where they need to stay away from their partner. This may happen due to work reasons on their part or their spouse, where they will have to go through a long distance relationship or some internal problems may also arise as a result of which they will have to deal with each other. face a number of problems that will eventually lead to psychosis.
Men born in Uttarashada Nakshatra will need to be careful with sharp objects as these carry the risk of causing large cuts and bruises. They will also experience many health problems early in life.	Women's health in this nakshatra is generally good without major problems. There may be cases where they will have to deal with issues such as uterine problems, hernias, or stomach problems. But most of the time everything will be normal.

SHRAVANA

Symbol- Ear, three footprints in uneven row

Ruling planet- Jupiter

Gender- Male

Gana- Deva

Guna- sattva/tamas/rajas

Presiding Deity- Vishnu

Animal- female monkey

Indian Zodiac- 10° – 23°20′ Makara

Favourable Activity: Buy automobiles, vehicles, beginning a journey or procession, travel, change of residence or job, and other major changes

This is called the "star of learning". Under its influence, the people are intellectually wise. They keep on looking for new things to learn. They are good at listening as well as teaching others. They tend to be restless and always go to different places in search of more knowledge.

Shravana Nakshatra Padas

1st Pada: People born in this pada have logical thinking and are also very ambitious by nature. In fact, these people are also very career-focused and quickly get frustrated when things don't go as planned.

2nd Pada: Those born in the 2nd pada of Shravana Nakshatra are intelligent, soft-spoken and very diplomatic. They are very active at work and do not leave work in the middle.

3rd Pada: Those born in the 3rd pada of Shravana Nakshatra, ruled by Mercury, have a little difficulty. They also have a desire to learn and succeed in jobs related to the media and communications fields.

4th Pada: Those born in the 4th pada of Shravana Nakshatra are very sympathetic and understanding beings. They like to mingle with people and are very open-minded. However, they can be rigid in the face of change.

Characteristics of People Born in Shravan Nakshatra:

Male	Female
Men born in Shravana Nakshatra have a strong Moon influence over them. And so these people are really gentle in nature. The native has established values in life and peer pressure cannot prevent him from following them. Men born under Shavaran Nakshatra are different from other men in many ways. These people are very concerned with the order and cleanliness of their environment. Unlike many others, the man born	Women born in the house of Sharavan Nakshatra are charitable in nature and contribute to society in the way they can. The woman has compassion for those in need and cannot see others suffering. However, the lady can also have a habit of showing off and she makes sure that whatever nice thing she does gets everyone's attention. In a way, this trait is not bad because it motivates others to do good. Women born in Sharavan

in Shravana Nakshatra is also very helpful to others and really does not expect anything when it comes to helping someone. Such people also believe a lot in God and his will.	Nakshatra are talkative but are also excellent keepers of secrets. These women can hide everything, especially from their husbands, which can lead to friction between couples in some cases.
The man born in Shravana Nakshatra goes through many changes in his life until the age of 30. Therefore, he may not have a stable career before this age due to his willingness to try new things often. Technically, the best period for those born in Shravana Nakshatra begins after 30 years and continues until 45 years. This will be a stable period for the native in which he can try professions like engineering related or any kind of import/export activities. When it comes to work, these people tend to get so caught up in it that they often forget that they need to be with their family.	Women born in Sharavan Nakshatra often have difficulty in studying, as she prefers to do other things in life. When it comes to the profession, these women are allowed to do whatever they want because only then can they excel in their careers. Women born in Sharavan Nakshatra have a great career after the age of 26. She can be a very good representation of the fine arts and above all a very good dancer.
If these people can bring work-life balance, then the native men born in Shravana Nakshatra will have a very happy married life. Your wife will generally love your caring nature, which makes you an irresistible husband. However, those born in Shravana Nakshatra must also be careful not to indulge in adultery, which they tend to do when they get a lot of attention from women after a certain age.	When it comes to family life, the woman born in Sharavan Nakshatra can make everyone happy and content. As these women strive for perfection, they don't want to give anyone a reason to mock them. Also, she accepts that other people are just as perfect as she is and can therefore let herself down. However, this perfectionist attitude does not apply to her husband, to whom she gives a lot of love and care, thereby helping her to have a very fulfilling married life.

Speaking of health, a person born in Shravana Nakshatra may complain of troubles related to ears. You need to take special care of your skin because you are prone to skin diseases and digestive system problems.	In terms of health, like men born in Sharavan Nakshatra, women can also face skin diseases from a very early age. The woman may also be susceptible to tuberculosis.

DHANISHTA

Symbol- Drum or flute

Ruling planet- Mars

Gender- Female

Gana- Rakshasa

Guna- sattva/tamas/tamas

Presiding Deity- 8 Vasus

Animal- Female Lion

Indian Zodiac- 23°20′ Makara – 6°40′ Kumbha

Favourable Activity: Buy automobiles, vehicles, beginning a journey or procession, travel, change of residence or job, and other major changes

It is called the "star of the symphony". It includes property ownership and material possessions. It brings harmony in everyone's life. It is the drum-shaped constellation that is considered the "most talked about". He derives his power from eight ruling gods named Apah, Soma, Dhruva, Pravasha, Dhara, Pratyusa, Anila and Anala. These eight gods provided the natives with good performing skills in dance and music and became the richest. According to Vedic Astrology, Mars is the ruling planet of Dhanishta Nakshatra. It seems to be a musical drum symbolizing complete wealth.

Under its influence, people have a lot of wealth and possessions. They favor music and dance. But like musical instruments, they tend to be empty inside and are always looking for things to fill that void. This often makes them self-centered.

Dhanishtha Nakshatra Padas

1st Pada: The 1st pada of Dhanishta nakshatra is governed by the Sun and falls into the Leo navamsa. People born in this pada will be successful in all aspects of life except their married life. The main emphasis is on material achievement.

2nd Pada: Ruled by Mercury, this pada of Dhanishta nakshatra falls in Virgo navamsa. Although like the previous pada, marriage will be quite difficult for those born in the 2nd pada but they will discover their talents as an athlete or a musician.

3rd Pada: This 3rd pada of nakshatra is ruled by Venus and is in the navamsa of Libra. Unlike the other two padas, these people will have a very successful marriage and will generally be in a very healthy state of mind. They will also grow spiritually with the performing arts and astrology.

4th Pada: This 4th pada of nakshatra is ruled by Mars and is found in the navamsa of Scorpio. The emphasis here is on physical strength and outdoor activities. People born in this pada have tremendous energy and will do well in sports.

Characteristics of People Born in Dhanistha Nakshatra:

Male	Female
Men born in Dhanishtha Nakshatra are said to be intelligent and have a good work ethic. They love to learn and accumulate knowledge. Therefore, whatever job they decide to choose for themselves, they will succeed in it. Dhanishta men take their moral values very seriously and will try to avoid any form of controversy that might affect others. They will never, in any way, by their words or actions, consciously hurt anyone. They will always stay away from arguments unless there is no other choice. It is	Dhanishta nakshatra women are generous and kind. Just like Dhanishta men, they are also very intelligent, high achievers and due to their very ambitious nature, they will easily get a job with a lot of monetary benefits. But along with that, they love to spend a lot and sometimes like to splurge on themselves and their loved ones. They can also be called empaths as they can feel the pain of the unfortunate and would love to participate in

believed that these men are religious in nature and prefer to stay in their comfort zone, hang out with the same friends, and do the same activities. If they've made a mistake, they'll never forget. Since they are very patient, they will wait for the right time to take revenge.	charity work. These females will generally have a dominant personality but they hold it back for the well-being of their family.
Dhanishta nakshatra men are high achievers. Due to their thirst for knowledge and intelligence, careers like historian or even scientist would suit them best. They can also work in an intelligence agency or as private secretaries to big businessmen, if they're interested, as they are very good at keeping secrets no matter how big. These men are more advanced than their peers intellectually and thus succeed faster than others. Their careers will flourish after the age of 24. Although they have to be careful in their work and at the same time trust their colleagues even when they are asked to trust.	Women in this nakshatra can choose anything as their profession as they can adapt to any situation and have knowledge of everything. These women can do jobs that are equally suitable for both men and women, as they are quite flexible and can easily adapt to many different situations. They may choose to work in teaching because they love to learn and share their knowledge, or choose to work in the field of literature because they are also good at words. Since there is no limit to their interests, they can also choose a career related to science.
Men under this sign will be extremely lucky to get married. Their wives will be like embodiment of Goddess Lakshmi and bring them a lot of luck. They will have the upper hand when it comes to taking on the family role but they will have a very good relationship with their siblings. Sometimes their loved ones create problems for them and they don't have the best relationship with their in-laws. But nothing too serious is there to be concerned with.	Dhanishta nakshatra women have a good sense of the importance of family. They are used to maintaining harmony among family members. Due to their controlling nature, they are most likely to be the main decision makers in the family and they are very good at managing household affairs.

Men in this nakshatra often don't feel healthy physically because they don't care much about their health and only seek help when there is no other choice, they will end up with illnesses like colds and flu, cold, cough or anemia.	Women of this nakshatra are also very careless when it comes to taking care of themselves. They rarely have routine check-ups and try to avoid medication as much as possible. As a result, they may experience many health problems such as anemia, cough or fever, blood problems or uterine disorders.

SHATABHISHA

Symbol- Empty circle. Thousand flowers or stars

Ruling planet- Rehu

Gender- Female

Gana- Neuter Rakshasa

Guna- sattva/tamas/sattva

Presiding Deity- Varun

Animal- Mare

Indian Zodiac- 6°40' – 20° Kumbha

Favourable Activity: Buy automobiles, vehicles, beginning a journey or procession, travel, change of residence or job, and other major changes

This nakshatra is also called the "veiling star". Under its influence, people are secretive and philosophical. They are good healers. They can be moody and lonely because they are not considered good communicators. They tend to overestimate themselves in terms of knowledge and consider themselves to know-it-all.

Shatabhisha Nakshatra Padas

1ˢᵗ Pada: Ruled by Jupiter and falling into the navamsa of Sagittarius, this first pada of nakshatra will focus on the optimistic and generous nature of people due to which they might be deceived by others.

2ⁿᵈ Pada: The 2nd pada of Shatabhisha nakshatra is ruled by Saturn and is in the navamsa of Capricorn. The main goal here is to achieve their goals. But they must be careful not to push themselves forward as that can stress them out.

3ʳᵈ Pada: Ruled by Saturn and living in the Aquarius navamsa, those born in this sign are clairvoyant and can be very aggressive and irritable at times. They have to make sure they don't get distracted often and practice meditation.

4ᵗʰ Pada: The importance of this pada is compassion and passion. Since this nakshatra pada is ruled by Jupiter and is in the navamsa of Pisces, the negative effects of the planets can cause addiction problems.

Characteristics of People Born in Shatbhisha Nakshatra:

Male	Female
Men born in Shatabhisha Nakshatra are very devout and sincerely follow the rituals. These males are very stubborn by nature and no one can change their decision once they have made a decision. They also believe strongly in their principles and their every action depends on what they think is the right thing to do. They are also very emotional and get angry very easily. Although they are extremely intelligent, they get angry at the slightest comment and immediately lash out. Due to their modest nature, they do not like to brag about their achievements and will be easily underestimated by others. But people will eventually recognize them when it's time for them to show off their talents.	Shatabhisha nakshatra women are calm and humble as they are very spiritual and devout and will not intentionally harm anyone. They are God-fearing and follow their spiritual rituals religiously. Because they have a calm mind, they are rarely seen arguing or fighting. But they can also defend themselves strongly if someone misbehaves with them or tries to harm them in any way. Although they will not get involved in controversies outside the family, they will face many conflicts and quarrels within the family that make them mentally unstable. They have a generous and friendly soul with a good memory.
These men will struggle a bit at a	The females of this nakshatra have

young age in terms of careers. Before the age of 34, men in this nakshatra will go through many career changes and face dilemmas over their choice, but after that age they can expect solid strides in their career and can move forward gaining strength from one to another. Jobs related to astrology, psychology, reiki and other healing arts will suit them best as they are very spiritual in nature.	very sharp brains and have sharp knowledge in the scientific field. They love to learn new things and accumulate knowledge as much as possible. This desire to learn will come in handy as they try to make important decisions about the career they want to pursue. Since they have an intuitive brain, the best career option for them so that they can put their knowledge into practice would be scientific research. These women should choose biological sciences and will make good doctors or surgeons.
The men of this nakshatra will face many difficulties regarding their relatives and families as their relatives will come to them about their problems. And because of their kindness, they will help them all the time. They may have to go through difficult situations because of their brothers and they won't get much help from their father, but they will be very close to their mother and the bond between them will be very strong. Their married life will also be unstable even if they get a very thriving wife.	Women of this nakshatra will have a husband who loves them very much and their compatibility will be marvelous. They will adore their husbands and they will have a very loving relationship. But the longevity of the marriage won't be the best. These women will suffer many disadvantages in marriage for many reasons, including geographical distance, long distance from their husbands, and possibly even losing their husbands at a very young age.
The health of these men will not be very good and they will suffer from many physical ailments such as respiratory problems, urinary tract infections and diabetes. Due to their weak immune systems, they are likely to get frequent infections.	In terms of health, these females will have to suffer a lot because their health is often unstable. They may suffer from urinary and uterine disorders as well as chest pain and gastrointestinal diseases.

PURVA BHADRAPADA

Symbol- Sword, two front legs of a funeral cot, Man with two faces

Ruling planet- Jupiter

Gender- Male

Gana- Manusha

Guna- sattva/sattva/rajas

Presiding Deity- Aja Ekapada

Animal- Male lion

Indian Zodiac- 20° Kumbha – 3°20′ Meena

Favourable Activity: Performing destructive deeds such as demolishing, poisoning, setting fire, and confronting enemies

This nakshatra is known as a "star of transformation". Under its influence, people are passionate and very forgiving in everything they do. They have two faces and secrets about themselves. They will face troubles and accidents in life so be careful. They are good at communicating and influencing people.

Purva Bhadrapada Nakshatra Padas

1st Pada: Ruled by Mars, the first pada of this nakshatra is in the navamsa of Aries. People born from this pada must practice patience and learn to control their emotions. Problems related to their aggressive mentality may arise. They must learn to channel their emotional energy to achieve their goals.

2nd Pada: Ruled by Venus and falling into the navamsa of Taurus, people of this pada will have an energetic nature that they will be passionate about exploring their dark side.

3rd Pada: Ruled by Mercury and falling in Gemini, those born under this sign are naturally curious. They like to explore the softer side of their nature and have a humorous personality.

4th Pada: This 4th pada of nakshatra is ruled by the Moon and is in the navamsa of Cancer. People born in this pada may have a dangerous feeling about them because they have both good and bad traits. They match the other three padas of this nakshatra

Characteristics of People Born in Purva Bhadrapad Nakshatra:

Male	Female
Men born in Purva Bhadrapada nakshatra are soft-spoken and peace-loving. They have very strict values that they follow religiously and they are easily provoked when others do something quite the opposite. Although they are not the most religious people, they are very humble in nature and are always ready to fight for others if they encounter injustice. They will be angry if belittled in any way and love a simple uncomplicated life. They have a very kind soul and like to help those in needs, but for some reason they always create misunderstandings that make them unloved. People respect them a lot even if they are not always strong financially.	Purva Bhadrapada nakshatra women are born leaders and are the most dominant among their peers. They have an authoritative way of speaking and are best suited to a leadership role in a group. The projects they lead will run smoothly and the people working under them will have no problem keeping up with their orders. Their morality is the most important thing to them and getting them to do something against it would be impossible. Although they find it difficult to trust anyone without assessing their intentions. Even if they have the financial ability to help others easily, they will only do so after carefully assessing the situation and making sure they really need their help.
Men of this nakshatra will be extremely lucky in business. They are naturally intelligent and business savvy. If they enjoy working in government jobs, this will also suit them perfectly, as it is likely that their monthly income will be higher than average and they will be regularly promoted and raised. wage. For this reason, these men will never	The women of this nakshatra have a desire to learn and discover. So professions related to science and technology will suit them best. Since they are extremely intelligent in their studies and excel in their studies, they can pursue their careers as scientists or doctors. They can also choose a teaching job if they prefer a

suffer a financial disadvantage and will be independent in all aspects of their lives. Their career growth period will be between 24 and 33 years. They will find themselves settling in between the ages of 40 and 54.	simpler and less stressful job. Other careers that might suit them are astrology, statistics, or research, where they can use their brains the most.
Everything will be normal when it comes to the relationship of Purva Bhadrapada nakshatra men and they will find loving wives and healthy children. But when it comes to love from maternal side, these males won't get much. Their relationship with their mother will always rest on fragile foundations. The cause of the gap between mother and son may be due to the working conditions of the mother.	Purva Bhadrapada nakshatra women will be blessed with a very happy and prosperous family after marriage. They will find a husband who loves them and they will have a very good compatibility. The women of this nakshatra will be very lucky in terms of children because they will have many children and they will have a very large family. These women are very good at managing the household and will be perfect for household chores.
The males of this nakshatra will suffer a lot in terms of health. Health problems such as bouts of paralysis will stress them out. They may suffer from acid and digestive problems and may develop diabetes later in life. Problems with the ribs, feet, and sides of the abdomen may also occur.	There are health problems that women in this nakshatra will have to go through. Some of the possible problems are liver problems, low blood pressure, stroke and pain in the ankles.

UTTARA BHADRAPADA

Symbol- twins, back legs of a cot, a snake in the water

Ruling planet- Saturn

Gender- Male

Gana- Manusha

Guna- sattva/sattva/tamas

Presiding Deity- Ahir Bhudyana

Animal- Female Cow

Indian Zodiac- 3°20′ – 16°40′ Meena

Favourable Activity: Build homes, plant trees, purchase property, lay a foundation, and buying agricultural property

This nakshatra is called "Warrior Star". Under its influence, people have good control over their emotions. They tend to be lazy. They have a kind and cheerful nature. They are extremely protective of those they love, love their home and family and the simple pleasures that come with it.

Uttarabhadrapada Nakshatra Padas

1ˢᵗ Pada: The 1st pada is dominated by the Sun and falls under the sign of Leo navamsa. Those born in this pada are intelligent and share knowledge gained through experience. These people have leadership energy and are very goal-oriented.

2ⁿᵈ Pada: This 2nd pada of nakshatra is ruled by Mercury and falls in Virgo navamsa. People born in this pada focus on the higher things in life and are often curious to make it big in life.

3ʳᵈ Pada: This 3rd pada of nakshatra is ruled by Venus and is in the navamsa of Libra. People born in this pada strive to keep everything under control and in balance. People in this category will be more attracted towards the target.

4ᵗʰ Pada: Ruled by Mars and falling in Scorpio, the goal of those born in this sign is to venture into the unknown. They will want to study the occult, through which they gain knowledge.

Characteristics of People Born in Uttara Bhadrapad Nakshatra:

Male	Female
Men born in Uttarabhadrapada Nakshatra are free from any judgment or prejudice and will have relationships with people of higher and lower status. They won't bother others with their problems and will likely find solutions on their own. They have a heart of gold and will sacrifice everything for those they love and trust. However, they may have problems with anger management. It is believed that they will get angry at the slightest provocation but are easily and quickly cooled down and will not hold grudges for long. They are said to be very intelligent and can be excellent speakers. They will overcome all obstacles to achieve their goals. Also, they are mostly very sexual people and will always want a friend of the opposite sex to accompany them.	The women of this nakshatra are considered the Lakshmi of the family, as they bring fortune and wealth wherever they go. Their personality is like that of a goddess, humble and kind. They tend to be very respectful to their parents and elders. They are the ones who will have the best solution to all problems in the family and they are excellent at maintaining family harmony. That is why the women of this nakshatra become very good housewives. Anyone who has to associate with it will never be inconvenienced as these females can adapt to any situation and will never be the one to complain. They are also brave and courageous and will fight for what they think is right and just.
Although these men in nakshatra do not have the best education and qualification, they will participate in many extracurricular activities through which they will learn many practical skills. Regarding their education level, their interest will be more towards fine arts. They are very ambitious people and they will win the top spot in any competitive situation because they believe in self-education as the best form of education. These men will have to	As conveyed earlier, the women of this nakshatra bring fortune wherever they go. Their career will flourish in whatever job they decide to do, which will make them rich. Another thing to notice about them is that they get along very easily with people. So, in addition to receiving praise from the elders for their hard work, they will also be very popular with their peers. However, they may have to travel a lot for work,

struggle a bit in terms of careers before finally settling down at 42.	which they don't like very much.
The male of this nakshatra may have to go through many hardships in his childhood as he may have been abandoned during his childhood and had to live away from home for most of his early life. Although he respects his father, for some reason he will not receive the love or support he deserves from his parents. But after marriage, all his difficulties and hardships will bear fruit and he will have a beautiful, talented, meek and loving wife who loves him dearly. He will also have very lovely and talented children.	The women of Uttara Bhadrapada nakshatra are ambitious people and whatever they do, they accomplish with excellence. And because of that, they will make their parents and loved ones extremely proud. Due to their hardworking nature, they will bring glory to their families. They will also never face financial problems after marriage due to their good luck and prosperous family.
Although they are not particularly concerned about their health, these men born in nakshatra maintain a healthy lifestyle, very disciplined and active. So they don't have to worry about their health and live virtually disease-free lives.	Women of this nakshatra will not face any major health problems. There may be problems here and there, such as joint or bone pain, menstrual cramps, or digestive problems.

REVATI

Symbol- drum, pair of fish

Ruling planet- Mercury

Gender- Female

Gana- Deva

Guna- sattva/sattva/sattva

Presiding Deity- Pushan

Animal- Female Elephant

Indian Zodiac- 16°40′ – 30° Meena

Favourable Activity: Learn music, conducting dance, and arts and marriages. They are also ideal for the enjoyment of pleasures, making new friends, and wearing new clothes

It is the last of the 27 Nakshatras. It indicates a journey, the final journey from one life to the next. Under its influence, people are loving, kind and helpful. They are happy and positive people. They like to socialize and get to know new people. They are creative and imaginative. They make great artists. They are caregivers and always help others.

Revati Nakshatra Padas

1st Pada: The 1st Pada of Revati Nakshatra falls in the sun sign of Sagittarius Navamsa and is ruled by Jupiter. People born in this pada are generally appreciated by everyone. They will be rich, knowledgeable and wise in nature.

2nd Pada: The 2nd Pada of Revati Nakshatra falls in Capricorn Navamsa and is ruled by Saturn. People born in this pada strive to ensure that all their wishes are fulfilled. They are much more concentrated and balanced in nature.

3rd Pada: The 3rd Pada of Revati Nakshatra falls to Aquarius Navamsa and is ruled by Saturn. People born in this pada yearn for spiritual learning. They can become a point of contact for anyone with their problems.

4th Pada: The 4th Pada of Revati Nakshatra falls on Pisces Navamsa and is ruled by Jupiter. The life of people born in this pada is quite unstable and natives can easily be carried away by illusions. It's not good at all.

Characteristics of People Born in Revati Nakshatra:

Male	Female
The native man born in Revati Nakshatra is a sincere person who likes to do things systematically. Natives are very practical and have a good understanding of how things	The native woman born in Revati Nakshatra is authoritarian in nature. She tries to control anyone and everyone, including things beyond her control. Due to her

work and feel. They use their own experiences in life to guide others and are therefore very helpful. Since childhood, people born in Revati Nakshatra have been used to independent living and as a result, he can easily get frustrated if someone tries to control him. His uncontrollable trait escapes no one, not even his wife. Men here also don't trust anyone easily. However, once he finally trusts you, he will become too attached to you. These people are also loyal and very ambitious, and even a small setback can depress him.	nature, she may not be very popular, but she will be a decision maker or influential in her personal and professional life. Furthermore, the woman born in Revati Nakshatra is a spiritual and God-fearing person. She may also have beliefs in superstitions and thus be able to follow all religious practices and rituals. It gives him mental peace. In life, the lady has the will to achieve great goals but laziness prevents her from reaching new heights. She is also afraid of taking unfamiliar paths, which prevents her from achieving great things in life.
Revati Nakshatra men believe in the will to work, not the experience under his sleeve. These people can take an opportunity, whether they have experience with it or not, and try to do it with all their might. However, this can lead to failure and frustration for him most of the time. Instead, if he does anything in a planned way, nothing can stop him from achieving greatness in his chosen field. Such people have a scientific inclination and are therefore able to create their own future in all that is related to it. However, his rewards are unlikely to match his hard work, as he will have to wait until age 50 to get the most out of his investments.	A woman born in Revati Nakshatra will have a natural inclination towards fine arts or mathematics. She could also aim for a profession that requires her to interact with the public, such as a flight attendant or administrator. Powerful planets, such as Jupiter in Revati Nakshatra, can bless you with the ability to engage in PR work or as a diplomat. However, to get the most out of her career, the Revati Nakshatra-born woman will have to control her nature of getting distracted. The best time for your career is between 27 and 38 years old.
The man born in Revati Nakshatra may not be lucky enough to benefit	Woman born in Revati Nakshatra will be blessed with love and

from his father or his close relatives. He is a self-made person and can be very different from his family members in morals and attitudes. This can become the reason why he is not compatible with the family. However, the same nature will have a strong effect on his wife. His married life and his relationship with his wife will be quite good as she will be flexible in nature.	harmonious married life. Nothing major interrupts his love; and she might even marry the first mate she fell in love with. The woman born in the year of Revati Nakshatra is a devoted lover and very supportive of her partner. Sometimes there may be minor disputes with the parents-in-law but will be resolved soon.
Male born in Revati Nakshatra has to worry about his health. Minor health problems like fever, dysentery or facial skin problems like pimples will be very common among these natives. You should adopt a healthy lifestyle and include yoga in your daily to-do list.	The girl born in Revati Nakshatra does not have any serious health problems. However, minor ailments of the stomach, feet, and ears can become a temporary cause for concern after the age of 24.

ABHIJIT NAKSHATRA

Symbol- Horse Head

Ruling planet: Ketu, Mercury

Gender- Female

Gana- Deva

Guna- sattva/sattva/sattva

Presiding Deity- Ashwini Kumars

Animal- Male Horse, Female Elephant

Indian Zodiac- 06° 40' to 10° 53' 20 in Capricorn

Abhijit Nakshatra lies between Uttarashada and Shravan Nakshatras as it begins from the last pada of Uttarashada and ends at the first 1/15th of Shravan

It is not an ordinary nakshatra like other 27 nakshatras. We may call it as an invisible star. The moon has 27 wives; they are the daughters of Daksha Prajapathi and his wife Panchajani (Virani). These 27 sisters have one brother and that brother is named as Abhijit Nakshatra. Abhijit is the Sanskrit name of Vega, the brightest star in the northern constellation Lyra.

The only time Abhijit is used is for Muhurta. Abhijit (lorded by Mahavishnu) indicates the direction in which the Sun (i.e. solar system) transforms in the universe and in Krishna marga, Abhijit Nakshatra faces west. Therefore, it symbolizes the eye (Chakshyu) of the zodiac Aratus.

Abhijit means "Winner" or "one who cannot be defeated". In the Bhagavad Geeta, Krishna says that He is Shiva among the Rudras; He is Arjuna among Pandava and He is Abhijit among classical Vedic texts of Nakshatra which mention Abhijit as one of the auspicious times to perform any auspicious activity except while travelling in South direction. His deity is Lord Brahma. Some Vedic texts also mention that 28 minutes before and 28 minutes after 12: 00 (both morning and afternoon) is also known as Abhijit Muhurta too.

Abhijit Nakshatra Padas

1st Pada: The natives born in this pada have the excessive qualities of this Nakshatra. They can be recognized by their small eyes and small nose. Moreover, there is a fiery side of these people, which needs to win over others.

2nd Pada: The 2nd Pada is located in the Taurus Navamsa and is ruled by Venus. People born in this pada are more resource-oriented and practical. These natives direct their efforts in the right direction and think realistically.

3rd Pada: The 3rd pada is in Gemini Navamsa and is ruled by Mercury. People born in this neighborhood are smart and have good decision-making abilities.

4th Pada: Those born in the pada of this Ashwini nakshatra learn the science of the body very quickly. They are very interested in body repair and dissection.

Characteristics of people born in Abhijit Nakshatra

Male	Female
Abhijit Nakshatra-born native is a loving person. They are loved by everyone for their simple and useful nature. Moreover, since these people are very positive and optimistic, they do not let any obstacle discourage them. In fact, if they encounter obstacles in their life, they are even more determined to overcome them. This nature also inspires them to try new things in life. And in doing so, their intelligence helps them a lot. Men born in Abhijit Nakshatra are very familiar with wealth and material comforts, therefore they work hard to accumulate it until the age of 37. Then their devotion can lean towards spirituality.	Abhijit Nakshatra-born woman is a kind-hearted person. They are very helpful and don't hesitate to reach out to you first if they find you in trouble or need help for themselves. Although the world is always judgmental, these people tend to be impartial and only form opinions about you after getting to know you personally. The woman born in Abhijit Nakshatra is also very selfless and believes that everyone deserves a 2nd chance in life. As for life in general, these people may not be too serious in their early years, but around the age of 18, an important event occurs that makes them become very serious and mature. The woman born in Abhijit Nakshatra is endowed with many skills but needs motivation to perfect them for her own good.
Men born in Abhijit Nakshatra are usually well educated and are quite intelligent. These people are more attracted toward business opportunities, but if they work in a corporate environment, they are more likely to reach the top faster than anyone else. If you are	Women born in Abhijit Nakshatra have many skills. However, she may have difficulty learning early in life. However, obstacles will not stop her. The career life of women born in Abhijit Nakshatra will be very generous from 28 to 39 years old. They can choose from a wide

interested in research work, you must pursue it as it will bring you career benefits. The best careers for these people are engineering, communications, hotel management and politics. The best period for career of people born in Abhijit Nakshatra is between 25 and 37 years of age.	range of options and often end up doing good work and making a good living. Whenever Jupiter is placed in Abhijit Nakshatra, she will rise to the highest positions and will achieve name, fame and power.
Men born in Abhijit Nakshatra are likely to get married early in life. The risk of separation is also frequent with these people. So you need to choose your partner wisely. Compatibility between husband and wife is normal. The two of you love each other very much but need to take steps to increase their bonding.	Women born in Abhijit Nakshatra must be brought up with due care until they reach age of 18 due to their fragile nature. Turning 15 will be an important period in a their life in terms of health. One must ensure her special care during this period.
Males born in Abhijit Nakshatra may face ongoing health problems but will overcome most of them as these problems are not too serious. All you have to do is adopt an active lifestyle.	Abhijit Nakshatra-born women often oppose marriage until a certain age, but this perception of them disappears after the age of 24. Rejection of marriage in the early stages is often due to their negative feelings and impressions they received in childhood. However, if a woman born in the year of Abhijit Nakshatra chooses to get married, she is likely to enjoy a happy and harmonious married life.

REMEDIAL MEASURES

In Vedic astrology, it is believed that the positions of the planets at the time of a person's birth can have a significant impact on their personality, health, and overall happiness. Therefore, astrological remedies aim to lessen the negative effects of adverse planetary influences and enhance the positive ones, thereby promoting better health and well-being.

As human beings, we all yearn for a life free of problems, worries, and suffering. Unfortunately, despite our caution and discipline, we end up doing things we shouldn't. We don't realize that we are all vulnerable to trials, temptations, mistakes, misunderstandings, and harm without knowing it, irrespective of our age. It is said that defects in stars and the adverse effects of planets on our lives often cause us to do things that are contrary to our personalities and characteristics.

In such a state, they think they can do magic with astrology and get rid of all their problems. People have a lot of misconceptions regarding astrology. They believe that the cure for problems according to astrology is to sit for hours in the temple, doing tedious things or even pouring money into idols and temples. There are countless kinds of problems in people's lives. Some face constant difficulties, while others have specific problems, and so on.

What is the astrological remedy?

Astrological remedies are antidotes that help remove the negative impact of planets or any other element in your life. Remember that astrological remedies won't completely remove pain from your life, but they will ease and release you from its effects.

Amazingly, astrology not only predicts aspects of life related to destiny, but it can also help to realign life and solve problems. In astrology, everything is a matter of time. We must understand that doing and wearing the right job at the right time is inevitable. Many people expect astrology and astrologers to completely eliminate the problem. Unfortunately, they are also humans, and they cannot change one's fate. They can only give advice, track the problems, analyze their effects, and help solve them to reduce their influence on your life. Another myth among people is that a cure can work for everyone. CERTAINLY NOT! Since each person has a unique birth chart, the frequency of problems, the type of problem, the position of the planets, so their impact also vary from person to person.

Astrology approaches the deepest layers of your personality, making you conscious and aware of the weak aspects where you need astrology's support and correction.

Karma plays an important role in the universe. Not only in astrology but in any study or creed, karma is at the core. Our past and present actions lay the foundation for the future. Your life and current events are the result of past actions without your knowledge. It's a vicious cycle that continues until your account is paid out in karma.

Some types of astronomical remedies include mantras and prayers, gems, mantras, rituals, offerings, and donations. Each of these remedies addresses different aspects of a person's astrological chart, and planets and houses are most strongly affected by adverse positions. The mantra is a prayer for happiness and personal growth and has great spiritual power. These invoke positive energies and lessen the negative effects of unfavorable planetary positions. Each planet is associated with specific mantras and prayers, and chanting these mantras is said to help bring about positive changes in an individual's life. Gemstones are another astrological remedy used to enhance the influence of the positive planets and alleviate the negative ones. Each planet is associated with specific gemstones, and wearing these gemstones is believed to have a positive impact on an individual's life. For example, wearing a ruby can enhance the influence of the sun, while wearing a blue sapphire can reduce the negative impact of Saturn.

Yantras are mystical diagrams or symbols used to invoke the energies of specific planets or deities. They are often used in meditation or puja (worship) to enhance the positive influence of the planet and lessen the negative influence. Yantras are said to have a powerful influence on an individual's energy and can help bring about positive changes in one's life. Rituals and offerings are other astrological remedies designed to appease or honor the planets. These may include various forms of puja, offerings of food, flowers, or other objects to gods or planetary energies, and other rituals designed to enhance the positive influence of the planet and reduce negative effects.

Finally, the gifts are astrological remedies that are said to create positive karma and reduce negative planetary influences. Donating to charitable causes or to temples or organizations that support the worship of specific gods or planets is believed to have a positive impact on an individual's life. In addition, it can help reduce the adverse effects of unfavorable planetary positions.

How astrological measures work

The basic idea behind astrological remedies is that each planet in astrology is associated with specific qualities, and its position in a person's birth chart can indicate strengths and certain weaknesses in the person's life. Therefore, if a planet is in a difficult position, it is believed that the planet's adverse effects can be balanced or neutralized by specific remedial measures.

However, it is important to note that the effectiveness of astrological measures is largely based on belief and faith. There is no scientific evidence to support the idea that astrological measures can influence the planets or change the course of events in a person's life. However, many people believe in the power of these remedies and use them to improve health and regain peace of mind. Ultimately, the effectiveness of astrological remedies depends on an individual's personal beliefs and willingness to make positive changes in their life.

Why do Remedies work?

Remedies are nothing but empirical, mystical, and metaphysical remedies that aim to ultimately reduce or neutralize past actions or negative effects caused by karma. Fortune is due to past karmic cycles. Solutions or remedies help an individual to continue or abstain from doing something. Even that particular action or inactivity seems to be karma in itself.

So when someone starts taking any remedy, he or she will do his best to undo the bad deeds committed in the past. However, when an individual tries to strengthen the weak beneficial planets, he will try to increase the effect by creating good karma.

Astrological measures can be broadly classified as follows:

1. Mantras:

There are classical Sanskrit mantras, which are energy-based sounds that provide a variety of vibrational and reverberant potentials. The mantra is a collection of Sanskrit words chanted to the rhythm. Mantras have the power to awaken the latent power of the soul. When a mantra is chanted, the mind gradually acquires a state of purity and serenity. All spells are associated with a particular planet or even seem to be immortal representations of that planet, and chanting different mantras has power. Moreover, mantra chanting is also known as "JAPA".

2. Yantra:

Yantras are mathematical symbols or diagrams. Generally, they are used in the worship of gods and lords of the planets as well as in tantric practices. The icons contain points, lines, triangles, squares, circles, and more. Yantras can be drawn on paper, engraved on metal, or even on a three-dimensional structure. When energized and worshipped daily, it can create a positive influence around you. Yantras appear to be geometric and mathematical graphics, signs, symbols, and designs.

However, all signs, symbols, and everything must have specific measurements. Even the yantras resonate with different energies and vibrations in a different way. The planetary yantras must be positioned in the right direction, because only then will they radiate positive and optimistic energy. It is extremely helpful in removing negativity and pessimism from life.

3. Remedial Products:

The various empowered astrological remedies also include the use of various products, including gems, rudraksha, crystals, charms, and herbs. A gem is a piece of crystal that allows specific colors of light rays to hit the body in an exaggerated manner. They are used to strengthen the planetary vibrations in the body. Also, wearing gems with jewellery increases the beauty quotient. Rudraksh beads are used for protection and chanting purposes. All of these products seem to be extremely helpful in removing negativity and inviting positivity. It also removes all bad effects from evil planets.

4. Service:

It is considered another form of remedy, perhaps the best in astrology. It is considered a kind of charity, gift, or offer to the poor and needy to uplift them and their way of life. Charity is very important in Hinduism. Dana means the act of giving something to the poor. Donate anything like food, water, grain, cows, land, gold, knowledge, etc. Depending on their individual abilities, each person can change a lot in attitude and karma. Different types of daans are mentioned for different planets.

5. Changes in attitudes and habits:

To improve your karma, this seems to be the most effective and impactful remedy or way to enrich or improve your karma. With this, one can also correct mistakes by developing good habits and positive attitudes. Due to the positions and alignments of the planets in the birth horoscope, many times situations turn out to be unfavorable and create chaos.

In these kinds of circumstances, it is advisable to admire and follow good habits and give up bad habits and attitudes, which are ultimately the result of alignment or positioning. You must learn virtues and moral principles. You have to be patient and let go of all your bad qualities, like anger. Also, avoid salt or sugar.

6. Fasting:

As the name suggests, you have to limit your consumption of food or some other thing(s) that are your favorites. Voluntarily limiting or sacrificing any desire to make you happy serves as a powerful remedy for neutralizing negative effects and reinforcing optimistic planetary outcomes.

7. Blessings:

One must receive the blessing of elders, including parents, teachers, or gurus. It is necessary to receive the blessing of the elders, which will eventually reduce the negative impact caused by the negative influence of various evil planets. If you have done something good, the elders will bless you, and it will have a positive effect on you. This is how your good karma comes into play.

8. Color therapy:

Color is used to balance the energy in the body. The seven chakras of the body are associated with different colors. Each planet has its own specific color that it resonates with and responds to. An imbalance of any color can create problems within that particular chakra and also on the planet. Color therapy can reduce this imbalance and act as an astrological remedy.

9. Totke

In North India, the word totke is widely used. It is basically a kind of remedy or ritual that helps people get rid of their daily troubles and problems. From a traditional point of view, this seems like a great activity to get rid of problems like inactivity or illness. If you say Totka in front of someone, that person will immediately understand that particular word is being used in a negative sense and will also think that it is being done to do something bad to someone. However, Totka is a traditional belief that is passed down from generation to generation and seems to be useful.

10. Religious:

It includes several actions, including prayer, ritual, worship of God and Goddess, performing yagya, which is sacrificial fire, and yatras to different spiritual places. Worship can be internal or external. External worship includes devotion to the deity in the form of a statue, idol, linga, saligrama, or any other symbol. Inner worship is done through spiritual channels without any physical entity. In addition, there are several religious sites that are decidedly places of worship that must be visited in order to neutralize the negativity of the evil planets. For example:Trimbakeswar Temple, Nashik. Apart from this culturally diverse land, India is also popular to perform puja and offer prayers to God to remove the evil effects of Rahu, which is the north node, and Ketu, which appears to be the southern node. In addition, it is an ideal place to reduce the pessimistic impact of Kaal Sarpa Dosha and Pitru Dosha.

11. Spiritual remedies:

In addition to religious measures such as prayer, there is another way, which is a spiritual remedy that includes yoga and meditation to help rejuvenate and strengthen the mind, body, and soul. In addition, it pleases and permanently strengthens the planets.

Specific Remedies:

Health: It is important to note that there is no scientific evidence to prove the effectiveness of these remedies and that a person should approach a licensed medical professional for treating their medical condition.

Approaching astrology and all related remedies is also essential with a critical and lucid mind, not relying solely on them for treatment. If you are experiencing any health problems, it is best to consult a qualified doctor.

In traditional astrology, each planet is associated with specific parts and organs of the body, and some astrologers may suggest remedies based on these associations. For example, if a person has stomach problems, the astrologer may suggest remedies related to the planet Jupiter, which is related to the digestive process. If you constantly have health problems, practice Rudra-Abhishek at home. To do this, chant the Rudra Gayatri, "Tat Purushaya Vidmahe, Mahadevaya Dhimahi, Tanno Rudra Prachodayat," and offer a sacred bathing ceremony for Shivling on any day of the week continuously for 11 weeks.

If your illness is not getting cured for a long time and doctor recommends the same medicine then shelve the old medicines, buy the same new medicine and start taking it from Poornima day or during the full moon phase (Shuklapaksh) on panchami, sashti, saptami, ashtami, or trayodashi.

If minor ailments keep bothering you from time to time, then chant 'Om Ganapataye Namaha' 1008 times on Thursday while holding golden mustard seeds in the palm of your hand. After singing, wrap these beads in a yellow cloth and tie them around the neck.

Career: Depending on your zodiac sign, certain days of the week and certain times of the year are considered positive for your career growth. These astrological measures for academic focus can help you succeed in your professional area of life. Today's predictions are based on astronomical calculations and planetary motions. An example of this is fasting on Tuesdays while worshiping Lord Hanuman, the God of Strength, which is considered auspicious. It means devotion to achieving a particular goal. If you can't get a job, give a spoonful of mustard seed to the sun god continuously for 41 days. Arrange to provide water on Sundays and maintain a free water dispenser at your birthplace for those who are thirsty. If your career is unstable with problems and frequent transfers, fill five copper cans with candies made of Bashan powder and give them on Sundays. Continue this practice for at least 11 Sundays. If you face obstacles in your formal work, chant the mantra "Om Vigneshwaraya Namaha" 108 times a day.

To succeed in your job, write the job description on a piece of paper, fold it, and place it in front of Ganesh along with some supari. Never start new work in Rahukalam.

Betterment in the Love Life: To improve understanding with your partner, here are the remedies of astrology.

- Worshiping the planet Venus: Venus is the planet that rules love and relationships. By worshiping Venus, you can attract more love and respect. You can wear a diamond or a white sapphire, chant a Venus mantra, or perform a ritual dedicated to Venus. These are also considered valuable remedies for finding love again.

- Wear gems: Certain gemstones are said to attract love and respect, such as rubies, emeralds, and diamonds. It is believed that wearing these stones can strengthen your aura and attract positive energy, which in turn can earn you love and respect.

- Take remedies for the 7th house: The 7th house of the astrological chart represents love and relationships. You can perform 7th house remedies like wearing 7 Mukhi Rudraksha, performing puja for Lord Shiva, or chanting Vishnu Sahasranama.

- Offering water to the Sun: The Sun symbolizes respect and authority, and by offering water to the sun, you can gain more respect in your life. You can do this by waking up early in the morning, facing the sun, and offering water while chanting mantras. These astrological measures for respect only work when you are devoted towards Lord Sun.

- If there are frequent problems between you and your lover, give rice and besan on Thursdays, especially to monks, nuns, or priests.

- If you and your spouse often have disagreements and quarrels, donate mustard or sesame oil on Saturdays and avoid wearing black clothes. Chant the mantra "Om pram preem prom sah shanischaray namah", facing east after sunset in the evening.

- Get water from a water source near the cemetery and put it in a puja or keep it in a safe at home. Also, give five almonds to the needy on Sunday to see a marked improvement in relationships.

Solving problems in marriage: If the marriage is delayed, chant the mantra "Om Jawal Jawal Shulani, Dushtgrahaan, Huun Phat Svaha" for 10 minutes in the morning and evening, and especially do it on Ashtami day in front of the image of Goddess Durga.

If repeated covenants fail, stand with your palms together in front of the moon at night and chant the mantra "Om Shram Shram Shrem Shrom Sah Channdramaseh Namah", every day for a year.

If you have a weak Mars in your zodiac sign causing problems in your marriage, there are astrological remedies. Chanting the mantra "Om ang angaarkay namaha", begins during Shuklapaksh (the waning phase of the moon), accompanied by a rosary of sandalwood.

Remedies for different Houses

1st House: When the 1st house is afflicted in the native's horoscope, then there will be problems in the areas related to the self. Problems can be mitigated to some extent by taking corrective action. Get more exercise and take a yoga class. Have positive self-talk in front of the mirror, praising yourself and all your good qualities before going to bed at night so that it sinks into your subconscious before you go to sleep. To activate the 1st house, natives can focus on the energy of the planet Mars. This can be done through various means, such as wearing gemstones associated with Mars, performing specific rituals or chants, and incorporating the qualities of Mars into your daily life.

2nd House: The 2nd house is related to accumulation of wealth. When the 2nd house is afflicted in the horoscope, then there will be problems in the areas associated with the 2nd house. Problems can be mitigated to some extent by taking corrective action. If the 2nd house lord is troubled, the native may have difficulty speaking, such as hesitancy. Native speakers sometimes have erratic or harsh speech. If you are having problems with family, food, or addiction, or are having trouble saving money, you need to perform appropriate remedies related to the planets. Find ways to save money every week, no matter the amount.

To improve and activate the 2nd house, you can sit calmly and quietly for a long time.

3rd House: Behaviour's should be balanced in a positive way. If you have sibling rivalry issues, you need to confront them and follow the group board to resolve them. If you lack the courage (benefics in 3rd like Jupiter and Venus), you may need to join competitive team sports, learn martial arts, or go on an adventure. If you really want to activate the 3rd house of the horoscope, leave your idleness behind and complete your unfinished tasks, especially those that benefit not only you but others. Don't get frustrated with your friends and loved ones for not keeping your promises. Help them a lot.

4th House: Happiness and healing problems with the mother are key. If your mother is still alive, spend time with her, take care of her, and nurture her. Practice forgiveness. Clean the house, get rid of the clutter, beautify it, fix it, and celebrate it. Add a security system to increase security. Practice cooking at home and feed others with your cooking. The 4th house is controlled by your mother, your godmother, or a woman you think is like your mother. Take care of her and try to spend enough time with her. The 4th house can be activated if you bring happiness to others. Blessings can take the form of words like "thank you". The 4th house brings happiness, so if you spread something positive like happiness, the 4th house will be activated. So be happy and keep everyone happy.

5th House: The 5th house deals with our enthusiasm and what we most enjoy doing in life. We must find a way to prolong joy and support Jupiter. If malefics like Saturn and Ketu are placed here, the joys of life will be extinguished. Find your passion and commit to it. Jupiter loves to be expansive and playful. To activate the 5th house, keep fast on Thursday. Jupiter is considered the lord and ruling planet of the 5thhouse. By keeping fast on Thursday, the planet Jupiter will be supportive, and for sure, the 5th house of the horoscope will be strong and dynamic. If you don't want to or can't keep fast, bring a banana sapling into the house. Take care of this young plant; it will also bring good results in relation to the 5th house. Sapling turmeric is also equally useful.

6th House: The 6th house requires us to find discipline (Saturn) and find time to exercise (Mars) to overcome health and dietary issues. The 6th house also requires us to have a healthy attitude towards work and our daily routine. Change your attitude. Make a list of the things you love about work and be grateful for them. Fully activated 6th house of the horoscope brings sickness, debt, and enemies, as these are the main results of this house. No one wants these things. So keep one thing in mind: the strong 6th house of the horoscope is futile. In fact, we must make the 6th house the weakest in the horoscope by performing some remedies. To get rid of sickness, worship Lord Shiva and chant the Mahamritanjya Mantra daily. To get rid of your debts, worship Lord Ganesha and chant any of his mantra. After chanting the Lord Ganesha Mantra every Tuesday, offer sweet Laddu to Lord Ganesha. You will get positive results in 43 days, and after a year, you will be out of debt. To win over the enemy, chant the Devi Baglamukhi Mantra. There is no greater and more useful mantra than the baglamukhi mantra. This spell can make a weak person strong. It starts working for the helpless from day one.

7th House: Learn skills that are related to listening and learning from your partner rather than speaking or telling something to them. Learn to say "yes" in relationships when your partner wants to do something so you can do something together. Take a class together, like an art class or a dance class. To activate the 7th house, you can focus on the energy of the planet Venus. This can be done through various means, such as wearing gemstones associated with Venus, performing specific rituals or chants, and incorporating the qualities of Venus in your daily life. An ancient remedy to strengthen the 7th house of the horoscope is to marry an earthen pot or a tree of aquamarine, berry, tulsi, etc. By chanting the mantra of Venus, you can activate the 7th house of the horoscope, but remember that if you are single, then immediately after activating the 7th house of the horoscope, the possibility of marriage will be very high, or a lot of marriage proposals will start coming to you.

8th House: The 8th house is very mystical and invites you to engage in meditation and spiritual practices that can help overcome some of the harsh karma the 8th house can bring. Performing transformational work allows your soul to discover and transform its deepest problems. Those who want to go abroad or who are already abroad should think about activating the 8th house. People suffering from stomach problems and people with life-threatening illnesses should also think about activating the 8th house. It is very easy to activate 8th house of horoscope by reciting the Mahamritanjya Mantra. Since the 8th house is the house of age, as soon as you start reciting the Mahamritanjya Mantra, the 8th house of your horoscope will get activated immediately.

9th House: The 9th house in astrology, also known as Dharma Bhava, is one of the trine triangle houses and prosperity houses. A favorable arrangement of a planet in this house or having this house without any harsh consequences indicates whether someone will have their fair share of wealth in this lifetime. To activate the 9th house, one has to start a journey to religious places, start studying Dharma, start serving your father, start giving 10% of your income to the poor, and carry out the remedies related to the 9th lord and the planet placed in the 9th house.

10th House: Ensure that you are noticed and recognized in the workplace by giving your best in everything you do. Show leadership, support, and recognition to your colleagues. Hire them and work with them in the trenches, and they will come back to you. Find a new job. Put your leadership in service to the community for recognition. To activate the 10th house, which represents career, fame, and public image, you can perform "Das Mahavidya Puja", which is a ritual to soothe malefic energies that affect the house. You can also recite the "Vishnu Beej Mantra", a mantra dedicated to Lord Vishnu and said to bring success and prosperity to the 10th house.

11th House: Do the work of humanity and service to help others. Find ways to increase your income by getting a side job or starting your own small business. Make new friends on weekdays and reach out to your own friends. To strengthen your 11th house, you can chant the mantra of the planet that rules your 11th house.

12th House: Take a meditation retreat, visit an ashram, or visit a foreign country. Perform service work without waiting for confirmation. Donate to your favorite charities. Surrender when things seem out of your control and pray to the source of your divinity. To activate the 12th house, which represents spiritual growth, liberation, and charity, you can perform "Bhagwan Vishnu Puja", a ritual intended to appease God Vishnu and remove any bad influences on the 12th house. You can also recite the "Mahamrityunjaya Mantra".

Remedies for different planets

It should be noted that the remedies mentioned for different planets are very common, popular, and proven and can be applied to both men and women. Moreover, spiritual remedies should not be taken blindly but must be properly consulted and analyzed in advance by an experienced astrologer. Maintaining good moral behavior purifies our inner health and helps us see beyond our imperfect senses. Furthermore, these remedies are spiritual in addition to ethics and morality and can be practiced without much effort, but the extent to which the benefits are obtained from these remedies depends on several other influencing factors, like the type of afflictions in the horoscope, the consistency of performing the rituals, the muhurtha, and the faith while doing it.

Remedies for Weak Planets

Weak Sun:

If the Sun is malefic or in a malefic house like the 6th, 8th, or 12th house, or is in conjunction with a malefic planet like Saturn, Rahu, or Ketu, or is debilitated in any aspect of Libra, natal chart, or zodiac sign, then strengthening the influence of the sun in the native and the world needs correction to lessen the suffering of the sun in his life. If the sun is weak in a person's natal chart, this may cause the person to lose self-confidence and may create many problems in life. Since the sun is weak, their relationship with their fathers is not good, and they face many problems. A weak Sun may be the reason of the following problems.

- Native will constantly feel insecure about their position and social status in the society. This leads to feelings of insecurity, affecting their relationships both within and outside of society and at home.

- An individual is likely to become dull and therefore less motivated. They need the support of others. The father of the native may not have a good luck.
- A weak Sun in the horoscope can also lead to business-related challenges or problems related to employment.
- Weak vision, intermittent headaches, weak bones, circulation problems, heart disease, and discomfort from inflammation.

Therefore, it is important to analyze the position of the Sun in your horoscope and take the necessary remedial measures when the Sun is weak.

Remedial measures of a weak Sun

- Worship Lord Vishnu daily.
- Feed monkeys and cows regularly.
- Offer Argya (water) to the sun in the morning.
- Surya namaskar at sunrise.
- Strictly observe fasting on Sundays.
- Eat sweets and drink water before leaving the house.
- Honor your father and have a healthy relationship with him.
- Recite Aditya Hridaya Stotra.
- Chant Gayatri Mantra every day.
- Donate wheat and jaggery to the poor.
- Eat sweets before starting any work.
- Cut a piece of copper into two parts. Throw one into the water and keep the other with you forever.
- Chant Beej Mantra of Sun Aum Hraam Hreem Hraum Sah Suryaya Namah for 7000 times in 40 days.
- Offer soaked crushed wheat and jaggery (gur) to a cow on Sunday or daily.
- Fasting on the days of Shivarathri and the 13th evening of the lunar calendar (Pradosham).

- Avoid eating non-vegetarian food, alcohol or any other unpleasant food
- Donate red color things
- Wear Ruby gemstone (A competent astrologer should be consulted before wearing gemstones).

Weak Moon:

The Moon loses its power substantially when it is aspected or conjuct by malefic planet(s) in the horoscope. It also becomes nearly powerless due to its placement in inauspicious houses. The emotional state of the native in such a case is affected and the level of comfort and luxury decreases. A weak moon can cause many problems in life. It also represents emotions, thoughts, and feelings, and when the moon is weak in a person's chart, it can create depression, mood swings, negativity, and even the brain. A weak moon can lead to the following:

- Causes the individual to have negative traits such as mood swings and emotional instability. This is due to his anxious mind and wandering thoughts.
- May cause mental disorders such as anxiety, depression and many phobias. This can limit an individual's ability to work effectively and they lack motivation.
- These people may not express their feelings clearly or hide them from others, which increases suspicion.
- The weak moon can cause weak eyesight.
- Possible problems at home, with home environment, land, property and savings.
- Lack of love and care from the mother during childhood. This may be due to the death of the mother or her absence for reasons beyond her control.
- Allergies to milk or dairy products occur when the Moon is weak.
- It affects the general health and well-being of individuals under the influence of the weak moon

- People with a weak Moon will always be annoyed by their neighbors.

Remedial measures of a weak Moon

- Worship Goddess Durga, Lord Shiva and Lord Krishna.
- Recite Shiv Chalisa and Durga Chalisa.
- You can perform Rudrabhishekam and also recite Shri Shiva Sahasranama Stotram.
- Never accept money as a gift or donation.
- Donate milk to the poor people.
- Try to give white clothes or rice to the poor.
- Fasting on Mondays, eat once a day.
- Avoid eating cold foods at night. Also, eat fresh and succulent fruits.
- Wearing a silver or gold ring on the index finger on Monday can remove negative energy from the person's life. (Try this remedy only after consulting a professional astrologer).
- Practice meditation and yoga every day.
- Placing peacock feathers in the house.
- Avoid having large clocks in the house.
- The Moon rules over water. Thus, avoid wasting water.
- Offering milk to Shivling every day and if not possible, do it every Monday.
- Offering dough to cows on Mondays or daily.
- To serve one's mother or elderly women in need.
- Feeding crows with boiled sugared rice.
- Keep a pot of fresh water for the bird.
- Japa Beeja Mantra of Moon: Om Shraam Shreem Shraum Sah Chandraye Namah – 10,000 times in 40 days to make the moon stronger.

Weak Mars

Mars is considered inauspicious, especially when it is weak, either due to deblitation, being combustible, or having aspects of malefic planets. Mars is considered malefic if it is placed in the 1st, 4th, 7th, 8th, and 12th houses. Also, if the planet Mars is the lord of the 6th, 8th, and 12th houses in your Kundli, it is considered a malefic placement. Some of the negative effects of weak and malefic Mars are:

- It may cause problems of aggression and anger. You may feel irritable most of the time and have difficulty focusing on family and work.
- You may feel exhausted most of the time and have less motivation to work.
- Delayed marriage is one of the worst effects of malefic Mars in Kundli.
- People with weak Mars in Kundli will often feel jealous and arrogant.
- The weak position of Mars in the horoscope also causes health problems. Oftentimes, the digestive system of natives can be affected. You may have trouble eating hot, spicy foods.
- Mars can also weaken you emotionally. You can become impatient and prone to depression and stress. That's when weak Mars remedies come in handy.
- Another weak adverse effect of Mars is that it can lead to obesity in the natives, because their metabolism is less efficient.
- If Mars in Kundli is malefic, you will lack consistency in life and you will regret the same. You will have a low resistance to pain and illness.
- Weaknesses prevent you from trying new things in life, thus making you a coward.
- You can also have an accident, cuts, burns and other similar injuries.

Remedial measures of a weak Mars:

- Reciting the Hanuman Chalisa daily is one of the best ways to strengthen the weak Mars in Kundli.
- Wear red coral gemstone.
- Feed monkeys jaggery and gram on Tuesday.
- Donate bel fruit.
- Grow plants at home that have red flowers. Use the same flowers to worship God on Tuesdays.
- Always try to listen before act.
- Mix belgiri into water before bathing. And when you shower, chant the Mangal Mantra.
- Keeping a square silver coin in your wallet protects you from financial problems caused by weak Mars.
- Have honey in the morning.
- When you visit a temple, remember to recite the Gayatri Mantra along the way.
- Help young brothers/servants.
- Offer milk to the Banyan Tree (Bargad Tree)
- Pray/meditate every morning for at least ten minutes.
- Provide Bhog to Lord Hanuman every Tuesday.
- Donate money for the causes related to soldiers and farmers.
- Offer water with sugar to the Sun in morning.

Weak Mercury

Mercury is one of the Navagrahas and is considered benevolent when associated with an agile mind. He is the lord of the two zodiac signs, Gemini and Virgo. If not beneficial, it will turn malefic when placed with an enemy or other malefic planet in the horoscope.

Then it begins to produce negative effects, called Pratikool in Vedic astrology. When giving pratikool, or the negative effects, the following problems arise:

The individual can become cunning, strongly objecting to those whom he does not like. He can also be a liar and a gambler. The person may have a boastful and ostentatious nature. He can be cocky and unprincipled. He may be someone who doesn't follow the instructions of others, spreading scandals and changing jobs too much. Moreover, it can also affect your vitality and fertility. People with low mercury often have unusual thoughts about sex. It also increases career and financial difficulties due to lack of co-worker support, excessive spending, frequent job changes, poor communication, and debt.

Diseases like improper speech, stammering, loss of speech, headaches, neuralgia, spasms, giddiness, hysteria, and insomnia are usually related to weak Mercury.

Remedial measures of a weak Mercury:

- Recite Vishnu Sahasranama.
- Water the tulsi plant in the morning.
- Feed the cow's green or leafy food (palak/spinach) on Wednesday.
- When buying new clothes, remember to wash them before wearing them.
- Chanting the Buddha's mantra or Jaap is one of the best ways to worship Mercury.
- Keeping a parrot to also calms Mercury.
- One of the most effective mercury cures is to feed cows at least once a day before you sit down to eat. You should mainly feed them green grass, spinach and other green vegetables.
- Feeding soaked green gram to feathered creatures also strengthens weak Mercury in the horoscope.
- Natives under the bad influence of Mercury should never disrespect their sister or sister-in-law.
- Maintaining good oral hygiene is in itself a remedy for minimizing the negative effects of mercury. Cleaning teeth and tongue twice a day will help.

- Place a pot filled with rainwater on the roof. You can also put milk in it.
- Provide an earthen pot filled with mushrooms in a religious place, such as a temple.
- Never receive a tabeez (amulet) from a sage.
- Avoid green color as much as possible.
- Donate green clothes. Donate to the orphanage. Help poor students financially. Wear copper coin in white thread.
- Wear stainless steel ring.
- Donate medicine of asthma to needy ones.
- Wear a tilak of kesar (saffron)
- Offee jaggery to monkeys.
- Donate green pulses to a temple on Wednesday.

Weak Jupiter

Jupiter's benevolence is well known, but weak Jupiter can cause problems like obesity, diabetes, and inflammation. One may have dry skin. Weak Jupiter can cause any disease, such as liver, kidney, or spleen problems; diabetes; jaundice and memory loss; ear diseases; diabetes; jaundice and memory loss; any tongue problems; calf problems; jaundice; dental disease; and so on. Therefore, if someone has any of these issues, the position of Jupiter in their natal chart may be to blame. Weak Jupiter can cause unhappiness and negatively affect the lives of native people. This can cause problems like:

- Jupiter can lead to loss of knowledge if it is in the weak spot of the horoscope.
- A native can choose the wrong path in his life, if remedies in relation to weak Jupiter are not done
- A weak Jupiter can damage a person's image and cause disrepute.
- The person may be unable or unwilling to respect their teacher or guardian.
- Such person may also have no wealth or children.

- People with weak Jupiter often lack confidence, faith, and focus.
- They are often pessimistic, financially and mentally bankrupt. Weak Jupiter can also lead to financial difficulties later in life.

Remedial measures of a weak Jupiter:

- To carryout ishtadevata puja.
- Recite Shiva Sahasranama or Shri Rudram.
- Water peepal tree in the morning.
- Give bananas in small pieces to beggars or crows.
- Give yellow candy (bundi laddu) to the crow.
- Wear gold jewelry.
- Help your brother or sister as much as possible.
- Use your father's items
- Start helping orphans and the poor more often than you are doing now.
- Serve your tutor.
- Do japa of the Guru Beeja mantra: Om gram greem groum sah gurave namah, 16000 times in 40 days.
- Donate Saffron or turmeric or sugar on Thursday.
- Do Fasting on Thursday.
- Wear a 5 mukhi rudraksha.
- Wear Yellow sapphire.

Weak Venus

Venus represents love, beauty, and passionate behavior. If Venus is malefic, these aspects will work against the individual. Love turns into lust, and acts of excessive passion can be very damaging. They may face relationship problems in their married lives and may even cause extramarital relationships. They may face business and sex scandals.

Remedial measures of a weak Venus:

- Jagadamba or Goddess Lakshmi should be worshiped regularly.
- Provide quality food items like sweet kheer(rice pudding in milk), burfy, rasagulla, etc. to crows.
- Donate brightly colored silk clothes.
- Donate sugar, rice, cooking oil.
- Use cow ghee at home and also donate to temples.
- Always carry a silver item with you, no matter what, this remedy has proven to be the quite beneficial.
- Use Venus' favorite white items on Friday. For example, try to wear white clothes on Friday or keep a white handkerchief in your pocket.
- Avoid painting walls with brown or beige colors.
- You must give a portion of food to cows, crows and dogs before your meal.
- Silver attracts Venus. Platinum is also beneficial. Wearing silver helps to get rid of skin problems.
- Include white foods in your diet. You can eat dairy products every Friday. If you do not consume salt on Friday, your Venus will be strong.
- Listen to melodious music with slow sound.
- Bathing with cardamom water strengthens Venus. Boil a large cardamom in water. Sieve and mix in your bath water. Continue reciting this mantra while bathing - Om Dram Drim Draum Sah Shukraaye Namah.
- The Friday fast is a great way to gain the grace of Venus. Fasting on Fridays, which alleviates deprivation or lack of worldly pleasures, can begin with the Shukla Paksha Friday of any month. However, starting this fast from the month of Shravan is considered very auspicious. At least 21 fasts must be performed on Fridays. To do this quickly, after bathing and meditating on Friday, after wearing white clothes, it is recommended to chant 3

or 21 garlands of the Venus Mantra. On this day, only milk and rice are used as prasad. It is considered auspicious to give curd to Divyang, especially to one-eyed beggars, if possible before receiving prasad. If there are no beggars, you can also feed white cows with curd. On the end of the 21-day fast, after feeding the Brahmin children, donate white clothes, white things like sugar, milk, rice, etc. according to your ability. By this quick observation, prosperity and happiness are achieved.

- Depending on your ability, give white things such as sugar, milk, rice, money, perfume, etc. on Friday.
- A diamond can be worn for the auspiciousness of Venus. The diamonds are expected to be worn in the Hora, Nanda Tithi and Rohini constellations of Venus on Friday.

Weak Saturn

If Saturn is weak in the horoscope, a person begins to form bad habits; people become victims of addiction. Their home electronics often seem to malfunction. A weak Saturn can cause fear, lack of courage, guilt, and apathy. Their house may be slightly damaged. Loss of honor and loss of wealth can be experienced. That person is not reaping the full fruits of their hard work. Due to the decline in karma, the situation related to Saturn deteriorates; people become very pessimistic, lack confidence, and lack vitality. One after another seems to fall prey to bad habits. In addition to economic damage, reputation is also affected. If Saturn is weak in your horoscope, such actions can ruin your life. Weak Saturn easily pushes winners into activities such as gambling, adultery, theft, and crime.

Remedial measures of a weak Saturn:

- The Maha Mrityunjaya mantra should be recited.
- Light an earth lamp (Mitti ka Dia) under the peepal tree.
- Water the peepal tree in the morning.
- Donate black grams.

- Nonvegetarian food should not be consumed if Saturn is weak. Alcohol, drugs, etc. should also not be consumed.
- Do not falsely accuse others.
- Keep your company good.
- Do not cut nails and hair on Saturday.
- Do not disturb animals.
- You should be careful not to get angry, especially on Saturday and Tuesday. Do not offend anyone.
- If you fill a bowl with oil on Saturday and give it to someone in need after seeing your face in it, Shanidev will be happy.
- You can apply oil to your body and nails while sleeping on Saturday night.
- If you worship Shanidev on Saturday, you should eat things made from jaggery and chickpeas.
- Wear black on Saturdays, because Shanidev likes black things.
- Offering salty rice with dal (lentils) to beggars and crows
- Provide salted roti (bread) with mustard oil applied to it, in pieces, to the crows every morning.
- Donate black pulses, salt, or mustard oil on Saturday.
- Take care of the servants and/or the poor.
- Recite the Shani Bija mantra, Om Sham Shanishcharaya Namaha.
- Chant Shani Tantrik Mantra: Om Praam Preem Proum Sah Shanaischaraya Namah. Chant 23,000 times in 40 days.
- Recite Shani Stotra on Saturday.

Weak Rahu

Due to a weak Rahu in the horoscope, confusion can be created in the mind, and a person can create a bad situation for himself. He will hear the bad and ignore the good. He may lose control of his tongue and say things that turn the relationship sour. It will make someone speak in a very direct way, making people forget their own principles. The person will cry, think too much about the past, and dream big about tomorrow. Being a victim of anxiety, fear, and agitation even when nothing is happening. A person may not make a decision or change their decision more than once. He or she will not trust others. Fraud, dishonesty, and lies are starting to happen. A person may suffer economic and financial losses.

A negative Rahu can even lead to health problems like depression, asthma, cancer, and urinary problems. Malefic Rahu can also cause cholera, skin disorders, dysentery, and uterine problems. It can also lead to suicidal tendencies, fears, and phobias. Phaldeepika says that the shadowy planet Rahu causes problems like brain disease, liver disease, and general weakness.

Remedies measure for a weak Rahu:

- Durga puja must be performed. Fasting on Ashtami Tithi for Maa Durga is done because Goddess controls all results of planet Rahu.
- Serving parents.
- Start wearing blue clothes more often.
- Respect father-in-law, grandparents and sick people.
- Do not drink alcohol or eat non-vegetarian food.
- Take care of a street dog or you can have a dog.
- Provide sweet parantha (Indian pancakes) with sugar stuffed in it and fry in small pieces for the crows daily in the morning.
- Charity and service to lepers.
- Consume coconuts in any form.
- Do not eat leftovers or expired food.
- Do not eat late at night, one should try to finish the dinner maximum within an hour after sunset.
- Offer black grams as a naivedya, to Rahu (located to the southwest, facing east), where the Navagraha gods are arranged

according to the Vaidika Prathishta system. Make this offering for 9 days.

- Donating Rahu foods like garlic, onion and mustard oil can help reduce its negative effects.
- Rahu Grah Shanti Puja is made to appease Rahu.
- Recite Rahu's Beej Mantra "Om Bhram Bhreem Bhroum Sah Rahave Namah" 108 times a day.
- For the best benefit of Rahu, chant the Vedic mantra "Om Kayanakshachitra Aabhuv Dooni Sada Budhah Kaya Shachishthya Vrata" at least 108 times a day.
- If you don't have time to visit temples or take other corrective actions, get Rahu Yantra, compile and load with poojas. Then wear it on the advice of your astrologers.

Weak Ketu

Ketu can create ruthless fanatics, immoral people, people with mental or physical inclinations, people with unusual and terrifying inclinations, people with strange tendencies or illnesses, virtuous fake people, executioners or beheaders, psychopaths, torturers, predators, serial killers, and point out problems and dangers through cats, poisonous insects, reptiles, etc. It has also been observed that the professions that Ketu represents are those that involve a great deal of risk, danger, and physical and mental fatigue. The most dangerous aspect of a bad Ketu in the horoscope is that it can turn a native experience into a gruesome near-death experience. It could be an accident, an electric shock, a fall from the roof of a building, a bomb explosion, or a terrorist attack.

Ketu also governs all viruses in our body and can even infect natives with viruses. Some of the signs by which you can determine that your Ketu is not in an advantageous or favorable position in your horoscope, and then you can take Ketu remedies along with other medication (as prescribed by your doctor) are:

- Poor hearing.
- Pain in joints

- Repeated Cough
- Nervous breakdown
- Spinal problems
- Stone problem
- Start smoking marijuana or tobacco
- Spending time on useless activities such as illusions about others, misunderstandings etc
- Getting into the strange habit of keeping beard and mustache for weeks and then suddenly shaving it off
- Dress up strangely, start talking about esoteric things

Remedial measures of a weak Ketu:

- Give food (slices of milk bread) to stray dogs.
- Light up the Ghee Diya under the Peepal tree every day, especially on Saturday.
- Donate dull brown items to needy ones.
- Worshiping Lord Hanuman Ji, Ganesh Ji and Maa Durga. You should chant Hanuman Chalisa every morning.
- Wear more white and yellow clothes.
- Avoid wearing gray or brown clothing.
- Serve the elderly and saints.
- Give green grass (normal) to donkeys.
- Keep a silver jar with honey in it.
- Worshiping Ganesha and chanting the mantra - "Om Gan Ganapathye Namah" 108 times on Tuesdays, especially in the evening.
- Chant the mantra "Om Ketum Karnavann Ketave Peshomayyam Apeshase, Samushdwirajaythah" or you can also chant "Om Hum Kem Ketave Namah".
- Try to keep and carry a silver ball with you.

- Wear anything made up of gold
- Donate blankets to the needy

Few significant things to be kept in mind while performing Remedies:

There are several points to keep in mind while performing the remedy:

There are no hard-and-fast rules regarding the remedy. However, there are some points to keep in mind, such as that it has to do according to Desh-Kaal-patra, Desh being the place, Kaal being the time, and Patra being the actor's specific personal identity.

To make it effective, one must take the remedy on their own. If you're sick, you're the only one taking the medicine or the treatment. No one else should do it for you. However, in some cases, infants, sick people, or the elderly cannot perform the remedy by themselves; they can ask someone else to do it. In addition, it includes recitation, attentive listening to mantras, careful use of mantras, gems, and Rudraksha, etc., which are suggested.

You should not lose patience and should not expect immediate results. It is the act of erasing your past, and it will take time because it depends a lot on the intensity of the actions you committed. To repay your karma, your patience may also be tested. You should only take the remedies when you have complete confidence and trust in them. Also, you shouldn't make any repairs just because someone suggested them to you. Also, don't experiment with it.

If you want to do some charity work or donate to the needy, make sure you do it with all your heart. Make sure you do it not just because you want to be blessed, but because it makes you and others happy and content. Your synchronization with your body, mind, and soul is extremely important. You need to stay positive and persistent while trying all these remedies.

In addition, you should keep in mind that it is not the remedies that will change your luck or fate. Ultimately, it's a better way for you to understand the pattern of things happening and the reasons behind them. It empowers you to change and empowers you to better deal with the situation and be less affected by it. Remedies help you turn a negative impact into a positive one.

Conclusion

Thanks for going through this book. We firmly believe that this book came into your hands because it was destined to be read by you at this time. In these pages, we have tried to be precise and simple and, side by side, delve into the mystical realms of Vedic astrology, discovering the profound connection between the universe and human life. As we come to the end of our journey, we hope that you have gained a better understanding of this ancient and fascinating science.

There are numerous books available across the market that offer a lot of information on astrology, but it was our endeavour that we may come up with something very basic and simple with which any person could easily connect, understand, and evaluate themselves and their loved ones.

Throughout these chapters, we have tried to convey the connection of a human being with planets, stars, the zodiac, and constellations that leave a unique mark on each person's soul. The position of the planets at the time of birth reveals each individual's potential, challenges, and life purpose. The planets in different houses, their aspects, and their transits all add depth and meaning to your personal story.

We've explored the zodiac signs and their archetypal qualities, as well as the impact of different types of constellations, or nakshatras that help you understand their precise influence on the life of a human being.

You can easily relate the chapters of this book to your life. Each chapter explores your journey in this universe. By this time, you must have realised that Vedic astrology is a vast science, not only about predicting your future with crystal ball accuracy. It is a tool for self-awareness, a map to help you navigate the complex maze of your life. This allows you to make informed choices, capitalise on your strengths, and overcome your weaknesses.

To conclude, let us remember that the influence of celestial things is not decisive. You have the ability to shape your own destiny. The planets may change, but ultimately you decide your direction. Your free will is the most powerful force in the universe, and astrology shows you the path and guides you to live a life of harmony.

We hope that this book will spark a lifelong curiosity about the cosmic forces around us and that you will be able to understand yourself and the people around you from a better perspective. The universe is a vast and wonderful place, and astrology is just one way to appreciate its beauty and complexity. Whether you continue to explore astrology for self-discovery, relationships, or personal growth, remember that the stars above are always there to guide you.

The mysteries of the universe are endless, as are the mysteries of your own soul. Keep looking up at the night sky, keep exploring your own birth chart and the birth chart of your loved ones, and keep seeking the wisdom that astrology has to offer. May your journey through the universe be a source of inspiration and enlightenment, guiding you to a deeper understanding of yourself and the world around you.

We encourage you to use the knowledge gained in this book as a springboard for further exploration of Vedic astrology. Your journey has just begun, and the stars above will forever be your companions in life's great adventures. Remember that you are a universe unto yourself and that the universe, in all its splendour, exists both above and within. We are always there for you to help you explore your journey.

Sanjay Vatts (vatts.sanjay@gmail.com)

Neena Jain (meghnaneena20@gmail.com)

www.ingramcontent.com/pod-product-compliance
Lightning Source LLC
LaVergne TN
LVHW061608070526
838199LV00078B/7214